Praise for *Just Call*

"The research into the life of a hobo and the times dating back to 1915, that author Linda Eddleston was able to infuse into the story of her father's hardscrabble life, is what puts the meat on the bones of this biography. Linda had the advantage of recording Frank's first-person stories of his life before he passed away. Frank's story, as told by his daughter, is a rich story of a man who lived through America's worst economic downturn, as well as hopping on, and jumping off of moving freight trains, in his search for work. The life of a hobo, while dangerous, was rewarding for a man of Frank's character, his strong work ethic, and a little bit of luck along the way. In his story we not only learn to admire Frank, but also the hard times the entire country experienced during the period known as The Great Depression."

> --*Ned Piper coordinator for advertising and distribution of the Columbia River Reader*

"*Just Call Me Frank, A Story of a Hobo* is an engrossing read… fascinating experience to learn about the history of the hobo culture and Frank's journey as delved into this lifestyle."

> *Sharon Ewing-Fix, retired elementary librarian/media specialist*

"Eddleston weaves an excellent story of a young man coming of age and experiencing the world while riding the rails before and during the great depression. I loved reading about the adventures and experiences Frank had. A great window into a different time period, and well worth reading."

> *Ridge McCoy Manager, Product Launch Training, Frank Rose's grandson*

"A superlatively written story of my father's life."

> *Daniel Rose, son of Gilbert Franklin Rose*

Acknowledgments

My writing support starts with family members and friends that encourage me to "just tell the story."

This story is my dad's story. Gilbert Franklin Rose was born on September 27, 1911 and died on August 22, 1994. Before his passing, he talked about the days he rode the boxcars. Ron Walker, an avid historical filmmaker, recorded my dad's stories.

I transcribed these tapes and kept both tapes and transcriptions. Years later, I decided to write a novel about my dad's life.

This book includes his troubled childhood days. At the age of seventeen, he answered his spirit of wanderlust and decided to jump on a freight train, explore the countryside, and find work.

His reasoning was, "Riding the boxcars is a convenient way to travel and safer than hitchhiking."

Just Call Me Frank
A Story of a Hobo

Just Call Me

A Story of a Hobo

Linda Eddleston

Linda Eddleston

Karin Bonaudi, Ink.
Renton, Washington

Just Call Me Frank, The Story of a Hobo
Copyright © 2023 Linda Eddleston

ISBN 978-0-9891430-4-2

Cover art and book design by
Poouster Graphics
Castle Rock, Washington

FIRST EDITION 2023
Published by
Karen Bonaudi, Ink.
Renton, Washington

Printed in the USA
National Color Graphics
Spokane, WA

Dedicated in memory of

Gilbert Franklin Rose

My dear father

> *Just because you're riding boxcars they label you as a bum, but just because you're broke and looking for a job, doesn't mean you're a bum.*
>
> Gilbert Franklin Rose

Just Call Me Frank
Table of Contents Book I

Chapter One

Chicago, Illinois 1933 Twenty-One Years Old

The event happened during mid July. Chicago was experiencing days of unbearable heat waves. On this train, there were many hobos. It was a slow-moving train, leaving the Chicago Train Station. They were following the harvest, going from town to town, hoping for a day's pay for a day's work.

Yet, when these men heard the call, "Water, there's water," they moved quickly. They were hungry, dirty and extremely thirsty. Many leaped off the train, as it started to pick up speed. They ran to a flowing stream of water.

Frank Rose was twenty-one years old. He was tall, thin, but muscular. Easily he moved, and slithered between the men to get to the doorway. He was ready to jump off the moving train, but a clip hanging on the door caught on his overall strap. As he leaned forward, ready to jump, a piece of metal tore his overall bib. These seconds of delay hindered his movement.

Instead of his usual successful leaps off trains, or rolls down grassy hillsides, this time he was unable to leap when the time was right. He hesitated. Then he gave himself an extra push of momentum knowing he had to leap away from the train wheels that were increasing in speed.

He didn't land on his two feet. He tripped, fell forward and landed with his face in the dirt, only semi-conscious of his surroundings. He was motionless, yet he heard a yell, "Move your legs man! Pull your legs in!"

In his stupor he thought about his haunted past. Who was yelling? Was it mean Mr. Steward's voice? It wasn't his kind mother's soft words. Was it his brothers protecting him as they had in the past? No, it didn't make sense. They were not here now.

Frank realized this was a stranger shouting a warning. Where were his legs? He had to think and get back to reality. In his mind, he heard his own commanding thoughts; think Frank, think. He saw visions of his teenage years riding on top of boxcars, feeling warm sunshine, but also fighting stormy weather. His troubled childhood, his mother crying, and a mean man flashed through his memories.

Suddenly, he clearly visualized the current situation. He didn't land on the tracks from which he jumped; these were adjacent tracks. There was another oncoming train.

He heard the roaring engine, and the long steady whistle blast. He struggled to focus. "Move those legs!"

Where were his legs? His mind whispered a quiet, stern voice, "Think Frank, think!"

The world was spinning in slow motion. He started to come to his senses. His heavy boots must be on the second track.

The whistle blew again. He knew the steady, long blaring sound meant something was in the train's way. He could feel the wind picking up dust particles in the air. He smelled the dirt, felt the sand in his eyes and tasted the blood from his cut lip.

The warning voice shouted one last time. "For God's sake, move your legs!"

Chapter Two

Portland, Oregon 1915 Four Years Old

Gilbert Franklin Rose did not know why his father disappeared. Gilbert did remember the day. He was four years old. He and his brothers were sick with whooping cough. The year was 1915.

During the week, Mary's three sons had been coughing; and at times gasping for air. This especially had been upsetting during the late nights. Mary had given them cod liver oil - a sure cure for anything. She had rubbed Vaseline on their chests, and encouraged them to breathe steam from a boiling water pot, but the hacking cough continued. Finally, she and her husband Sylvester, agreed to call Dr. Smithson. He checked on each child. Then he placed a "House Quarantined" sign on the front door. There was no sure cure; the sickness would have to run its course.

That day, Sylvester was at work. When he came home, in the early evening, it was still daylight. Despite not feeling well, Gilbert played with his toy horses on the big davenport and often peeked out the porch window. He heard his dad's heavy footsteps climb up the stairs. He was so excited. He saw his dad look at him through the glass. Gilbert decided it was a good time to play peek-a-boo. He hid under the covers. His dad tapped on the window and Gilbert jumped up, and he shook the covers off his head. His dad laughed and Gilbert laughed.

Abruptly, his dad stopped laughing. He had a serious look. He took his hat off and ruffled his thick blond hair. He pressed his large hand against the window pane. Gilbert pressed his small hand against his side of the window pane. Each held their hands there for several seconds.

Instead of his dad coming inside the house, he took the gold chain off his belt and pulled his watch out of his pocket. He studied his watch, like he could change the time if he looked at it long enough. Then he blew a kiss toward Gilbert and waved a good-bye.

Gilbert continued to play the hide and seek game. Maybe, his dad was going to hide on the porch. Gilbert covered himself in the blankets again, his horse toys dropped to the floor. He waited for his dad to tap on the window. There was no tap. Gilbert climbed off the davenport and went to the locked door. He stood on his tip-toes unlocked the latch, and opened the door.

He was barefoot, but he walked across the wooden porch and called for his dad. His dad was nowhere to be seen. He ran back inside to tell his mom. In a slightly worried, crying voice he pulled on her apron strings and said, "Daddy is gone."

Mary looked into her son's eyes. They were red, from sickness, but now also wet with tears of worry and concern. "It is okay, daddy will be back." Mary said the reassuring words, but in her heart she too felt upset. She feared the worst. Her husband would not be back.

Late that night, she looked in her husband's top dresser drawer - a drawer that she had never opened before. Then she saw the note addressed to her: *My dear Mary, I cannot stay here in Portland any longer. When you read this note I will have already been on the train for hours. I will return to my homeland, Florida. I cannot raise three boys. I am a disappointment to you, I know. The loss of our baby girl, Rose, was so sad. I can not handle the grief nor can I handle your grief.*

I left our money in the bank. Your name is added on the account. I know you will have to give up renting this home, but you are a wonderful, strong, determined woman and I know you will find a way. Sylvester

That was all he wrote. There were no words for his sons; no "I love yous." Mary felt weak. She leaned back against the side of the bed and collapsed on the covers. Sitting on the edge of the bed, she lowered her head into her cupped shaped hands, sighed and rocked back and forth. She felt an extreme loneliness, though she was not alone. She had three suffering sons in the nearby rooms. She heard one coughing as she fought back the tears.

She remembered the day that she left Long Island, New York, to be with Sylvester. It was nine years ago. Her parents were not happy with her decision to come out west to find work, to get married and to live in NE Portland. She was only nineteen. She made her choice and her promise of "for better or worse." There was no turning back now.

She tore the note in half and put it back in Sylvester's drawer. Odd, but his clothes were still neatly stacked in the drawer, just as he had left them. She slammed the drawer, harder than she expected. The noise might awaken the two boys that were asleep.

Mary mumbled and sobbed quietly. She asked questions to no-one. Questions that only Sylvester could answer, but he was not there to explain. "How could he blame the death of our new-born daughter as a reason to leave? Didn't he understand my grief of having a still-born child? Our tiny baby girl born too soon, born before we decided on a first name; buried as baby Rose. I tried so hard to comfort him. Is his pain more painful than mine?"

Mary sat on the edge of the bed. She quietly wept until she felt she couldn't breathe; she stopped sobbing and grabbed her handkerchief. She advised herself to take deep breaths, knowing that she had to be well for her boys.

Running away as Sylvester did was not the answer. Anxiety and grief cling to one's soul. There is no healing just because one leaves a place. She would stay and care for her sons. How she would manage she didn't know. Sylvester was right about one statement: she was a determined woman. Tomorrow she would have to explain to Millard age eight, to Lewis age six and to her young Gilbert age four why... no, where their father was.

Chapter Three

Portland, Oregon 1916 Five Years Old

A year passed. Mary tried carefully to manage what money Sylvester had left to support her and the boys. She wrote on paper how long she could pay her house payment of fifty dollars a month, and buy needed food for her family. No extra funds were available.

She consistently read the "Oregon Daily Journal" searching the job and education ads. The only ad that appealed to her was an ad that gave the notice of how a young woman could receive a practical nurse's license. The program required attending classes at Good Samaritan Hospital. This seemed like a career opportunity and one that struck Mary's interest. There was one main drawback: the training required live-in residency.

Mary knew that her rent allowance was almost non-existent so leaving her current "home" was becoming a reality. She would be housed at the hospital dorm, but her boys would have to be placed in foster care until she could find a job and purchase her own place. She told herself it would only be a temporary situation.

She decided she would speak to the social workers at the department of foster care. She knew what her demands would be: her sons would have to be placed together, not separated, and be in a home that was nearby where she could visit often. Her demands were met, but there would be future overbearing challenges for her sons, that at the time she could not even imagine.

The first foster home seemed to be a loving, caring place. The foster mother's name was Anna. She was a timid, shy woman in her early thirties. She had no husband, no children of her own, and no pets.

Mary was impressed with how Anna kept the house neat and clean. Anna showed her the upstairs where there was one big room with three beds. That is where her boys would be staying. Mary was glad that they would have a large space and that they would be together. There was also a large trunk full of toy cars, trains, balls and wooden blocks. A tall book shelf was stacked with kid books. Mary felt sure the boys would be comfortable at this house.

Mary became immensely involved with her education. Each time she visited the boys they seemed happy and busy too. Then a drastic, unthinkable, complication happened.

Anna had a sister named Ruby. Ruby came from back east, a city in Massachusetts. She came for a visit and stayed for several weeks. During that time, she spent time with Lewis, Mary's second son. Ruby adored him, watched his movements and wished he was her child. Lewis wasn't a baby. He was seven years old.

Unable to a have a child of her own, Ruby, for years, had longed for a child. She recognized that Lewis was a strong, healthy, obedient lad. Lewis was comfortable being the middle son. He was always helpful and quickly did whatever his mother, Mary, asked. Ruby realized that this boy could be hers - after all, Mary wasn't even around and wasn't raising her own children. She decided, she could raise Lewis and give him all he wanted. Her husband had inherited a great amount of money; they were rich and able to provide whatever was needed.

In her distorted mind, she decided to take Lewis to a new environment, far away from Portland. She figured it would be a good solution for her and for him. Hours before her visit with her sister ended, she lied to Lewis.

"Lewis," she called, "come, let us sit on the davenport and talk awhile." Lewis was just about ready to run outside, but he sat on the cushion and waited to hear what Ruby had to say. The last few weeks he and Ruby had played card games, tossed a baseball back and forth, and even went on some long walks. He felt okay visiting with her for a short while because he heard she was going to leave soon. He figured she wanted to say a decent good-bye.

"Lewis, your mother and I agreed that it would be great for you to have the opportunity of going on an adventure with me. We will ride the train. You'll be able to see new sights and play in the fields near my home. It will be a great experience! I'm sure you like seeing new places, and taking a trip is so much fun. It's an exciting way to travel. We will hear the whistle blow and we will go through long tunnels!"

Lewis had never been on a train. He hadn't been out of the city of Portland. He was curious about taking a trip and especially about riding a train. Yet, he was troubled. Why would his mother talk about this with Ruby and not tell him?

He sighed and then he asked, "Are my brothers coming too?" He quickly added his reasoning, "Because I have to help watch Gilbert. Also, Millard always wants to know where both of us are. I can't go anywhere without my brothers, except for school. Gee, Gilbert isn't in school yet; he'll miss me if I'm not around."

"Yes, I understand," answered Ruby, "this is only a temporary trip you will be back here soon. Your mother and I agreed just you get to go on this trip. I have your bags packed for you and we will be leaving now. We will ride to the train station by horse and buggy. Think about the fun adventure, Lewis. Remember, your mother really wants you to go and learn about new places. I told her I would take good care of you. It won't be forever just a fun trip."

Lewis was near tears; he wasn't prepared for any trip. He needed to talk to Millard and he definitely needed to say good-bye to Gilbert and to his mother. Why would his mother let him go without saying good-bye to him? He saw a big extra bag that he assumed was filled with his clothes, but what about his baseball mitt, his deck of cards, and his teddy bear?

Ruby took Lewis' hand and almost dragged him to the carriage. The servant of the household was ready to go. Ruby pushed Lewis into the carriage, and then she climbed aboard. The servant grabbed the luggage. He wondered why the boy was going too, but he wasn't in a position to question what took place in this household. He pressed his tongue against his teeth and made a clicking sound to get the horses to move and away they went straight to the train station.

It was days later, when Mary came to the foster home that she discovered Ruby had taken her son.

"What?" She screamed at Anna. "You let my son go with your sister to Massachusetts - over a thousand miles without my permission or even my knowledge? Are you crazy?"

Anna was shaking in fear, "I know she should have asked you, but the day she left she hurried away, while I was gone. I didn't know she was serious about taking Lewis. I saw no harm because she just wanted to care for him: not hurt him!"

"You've committed a crime! Aiding and abetting a criminal! Your sister has kidnapped my son. Do you understand that? Don't tell me she was just being loving and helpful - she's a criminal - of the worse kind! I will talk to the police. And you will never, never be a foster parent again. My son has been stolen - right from this house!"

Anna stood back trying to avoid Mary's wrath, "I don't know what to do. Ruby doesn't have a phone. I don't know how to reach her."

"Well, I do. She will be reached by the police. Give me her address!"

Anna went into the living room and looked through a pile of papers. She found Ruby's address and handed it to Mary.

Mary looked behind her. Millard and Gilbert were standing in the hallway overhearing the battling conversation. Mary was still shaking and her tears were hard to control, but seeing her boys looking fearful, she composed herself. She took their hands and hurried out the door. She did not stop to pack up their bags of belongings. With the borrowed auto, that she had to crank up to start, she told the boys to sit in the back seat. She wiped her tears and then sped up to 30 miles per hour to the police headquarters.

She stopped the auto by the front steps. Once again she held hands with Millard and Gilbert and marched into the police station. In tears, and with her whole body shaking, she started to speak. Her words were stuttering words: "I, I, I, need, need, to speak to an officer immediately: my, my son..." She could not speak the words. She collapsed on the nearby chair. An officer came closer. He looked directly at her. "What about your son?"

Mary continued to sob, but finally was able to speak the horrible words. "He's been kidnapped!"

The officer motioned for another officer to come. They grabbed paper and pencil; they asked Mary question after question. All the while, they quickly recorded on a note pad the painful details Mary shared.

Gilbert and Millard quietly sat on nearby chairs. Gilbert only moved his legs, swinging them back and forth in a nervous fashion. Millard was still like a young soldier on guard.

Finally, the questions stopped. The officers reassured Mary that they would do their best to get her son, Lewis, back to Portland. They told her it would take time. She was to call them tomorrow.

The police took Mary's statement seriously. They moved fast thinking Ruby might harm Lewis. In reality, Ruby had no intention of harm. In her misconceived mind, she really thought this was the best for Lewis.

Mary called the police station every day for a week and two more days, before she received a phone call from them saying her son was okay. She was directed to be at the train station at noon the next day to meet him.

Mary arrived an hour early at the train station. She was alone. Finally, she heard the roaring sound of the arriving train. The train slowed. She stood on the platform looking for signs of her son. The train came to a complete stop. People were stepping off the train. She saw a man in a suit holding her son's hand.

He nodded in her direction and released his hand. Then with a nudge on Lewis' shoulder he gave him permission to run to his mother's arms. Mary also ran to meet Lewis. Mary held him tight. Lewis didn't seem to mind her tight hold or the long hug. She released her hug. She looked at him as he quietly talked: "I missed you mommy so much. I missed Gilbert and Millard too. I wanted to show them what I was doing."

"I missed you too Lewis I love you so much. And your brothers asked about you every day."

"I rode a horse mommy. Is that okay? Did I do anything wrong Mommy? Was I wrong to ride a horse?"

"Oh, no, Lewis you did nothing wrong! It was wrong of Ruby to take you to her place without my permission, but you did nothing wrong my dear Lewis. You did nothing wrong!"

"I tried to be a good boy, but I cried at night because I wanted to know if you were okay."

"I know dear. I was crying too." Mary still had to wipe tears from her eyes, but now they were tears of relief. She turned to the officer, who had been patiently standing nearby.

She reached toward him, to shake his hand. "I am so thankful, so thankful." He shook her hand and patted Lewis on the head. "My job is finished now. Do you have transportation?"

"Yes, I've borrowed an auto for the day." He smiled and turned to leave.

Mary and Lewis walked to the automobile. Before she cranked up the auto she looked directly at Lewis. "I have to return to the hospital this afternoon; however, your brothers are waiting for you. You will be staying at a new foster home. The foster mother's name is Mrs. Grundersen. She is an older, nice lady. She plans to have a big lunch ready for you to eat when you arrive. I know you will like her."

*****

Mrs. Grunderson was a professional singer. She practiced every day singing the solfege scales on her piano. Away from the view, in the hallway, the boys mouthed the syllables" "do, re, mi, fa, so, la, ti, do" – only in silence. They also danced around, acting as singers too. When her voice hit the high notes, from one of her Irish tunes, they would jump in the air with their mouths open, as if they too sang the soprano melody. Then they ran outside and laughed. It was making fun of her, but not in a mean way because she was a likeable lady and cared for the boys, in a manner that they respected.

Mary came for one of her weekly visits. She waited in the living room while Mrs. Grunderson called for the boys. Lewis and Millard quickly appeared. Mary greeted and hugged them. Then she asked, "Where is Gilbert?"

Lewis answered, "Well, Mom…," he hesitated and spoke softer because he didn't want Mrs. Grunderson to hear his explanation. "Gilbert heard Mrs. Grunderson say that three boys were too much and she was going to call the foster care place and ask for a change. Gilbert heard this and then he ran off."

Lewis noticed his mother's worried look so he quickly added more information. "But, I know where he is. He's in the field behind the shed. He's not far."

Mary sighed. She believed Gilbert would run back as soon as he realized it was her visiting day, but she only had a few hours to visit. Spending time looking for her son was not an option.

"Lewis, go and look for Gilbert. Millard you stay here: we can visit until your brother returns."

Millard was anxious to tell his mom what he had learned in school. History was the subject that excited him the most. He knew a list of names of explorers. He was eager and excited to share this list: "Juan Rodriguez Cabrillo sighted the Oregon Coast in 1543, Juan de Fuca mapped the ocean currents in 1592, James Cook made maps of the seas, and Robert Gray went to China when he was young, and then he went around the globe and explored the Columbia River."

Millard paused for a long needed breath. "And…George Vancouver entered the Royal Navy at the age of thirteen. He also explored the Northwest Coasts!" He waited for his mother's reaction.

"Very impressive! You must be studying hard in school!" She reached over and gave him a hug. Questions crossed her mind, was Millard so interested in sea voyages that someday he might take off and go on a sea voyage? She released her hug and shook back a strand of her hair from her face. No, she would not consider such a thought of her son traveling miles away. Millard had not even been on a boat.

Millard wasn't able to share more of his knowledge and dreams about the sea because they both heard Lewis and Gilbert coming in the back door. Lewis was pulling Gilbert by his ears. Gilbert was screaming, "Ouch! I would have come on my own. I don't need you to pull my ears!"

Lewis released his grip. Mary looked directly at Gilbert. "Gilbert, you need to stay in the yard area, not run off in the fields. I need to know where you are at all times. This made my visit time an upsetting experience. Do you understand?"

Gilbert hung his head; he didn't like being scolded, especially from his mother. "I will try harder," he mumbled.

Mary hugged each child and said her good-byes. She told the boys she would have to speak to Mrs. Grunderson before she left.

They did reach an agreement. Mrs. Grunderson agreed to allow the boys to stay: at least until Mary could make other arrangements.

Mary went back to say a second good-bye. She kissed and hugged her sons. Reaching into her pocket she pulled out three lollipops and gave them to her boys. She told them not to worry there would be no sudden changes. She promised them she would see them the following week.

Chapter Four

Portland, Oregon 1919 Eight Years Old

The boys stayed at Mrs. Grunderson's home until Mary completed her training at Good Samaritan Hospital. It was after her training, that Mary realized that her job offers would also involve a commitment where she would be separated from her sons.

The opportunities available were nursing duties overseas to help the military men or in-home care positions in the city. Mary selected an in-home care position. She moved her belongings into Mrs. Standton's home. Mrs. Standton was an elderly lady (in her late eighties) living alone and needing constant care. This decision meant that Mary would be working in SE Portland. Mrs. Grunderson's home was in NW Portland near the Good Samaritan Hospital. Also, Mrs. Grunderson still was not willing to make a long term commitment with Mary. It was time for changes.

It would be the last foster home that her boys would have to stay in, but also the longest and the worst stay, especially for Mary's youngest son Gilbert. The year was 1919, Gilbert was 8 years old.

The boys were taken to the "Steward's Place" out on 105th Street in SE Portland. The house sat on its own hillside about 1/2 mile down a private dirt driveway. It was surrounded with fields. In front was a large covered porch. Several rocking chairs and a wooden swing hung with chains attached to the porch roof. To Mary the place appeared peaceful, pleasant and inviting.

Mr. and Mrs. Steward were foster parents taking in several children at a time. Mrs. Steward loved children and felt she was doing a worthy service caring for these needy youngsters. Feeding the entire group did not seem like a chore because she enjoyed cooking.

But, Mr. Steward only accepted being a foster parent because he saw it as a way to get these children to help with the chores. He cared less about their personalities or their needs. He also liked the idea of getting monthly checks, which came from parents or the government.

There was a definite financial need. Mr. Steward was not capable of maintaining a full-time job. He had lost his left arm and his left leg years ago from a train wreck accident. For an arm he only had a steel hook. His missing leg was now a wooden leg.

Amazingly, despite his condition, he was quite capable of doing many chores and activities. He used his hook arm to do some tasks, but also as a weapon, if needed. Using his wooden leg he walked with only a slight limp.

As long as Mrs. Steward was willing to feed their whole crew, he reluctantly tolerated having children at their home. Yelling out orders and demanding that the kids do chores was his specialty. He also raised Great Dane dogs for money; not because he loved dogs.

Mary had no idea of Mr. Steward's attitude or his behavior. She saw the situation as a safe place to board out her sons. She especially appreciated Mrs. Steward's kindness. Without hesitation she left her three boys in their care.

"Gilbert get over here!" Mr. Steward called each boy to his side, one at a time, to get information. "Okay, Gilbert, how old are you?" Gilbert hung his head feeling extremely shy in front of this gruff looking man that was missing one arm.

"I'm eight."

"Well, that means you can go to school. Have you been to school yet?"

Gilbert thought about it. He knew his brothers had gone to

school, but no one even suggested that he attend school. He didn't know much about it and really thought it was never something he would do. Mr. Steward was not patient about getting an answer. He yelled his command and question. "Give me an answer - have you been to school or not?"

Gilbert was near tears. Not only did he fear Mr. Steward he also feared the thought of having to go to school. He was use to having free time.

Gilbert mumbled, "No, haven't been to school."

Mr. Steward corrected him, "That should be 'No Sir!' Well, tomorrow you will start school."

Then he looked at Gilbert's dirty small feet. "Do you have any shoes?"

Gilbert looked at his feet. He had been going barefoot for a long time.

"No sir!'

Mr. Steward sighed, "Well, I guess that don't matter. Up early tomorrow and you can walk to school with your brothers. Now get back to the chores I told you to do today! Pick those beans. Get the basket full for Mrs. Steward."

That was Gilbert's introduction to Mr. Steward.

The nearest school was two miles up the dirt road. It was Russellville School.

The next morning Lewis woke Gilbert up. Gilbert tagged along behind his brothers following them to school.

Gilbert probably would have been teased at school for not wearing any shoes, for not knowing anything about school, for not being able to recite his numbers or letters, but he had two older brothers. No one wanted to mess with Lewis or Millard. Also, Gilbert had an eagerness to learn. It was an outward, visible excitement in his demeanor that the other children and his teacher noticed. Surprisingly, he was glad to be at school. If someone would have teased him he probably would have ignored it: being oblivious to anything negative happening at school. His teacher was fond of this new pupil, though she also realized it would be a challenge to get him (now a third grader) caught up with the other learners.

He enjoyed games and devised his own rules and methods of how to play during recess time. He didn't own a bag of marbles, but he was quick to play with the other boys and to figure out how to shoot those marbles across the circle marks in the dirt. His techniques enabled him to win a few marbles: that he put in his pockets.

It was at school, that the kids called him by his shorten middle name, Frank. He liked being Frank. Frank was easier to write than the letters spelling Gilbert and the name change distinguished him from the boy Gilbert that Mr. Steward ordered around. He could be Frank, an easy going child that was about to learn all that school life could teach him.

A slight name change happened with his brother Lewis too. He was called Lou at school, but Millard was always called Millard. The students respected and looked up to Millard because he was one of the older students in this one room school house.

*****

One of Frank's friends at school was an Indian boy that lived close to the Steward's place. His real name was Brave Heart, but he too had a name change at school. At school he was called Tommy. Not a variation of his real name, but a different name entirely.

21

When they were not in school, Frank and Tommy enjoyed a favorite pastime activity; they enjoyed looking for Indian arrowheads. The seven acres of property that the Stewards owned was an area where Indians used to have their campsites. To find these treasures they had to dig holes from under the plowed dirt. Frank and Tommy collected these arrowheads and hid them in a wooded box. They buried the box under dirt by the tall oak tree.

When Mr. Steward discovered all these newly dug holes in his fields, he was not happy. He figured that not only was dirt displaced but newly planted seeds were also scattered and unplanted. He considered the display to be an act of deliberate mischief. He didn't give the boys a chance to explain or to make amends. Instead, he decided that Gilbert needed a lesson in obedience.

When Gilbert got home from school, Mr. Steward met him at the end of the road. He ordered Gilbert's brothers to head to the house and start their chores. Then he dragged Gilbert to the nearest tree. Behind the tree he had a leather whip. He grabbed the whip with his hook arm. He continued to pull on Gilbert's shirt taking Gilbert to the barn. Then he swung that whip and whipped Gilbert until Gilbert's back and his back legs were bleeding.

Gilbert was a stubborn young lad and strong for his age. When Mr. Steward quit swinging the whip Gilbert grabbed his torn shirt and ran back to the house. He did not cry nor did he limp. He ran like the speed of a fury wind. He kept his mind alert and focused on only one thought. He hated Mr. Steward. He would not let anyone know how much he hated Mr. Steward. He would not tell his brothers or his mother. But, now he knew Mr. Steward was a mean man and Gilbert would always hate him.

Gilbert and his brothers were not the only children at the Stewards; however, after that whipping experience somehow word got out that Mr. Steward abused the young boy Gilbert. Not too long after that incident the Rose boys (Gilbert, Lou and Millard) were the only foster boys that were placed at the Stewards. Mary did not know why there were fewer children at the place. She only discovered the real reasons years later.

Unfortunately, it wasn't to be the last major punishment Gilbert experienced. The whipping caused physical pain that did heal, but the next punishment would be an emotional pain that would never heal. That pain would be so unbearable it would prompt Gilbert to plan revenge.

Chapter Five

Portland, Oregon Early School Days

After this incident of harsh punishment, Gilbert decided he wanted everyone to use his middle name, Frank. He liked the name Frank. When he was at school this was the only name his teacher called him; this was the name his fellow students used when they wanted his attention. He liked school. School was a safe, comfortable place.

From that day on, he only answered to the name Frank, even when his mother called him. When Mr. or Mrs. Steward addressed him, he waited, until they said Frank; then he reluctantly responded. There was one exception, when Mrs. Steward called him for dinner he quickly came no matter which name she used.

After the whipping, Frank stayed around the house less than before. He went to school with his brothers and then came back to the Stewards place (a place where he lived, but never called home.) He did his chores as quickly as he could so he'd have time to wander off with his friend Tommy. There were dirt trails around the Steward's property and plenty to see and places to dig and look for buried treasures.

One afternoon Tommy had an idea. He had been helping a neighbor down the road by taking care of his horses. Tommy got close and friendly with one horse. The neighbor told Tommy he could ride that horse around the neighbor's field to give the horse exercise.

Tommy had never taken the horse further than the neighbor's field, but now that he had Frank with him, he thought they could take the horse for a longer ride and still get back before dark.

"What do you say Frank? Want a horseback ride? See what's down the road?"

"Sure, why not?"

"You wait here and I'll go and get Old Blue."

Frank sat along the dirt roadside waiting for Tommy to return. Frank only rode a horse once before. That time Tommy was riding Old Blue in the neighbor's pasture. Frank happened along and Tommy let him ride Old Blue alone around the field. But this time they were going to follow through on an adventure beyond the field.

Frank quickly stood up, because Tommy and Old Blue were racing down the dirt road. Tommy barely slowed down and grabbed Frank's hand. Frank leaped up behind Tommy and hung onto Tommy's flying shirt tail and then slid across Old Blues' bare back.

Tommy kicked his bare heels into Old Blue's sides. Old Blue trotted down the road at a rapid pace. Frank loved the feel of the wind racing across his face and tossing his hair. He felt a sense of complete freedom, a feeling that he wanted to experience forever.

They rode Old Blue further than five miles, running along the same long dirt road. Suddenly, a farmer flagged them down. He waved his red plaid handkerchief and yelled at them to stop.

Tommy pulled on the reins and Old Blue stopped while neighing and pulling his head up and down.

"Hey you boys, you need to give that horse a rest." He patted the side of Old Blue and showed the boys his hand where he had swiped sweat from the horse's skin. He continued his reprimand "This horse needs to rest. You can't run an old horse to death!"

Tommy and Frank climbed off the horse's back. They both loved animals and had no intention of harming one. They had no idea that Old Blue was tired especially since they felt so energized from the ride. It was a warm day. The windy breeze felt good, but obviously to Old Blue the heat and the run was too much.

"You better head that horse back to home and get that horse some water."

"Sure, we will do that" Tommy answered. Now he was worried not only about the horse, but about his job with the neighbor that trusted him to care for his horses.

Tommy looked at Old Blue. "Don't worry Old Boy. We will ride you slow."

But Old Blue had no intention of riding anyone. Every time Tommy tried to climb on, Old Blue started to buck, and even attempted to nip Tommy. He was willing to let Tommy lead him with the reins, but definitely wasn't letting anyone ride on his back.

Frank tried too. He gently talked to the horse and patted his side. But the minute he started to get on Old Blue - Old Blue shook his head in a frantic manner and started to kick his hind legs.

"Guess we're walking," mumbled Frank.

The joyous ride was over. Tommy and Frank walked Old Blue back to his field. Frank watched as Tommy started to treat Old Blue. Tommy knew enough about heated horses to know what to do next. He took the hose and gently sprayed cool water over Old Blue and then gave him sips of water, a small amount at one time, until he felt Old Blue looked and acted more like his normal self.

Frank had been gone longer than he planned. It was beginning to get dark. He knew it would be dark when he reached the Steward's place.

When he got to the driveway, Mr. Steward was waiting for him. "You've been gone all day." He yelled. "The neighbor down the road thinks you and your Indgin friend stole his horse. What you got to say about that?"

Frank didn't answer and started to walk toward the house.

"You don't go stealing horses - you hear me? Get back here. Don't you take off when I'm talking to you."

Frank stopped. He wanted to remember the feeling of flying in the breeze. He wanted to run away.

Mr. Steward limped up beside him and handed him a shovel. He looked him in the eye. "Go down to the left side of the barn. You'll see an animal near the barn. You go and bury that animal. You need a lesson in how to take care of animals. Maybe starting with a dead one will teach you a lesson."

Frank didn't understand Mr. Steward. How can one learn about animals by burying a dead one? Then fear gripped him. He knew Mr. Steward had a rifle and that he and one of his friends shot animals for the fun of it - like opossums, raccoons and snakes. But they didn't bury those animals. The only tame animal Frank ever saw buried was a sick dog that died. Mr. Steward raised dogs. He never knew Mr. Steward to shoot a dog.

There was one dog that Frank had befriended. Did something happen to the one dog that he cared about? Did something happen to the same dog that followed him to school and waited for him to return?

He ran toward the barn. There was a dog lying on its side so still Frank knew, even from a distance, the dog wasn't breathing. Frank had named the dog Pity because it was a pit bull. He gently turned the dog. When he moved the dog, the dog's head rolled from its body. His head had been shot off!

Frank heard a piercing scream. He didn't recognize his own sounds. He wailed until his throat hurt. Then he hysterically sobbed in anguish. He collapsed on the dirty ground. He relentlessly cried until it was near midnight.

He didn't know how long he had been there in the dirt. It was his brother Lou that finally found him. Lou looked at the dog and immediately knew that it was an act of cruelty by Mr. Steward.

Lou started to shovel the dirt and to make a huge hole. Frank woke to the sounds of Lou scraping the shovel. Frank stood up and without saying a word started digging out dirt with his hands. Together they dragged Pity into the hole and then placed the blood-stained head into the opening, and covered it with dirt. Frank gathered dried leaves and placed them on top of the flat dirt. It was like creating a blanket for Pity and making his last rest a comfortable place.

For several minutes, it was quiet. There were no words that seemed to fit. Lou could think of no way to comfort his younger brother. Frank had an anger and resolution about him that Lou had never seen before. Frank stood up and brushed off the dirt from his hands and trousers.

Lou put one arm on Frank's shoulders. They started to walk back to the house. Frank's words were barely audible, but Lou heard, "I'm gonna learn how to fight."

"Sure, someday, Frank," Lou answered.

"No," Frank continued, "It will be soon. You know those boxing matches in town. I'll fight like them. I'll learn to do it the right way. Then I'm gonna beat up Mr. Steward."

Lou thought about Frank's idea. He could not blame Frank for wanting revenge. "First, little brother, you got to get through school and grow up."

"I will, Lou, I'll go to school. I'm gonna learn to read, write and do my arithmetic. I'll show him. Then I'll learn to fight. I'll treat him like he treated Pit... Pit..."

Frank's voice changed to a sob, but his tears were all dried up. He was so exhausted he could barely walk. Lou put his arm under Frank's arms and almost carried him back to the house.

Quietness penetrated the air. After several minutes, Lou said promising words that he knew would be long time coming, "You'll be okay, little brother. You'll be... okay."

*****

Frank kicked the dirt clogs as he walked to school. He kicked them in anger and determination. Anger - remembering his sad experience of losing Pity and anger toward mean Mr. Steward. Yet, he had a determination that school was important; it was a way toward his future revenge.

Today he headed to school later than usual. Lou and Millard got tired of waiting for him. Lou knew the problems and struggles Frank was experiencing. He understood why Frank missed school entirely the day before, and why Frank was late today.

Lou was sworn to secrecy. He was not to tell anyone, including Millard, and especially not their mother. No one was to know why Frank was so sore and so sad.

Surprisingly, Mr. Steward did not bother Frank the previous day. He was the source of Frank's devastation. He was the reason that two nights ago Frank and Lou had to bury Pity.

The next evening, Mrs. Steward begged Frank to come to dinner. She realized something was wrong, but she got no reply from Frank. After several pleading calls, she gave up. She shook her head in disbelief; she had never seen Frank so depressed that he refused to eat.

Today, though, Frank woke up ready to gobble some morning mush, drink some milk and head off to school. He had listed in his mind goals that he would achieve. One goal included having an education. He resolved to learn how to read, how to do arithmetic problems, to spell words and to grow strong. Then he would be ready to tackle Mr. Steward in mind and strength. He visualized how he would out-smart Mr. Steward and then hit him. He would hit him to the ground and leave him helpless like Mr. Steward left Pity.

He kicked the dirt clogs harder and further down the path, and mumbled out loud, "I'll get back at Mr. Steward. I will!"

This outburst of revenge gave him extra energy. He ran down the path, fearing he would be late, but hopefully not so late that he would be punished.

His teacher, Miss Brown, never really punished Frank. Frank was her favorite pupil; however, she might have to set him apart, as an example, if he came in late and disrupted class time. She would probably ask him to write sentences on the blackboard during recess.

He didn't want to miss recess. It was during recess that he won lots of marbles. Also, he was one of the most needed players on their baseball team. He picked up his pace and started to run. He was panting when he finally arrived on the school grounds.

The scene was odd, he could see the teacher and the kids on the playground field, but it wasn't recess time yet. Then his eyes gazed further and he saw the disaster. His heart broke. He saw a big dirt area of land with black, sooty ashes, broken boards and scattered burnt debris. There was no wooden school house with a porch, stairs to the porch, windows and a door. All that was left was a standing brick chimney and a border of cement foundation. The air had an odor of overly burnt, smoke ashes. He brushed his hand over his eyes and looked again. There was no school!

Miss Brown called the children to gather into a circle formation. She directed them to sit on the grass. Frank came just as they sat in one big circle. No one seemed to notice that he arrived late. The kids were chattering all at once, asking questions about what happened to their school. Where were their chalk boards, pencils, erasers, the big wall maps, and the globe of the world, their wooden desks and attached seats?

Miss Brown turned her head and looked at each student, in the same way she usually did when she took role call. Only this morning she didn't call out their names. She knew they were all present. She wanted each one to know that she was acknowledging them and that she cared. School was like a second home for many of these children and she was preparing to explain to them why they lost this home.

She drew in a deep breath to compose herself before she spoke. The children watched her. They understood that she was upset. She didn't have to give them a quiet signal as they became silent. They waited for her to solve this horrible predicament and to tell them the solution to this mystery of the disappearance of their school.

"My dear boys and girls. I have to tell you some sad news. Sometime late last night, during the windstorm, there was lightning. You remember what we learned about lightning and how dangerous lightning can be. Do you remember the big fir tree?"

The children nodded their heads. They knew the tree well, some had climbed that tree and it had a swing on it. It became part of their playground. They turned their heads to see the tree. The tall tree was split down the middle, there was only half of the tree, and the swing was gone. Its branches were broken. The branch sticks were part of the ashen heap on the ground.

"Well," Miss Brown continued, "that tree was struck by lightning last night and it caught on fire. Sparks must have flown to the school roof and that caused our school to burn. No one was around to see the flames until early this morning. Some nearby farmers tried to pour buckets of water toward the fire, but it was too late."

The children started to mutter their complaints and worries. "Hush, hush," Miss Brown directed. "This is sad for all of us, but our Mayor, Mr. Flagel promised that he would make sure another school would be built for us. First, we will start with a temporary shelter. So school will continue, but for a few weeks we might have time off, a short vacation."

The children started their conversations again. "Time off?" Some were happily excited.

Frank put his hands over his face and he slumped his shoulders down to his knees. He felt terrible. School was his place of safety and peace. He did not want time off. He didn't want more hours at Mr. Steward's. He wanted to be at school.

Miss Brown, too, lowered her shoulders. She felt overly tired and extremely sad. Then she raised her head. She looked toward Frank. "I have one more announcement." She clapped her hands to get the student's attention. "Since we are already here on the school grounds we will have class today, only it will be different than usual."

The children started to mumble, "How can that be?" "We don't have a school house!" Frank raised his head. He too wondered what Miss Brown was saying.

"We will have an all day recess, except for a picnic lunch time, of course." The kids jumped up and started to scream, "Yay!" They started to run to the field.

Miss Brown stood up and clapped her hands vigorously and pointed with her hand directing them back to their circle spots. The students reluctantly came back to their grassy seats. Miss Brown stood and waited for their attention. "It will not be a free for all recess," she announced. "Instead, it will be an organized recess time. We will start with a baseball game. All of us will participate, including me. I will be the umpire! Frank and Lou will be team captains."

32

The children looked toward their dirt baseball diamond. Their bats and some balls were still in the field.

Then she looked directly at Frank. "Frank, I want you to select one person who will be on your team. She turned to glance at Lou. "Lou you pick a person on your team. Go back and forth calling out teammates until every name is called."

Frank could not believe that now he was in charge of selecting a winning (he believed his team would win) baseball team, a team that would play against his older brother's team.

Frank stood up. Momentarily, he forgot his previous accumulated sadness. He looked over his classmates. He knew Lou would want an all boys team. Frank didn't really care. He had watched when the kids played baseball before. He knew that some girls could play baseball too. He looked toward Della. She could not catch a ball, but one time he saw her hit the ball across the field. He needed a good batter. He stood before the class and shocked them when he first chose a girl on his team. "I want Della," he said.

Then it was Lou's turn, "I choose Kenneth." Kenneth was the tallest, strongest kid in class, but Frank knew Kenneth was clumsy, still learning how to deal with his growth spurts.

The selection process continued. Frank added several girls. He knew which ones could run, catch a ball or distract the other team.

Lou kept calling boy names including their brother Millard. Frank felt slightly sad that he hadn't picked Millard first. It was going to be hard to win this game.

Finally it was down to the last two boy names. Frank and Lou called out the names.

Frank was satisfied with his team. They might even win this game.

Lou and Millard gave him a look that indicated watch out Frank we intend to slaughter your team.

Miss Brown in her long skirt and high boots stood behind the batter. She started to call out in an unusual commanding voice, "Strike One!"

Everyone looked at her. They had not heard her voice that loud or deep before. They had never played with an umpire before rather they were use to arguing out the plays. This game was going to be different. It was going to be a serious game!

Chapter Six

Portland, Oregon 1921 Ten Years Old

Frank rolled over in the lower bunk bed. He thought someone was near him, but he was too tired to even open his eyes. Then he heard the whisper. "Frank, wake up I've got something to tell ya."

Frank turned his head toward the sound. He was surprised to see his brother, Millard, leaning over his bed. Millard had his own bedroom space. He was four years older than Frank. He didn't like Mr. Steward any more than Frank did; however, Mr. Steward did not bother Millard nor did he ever punish Millard like he had with Frank.

Mr. Steward actually ignored Millard most of the time. Millard was a boy that even Mr. Steward didn't want to mess with. Millard was tall and heavy for his age. He had the look that meant 'don't mess with me.' He also was the one that if he did tell his mother about any mistreatment, the boys would have been out of the Steward's house. Despite the abuses, Frank and his other brother Lou did not share these experiences with Millard. Frank decided not to bother his older brother. He did not want his mother to be upset nor did he want Millard to take any drastic action, which he might have done if he knew Mr. Steward was mean to his younger brothers.

Millard did know one truth. He did not like staying at the Steward's place. He also knew that when he finished eighth grade he was going to leave. Now that the school had burnt down, Millard decided to leave slightly earlier than he had planned. He was in seventh grade and he decided it was time to be on his own.

He waited for Frank to be more semi-awake before he whispered his words. "Listen Frank, I'm leaving." Frank now realized what was going on. He sat up straight in the bed. He knew that whenever Millard said something or had a plan he meant it.

"No, Millard, don't leave. You can't just take off and leave Lou and me. Besides you don't even know where you are going."

Millard looked directly at Frank. "Yes, I do know where I'm going. Remember last week when I was late getting back. I was down at the shipyards in Portland. There is a ship at the dock. It needs deck hands. I lied and told them I was 15. They believed me. They said they need workers and I can get a job, right on the ship. It takes off late this afternoon. I can live and work on the ship."

Frank was near tears and desperate to plead his case. "No, you can't just take off like that without telling Lou or Mom." Millard sighed. "I already told Lou and I wrote a letter to Mom. She will read all about my plans once she receives the letter."

"No, Millard don't go. We need you here. Mr. Steward is going to have a fit when you leave."

"Don't worry I wrote a letter to him too. I told him to leave you and Lou alone, no more whippings or threats. He is to treat you kind. If not, I told him I would write to the foster care workers and I would tell Mom. Yes, Frank I know how you've been treated. No, I didn't hear from Lou. I figured it out myself. Especially on the days you missed school. I knew you weren't sick and I figured you got beat up and it was from mean Mr. Steward. I don't think it will happen again. I kept a copy of my note, and by God, I will report him if he harms you again."

"But, you won't even be around. How will you know what is happening around here?"

"I'll be back, little brother. I'll be back. The ship will be at sea, but it will come back to the Portland dock. When it does I will come back and check on you guys. Mr. Steward knows that. I will be back."

Millard had a pillow case packed with some of his belongings. He had on his high boots, his heavy jacket, extra pants and shirts. He was dressed to leave and to be gone for weeks.

Frank knew this was a definite good-bye. He was not going to be able to convince Millard to stay any longer. "Wait!" He commanded. "I have something to give you." He reached under the bed and took out his small leather bag. It was a bag that his Indian friend, Tommy, had given him. Inside the bag were the items that meant the most to him. "Take this bag and keep it so you can think of me while you are gone."

Millard opened the bag. Inside were two Indian arrowheads that Frank had found - on Mr. Steward's property. Also in the bag were three of Frank's favorite marbles.

Millard held the bag with respect. "No, Frank I can't take this bag. I know how much this means to you."

"Take it. I want something of mine to be with you as you travel the seas: this way I will feel that I am with you. Also, late at night you can look inside the bag and think of me. You will know that I am thinking of you because I really will be thinking of you. I love you Millard."

Millard leaned over the bed sheets and hugged his younger brother. He knew Frank would be okay. Frank was a kind boy, but also tough for his young age, besides Lou would watch out for him. Lou was two years older than Frank. He also, had always cared for his younger brother.

The sun was near rising. Millard knew his time was short. He wanted to sneak away before everyone woke up. He had to hitchhike into town and he best get on the road. He covered Frank with the blankets and told him to go back to sleep. Frank whispered a final question, "Where is the ship going, Millard?"

Millard stood still for a complete minute. He quietly said one word, "China." Then he crept out the door.

Chapter Seven

Portland, Oregon 1923 Twelve Years Old

The day was special! Frank was going to get his 8th grade diploma. His mom came early that morning with new pants for him to wear. Parents were invited to come to the school.

There were planned activities to show the parents what the students had been learning. Frank had made a display of Indian arrowheads. Arrowheads were made from flint, animal bones, antlers and hard stones that could flake easy. Then by using another stone and hammering it or chipping away on the flint (a process called flint knapping), a sharp projectile point was made. A slit was made in the arrow to hold the arrowhead. Frank and Tommy had a collection of these arrowheads and they had made some of their own. There were many in Mr. Steward's fields.

Tommy had helped Frank write this report. Together they pasted the arrowheads on cardboard. Then Frank used his best printed handwriting to explain how arrowheads were made.

Every eighth grade student had a finished project to share. There were only eight eighth graders so it was not a long presentation. After the presentations Miss Brown had planned that all the students would participate in a spelling bee contest. The winners would receive a certificate for 1st, 2nd and 3rd place winners.

Frank didn't much care for spelling. He had a hard time doing his spelling lessons and even though he could read well and he took pride in printing his letters, he never felt sure about his spelling abilities. Despite his doubts, today he felt grand. Mary had pressed his pants. She and Lou would be at the program to watch Frank receive his diploma.

Miss Brown lined the students up against the wall. She did not line them up in order of their grade level or ages. She did include every child from first graders to eighth graders. This had always been a one room school house. Even their desks were arranged in a haphazard order not according to grade levels. This was Miss Brown's intent with her 25 pupils - to encourage them to get along and to help one another in their studies like siblings helping each other; however, this was a spelling competition so for this contest each student was on their own. She had given them one hint especially as to how the younger children could compete.

Listen to each other she said. If someone misspells a word think about what mistake they made and see if you can figure out the correct spelling. Try to learn from their errors.

The list started out easy: spell school, spell bus, spell house, spell horse. Then the words got harder: spell America, spell country, spell education. Education got misspelled several ways, eliminating students. The list continued. Several students spelled their words correctly. So far, Frank had received easy words. He enjoyed the competition.

Next word: spell constitution. One of his fellow students got it right. Frank was glad; he didn't want to try that word. The next word was disadvantage. Disadvantage - Frank knew what this word meant: unfavorable condition - damage or harm. He had felt disadvantaged many times, but he no idea how to spell the word. He looked at his Mom and Lou. He didn't want to look like a fool. A fourth grader tried the word d-i-s-a-n. Then a fifth grader tried d-i-a-n-d. Frank listened. Now he knew d-i-s had to be the correct start. The next student tried: d-i-s-a-d-v-a-n-g-e-d. That student missed the word too. Now there were only two students left and Frank was one of those students.

He listened closely as the next student tried: d-i-s-a-d-d-v-a-n-g-e-d. Surprising to Frank Miss Brown said that was incorrect. Now it was Frank's turn. He had one chance to be the winner of this spelling bee. He knew the letters d-i-s-a-d-v-a-n were correct he slowly whispered the word one more time disadvantaged. It had a t sound! Slowly, still questioning his ability, he spelled the word, "d-i-s-a-d-v-a-n-t-a-g-e?"

Even Miss Brown looked surprised raised her eyebrows in disbelief and smiled in relief. "Frank, you just won the Russelville School yearly spelling bee award!"

Miss Brown told the students to be seated except for the eighth graders. She called them by name, one at a time, to receive their diplomas. The parents clapped and cheered for each one.

Then she picked up three more certificates and wrote full names on these certificates. She handed out the 3rd place spelling bee award winner that went to a third grader. The second place winner went to an eighth grade student. Last she gave Frank his first place certificate. Everyone clapped. Frank's mom stood up and clapped the loudest. Lou came up and patted Frank's back. He leaned close to Frank and mumbled, "I didn't think you could spell at all - boy what a surprise!" Frank accepted those words as a sure compliment from his older brother.

Food was served. Frank stood off to the side watching everyone eat. He wasn't even hungry. He felt so much joy because of his achievements, but he also felt sadness because he had a plan that didn't include any further schooling. He thought to himself, "No more education!" Then he realized education was a word that he had yet to learn how to spell.

Chapter Eight

Portland, Oregon 1925 Fourteen Years Old

Mary came to the Steward's house excited to tell Frank the news. When she arrived she had to wait. Frank was out running in the fields with his Indian friend Tommy.

The July days were sunny and warm. Mrs. Steward offered Mary a cool glass of lemonade. They sat and visited.

Finally, Frank appeared. He was hot, sweaty and anxious for something to drink. He was surprised to see his mom right there in the Steward's living room sipping her lemonade.

At first he had a terrible thought. Maybe she had heard something bad happening to Millard. Even Lou had left Steward's house now. Lou was working on a job at the meat plant in town. Only Frank was still at the Steward's. Secretly he had been planning his get-away.

Maybe his mom came to encourage him to stay at the Stewards. He greeted her with a warm smile and a kiss on her cheek. He still wondered though why she was here when it wasn't her normal visiting time. It was actually during her work schedule.

She still worked full time caring for elderly Mrs. Stanton. It meant staying at Mrs. Stanton's home, but the pay was good and she often had weekends off. It also meant that she was able to save her money so she could get her own place.

Quickly, Mrs. Steward went into the kitchen and came back with lemonade for Frank. His mom pointed to the end of the sofa cushion and invited him to be seated.

"I have something I'm excited to tell you. Don't worry it is good news. I bought a small house on 7th Street. You can leave the Steward's place and stay at my house. It is only a one bedroom, but I've made a private space for you on one side of the room. I can't be there all the time, but sometimes I can be home on the weekends. It will be a home for us!"

She was so happy to share this news she was near tears. She wanted to call her son Gilbert, his Christian birth name, but she knew he preferred the name Frank so she called him Frank. "What do you think Frank; a time when we can live in the same house?"

Frank hesitated. He wanted to make sure he heard his mother right. She was telling him he could leave the Steward's place and come live with her. He could not believe his ears. He was 14, going to be 15 in September.

He had waited all these years to live with his mom, and finally, it was coming true. He only wished his brothers were part of this new arrangement. Despite that separation, he felt happy.

He wanted to do a cart-wheel, but he was awkward at mastering those movements. Instead, he just jumped up and down. "Yes, yes, yes," he said over and over. Even Mrs. Steward clapped her hands seeing Frank's joy.

 Mary was as excited as Frank. "Then it is settled. Gather all your things. You are coming with me!"

Frank didn't hesitate. He gulped down the rest of his lemonade. Then he ran upstairs to gather his belongings. He had one major regret. He probably would not have time to say good-bye to his friend Tommy. He liked Mrs. Steward and he would take time to tell her so.

*****

Frank was happy at his mom's place, but it also meant a lot of alone time with nothing to do. Mary gave him a list of a few simple chores that she expected him to do. What she didn't leave was a list of restrictions.

When Frank was at the Steward's he wandered in the fields; now his free wandering time was on the city streets. Near his mother's home, there were bridges to downtown, busy outdoor markets, various shops, neighborhood homes and groups of young boys lingering on the street corners.

One summer sunny afternoon, while Frank was touring his new neighborhood, he met some of these young teenage boys. They greeted him like he was someone important. Yes, a new neighbor, but also a young strong lad that maybe they could use.

"Hey Kid," yelled the tallest boy, "What's your name?"

"Just call me Frank," he yelled, as he kept walking.

Five boys came close to him and surrounded him as he tried to continue his pace. A couple lads even walked backwards, in front of Frank, so they could look directly at him. The one speaker kid asked another question: "Ya hanging around here?"

Frank still thought they were only trying to be friendly. "Yeah, up on 7th Street."

"Well, Frank, we think you look like a tough guy - we think we could be good friends with ya, if you want."

Frank was flattered that they thought he was a tough guy and "friends" was exactly what Frank wanted. "Okey, dokey" he replied.

"Great! You see…," explained the talker kid, "we are a..." he hesitated, "…an established group. We hang out together and we

44

are loyal to each other. Like good friends should be. Do ya agree, Frank?"

Frank was quick to agree, "Yeah!"

By now they had stopped walking; however, the boys still surrounded Frank's space. It was hard to tell what each boy was thinking because only one did the talking. The others nodded and in that way showed that they agreed with everything that was said.

They were different ages. Two appeared to be older and the other two were younger, and one obviously the youngest. They all wore gray newsboy caps. Three of them wore long loose fitting breeches and loose baggy shirts that were opened at their neck lines. Two of the boys wore knickers, shorter pants that only went to their knees. They all had leather ankle boots.

They were near Frank's age 14, 15, maybe 16 at the most.

Frank definitely needed some friends and here were five boys offering him friendship and loyalty. Yeap, he was definitely interested.

"You smoke Frank?" Frank looked surprised.

"No," he answered. He didn't smoke, neither did his older brothers. He never had any money to buy smokes nor did anyone ever offer him a cigarette.

"Well, look Frank we'll teach you how to roll your own cigarettes and then you can try one."

Frank heard their names as they handed Nick the pouch of tobacco and then Dutch handed him the thin paper. There was Scott and Alfred that appeared to be real brothers, and Herb definitely the youngest and quietest kid.   They were guessing that Frank would cough, or get sick from his first cigarette, or that he would not be able to roll one himself.

They all stooped down on the sidewalk. Nick flipped some tobacco on the paper sleeve. Then he gently rolled the paper over the tobacco. Next, he licked the end and there was a cigarette. He took out a match box from his pocket and lit the end of the cigarette. He put it into his mouth and inhaled his breath. Out blew a whiff of smoke. He handed the cigarette to Frank. "Have a puff," he encouraged him.

Frank took a deep inhaling breath and also blew out a bellow of smoke. He immediately started gagging and coughing. Now they knew he was truthful, he really hadn't smoked before. They started to laugh at his helpless state.

When Frank quit coughing, Nick grabbed the one cigarette out of Frank's hand and said, "Okey dokey, this time you make your own."

They gave Frank what he needed, and he carefully followed the steps that Nick had shown him, and he rolled his first own cigarette.

"Great, Frank, now you can keep that one - as your own smoke."

"You guys buy these cigarettes?" Frank asked his onlookers.

The boys started laughing and repeated Frank's question in a mocking way. "Buy this stuff?" After their laughter subsided, Nick looked him in the eye. "Frank, we don't buy anything. We steal everything. We don't have any cash. Even our dads are either gone or broke."

Frank knew what it was like to be broke. Now that he was with his mom she gave him a little spending money now and then. Even when he was broke, he didn't try stealing. This was a new concept for him.

"Do you steal Frank?" Nick asked.

Frank was quick to answer, "No!"

He rethought the question in his mind, he had not stolen anything and, before today, he had not smoked.

Nick continued his speech. "In town it is easy to steal whatever we want or need. Right boys?" They all nodded their heads and said "yeah" in agreement.

"We'll teach you and you can hang out with us. We call ourselves the 'Rain Pack,' it rains a lot around here. You can be king of our Rain Pack Group. All you have to do is steal more than the rest of us. Think ya can handle that Frank?"

Then Alfred spoke up, "Imagine Frank, now you are just Frank, but if you become 'king of the pack' you could be the big cheese - have a name and title for yourself."

His brother continued, "We'd respect you Frank. We'd consider you like a royal King."

Nick added a last convincing plea: "You'd be a leader right next to me. These boys will do whatever you say. Want to be part of the group, man?"

Frank wasn't sure how to say no while all five of these boys gathered around him ready to pounce on him if he went against their reasoning. He was still holding his lit cigarette that he had rolled himself. He figured the only answer he could give that they would accept was, "Sure, I'll hang around."

"Ok! Now you're on the trolley." Nick seemed excited like he had made a new friend. "Meet us here at this corner tomorrow morning at 11:00. Before the day is over, you will be supplied with whatever you want."

They staggered down the street, looked back once or twice, and yelled at him to remember the time and place.

That night Frank was alone. His mom was at work. He sat up till the wee hours thinking about his encounter and the answer he had given. He had said "sure." Sure he would be there and sure he would try stealing. He always tried to be true to his word. So he could not think of any way out of not meeting these guys tomorrow morning.

When he woke up it was already 10:30 a.m. He only had a 1/2 hr. to do his chores, eat something, and meet his new friends, who were probably waiting for him only blocks away.

He splashed cold water on his face, popped one piece of bread in the toaster and ate quickly. He had slept in his clothes. His only goal was to run to the designated corner and meet his pals.

The few chores, that his mom had requested, he hurriedly finished. Then he left the house and ran down the street. He could see them, even from a distance. He had no other option in his mind except to join them.

Frank was dumfounded when he arrived because several boys said they were surprised that he showed up. A couple even said they didn't believe he would show. Maybe, he really did have a choice.

Nick asked Frank if he had any money. Before Frank could answer Nick explained, "You see Frank, we share whatever we have - equal sharing. Even if we steal we share what we steal. Also, we need a little cash. See, what we do is one person actually buys something while the rest of us do some shop-lifting. You know what I mean by shop-lifting?"

Frank had to admit, "No" he had no idea what Nick meant by "shop-lifting."

"It means," said Nick, "that we take some items we want and stick them in our shirts and walk out of the store. We don't pay for it - just quickly make a decision, take, walk out, and then run like some monster is chasing ya. Got it?"

Frank knew he was a fast runner so he decided he could maybe do this. He dug deep into his pocket, "Here, I've got 45 cents."

"Great," said Nick as he grabbed Frank's change. "Let's go. Okay guys we're going to do an easy one today, the outdoor market." They only walked a few blocks and there was the market. Outside were bins of apples and bananas just for the taking. Nick gave Dutch the 45 cents. "Go in there Dutch and get us some pop and candy bars. I'm going to give Frank his first stealing lesson."

Dutch did as he was told. He slowly picked out 3 five cent candy bars and then grabbed three soda pop bottles for ten cents each. He was up paying for his purchases. Meanwhile, out front, the five other boys were handling and looking at the apples and bananas. Each one grabbed one piece of fruit, including Frank.

Then they ran in different directions. This part Frank didn't really understand. He soon realized he was now on his own. He raced up two blocks back in the direction where they first met. Then he sat on the grass and waited to see if any of them had followed him. He was alone - with one stolen apple in his pocket! He didn't know what to do - was he to eat it? Did they share it? Where were these guys? The race caused an exciting rush. Feeling proud of himself he thought: I stole and I didn't get caught. His proof was a free apple in his pocket. He forgot that he had lost his 45 cents. For 45 cents he could have had nine apples in his pocket - they were only 5 cents each.

Oh well, he reasoned it was a fun day doing something adventurous with his new friends. He wandered home. He wondered, would he see them again or not?

Days went by. It had been two weeks, and Frank was meeting his friends at the same corner every morning. Now he knew his friends better. He discovered it wasn't all true what Nick had said about their parents. Dutch said his dad was working for the railroad, and he wasn't home, but he did send money to his family every month. Scott and Alfred were brothers and they both wanted to go to secondary school when the fall classes started. Herb was a loner and he admitted that in school he was teased so much that he changed his name from Herbert to Herb thinking it would help his status. Nick often was left alone at home. The only family he had was his mother. She was either at work or at the beer parlor drinking.

Frank was on a regular morning schedule of getting up early, eating, and doing his chores so his mom would not suspect anything out of a normal routine. Not only was he stealing food items and tobacco - he also stole some money that his mom had been saving to pay the gas bill. He wasn't keen on that idea but the boys needed some extra cash to keep up the charade.

The day came when they told Frank they were going to steal later that evening. They asked if Frank could come along. He was ahead of stealing compared to the other boys so he thought - why not, maybe I'll get to be "King of the Pac." So he agreed. He knew his mom would not be home; it would be fun to be out late.

The boys had a plan. In the evening, they were going to steal some fishing equipment down by the water front. Frank didn't know about this plan. They walked along the wooden board docks near the Hawthorne Bridge. They told Frank, "See those boats, they keep fishing rods near there, and we're going to get some. We know a warehouse that will buy them from us. All we have to do is get about twelve of those fishing rods. So each of us will steal two. Just grab two rods and run. Run in different directions like we always do."

Frank knew police were around the fishing docks. He didn't like this idea at all. But he decided that he wasn't going to argue; just do it quickly and run like the wind. The problem was the fishing rods hung on boards held by high hooks and not easy to grab.

He started to grab one when he heard noises and saw lights shining in his direction. He didn't grab anything. He just ran. All the boys ran in different directions, but there were several officers and they also ran in different directions. Two of them took after Frank. Frank ran down by the river and hid in some bushes. He could hear the officers talk.

He saw their light beams zooming over the grassy banks. He stayed close to the ground as still as a rock. He didn't even feel like he was breathing. The light was bright on the bush he was hiding under. Then to Frank's surprise he heard the same officer, that held the light near him, say "He went that way." He heard them running up the path back toward the dock. Still he stayed hidden and stayed there till late into the night.

When he finally made it home he took a bath, ate and sobbed with relief that he hadn't been caught. An idea came to mind. He remembered that when he was at Mr. Steward's place he had heard that dairy farmers needed some young boys to work at their farm houses. He thought that might be a way to escape before the police came looking for him.

The next day his mother came home. She didn't know what had happened the night before. Frank decided not to go into details.

"Hey, Mom, I got the morning chores done."

"Thanks Frank. Please, bring the groceries in from the car?

"Sure!" Frank loaded all the groceries into the house and placed them on the kitchen table. He started to put them away as he continued talking, "When I was back at Steward's place I heard about a farm house that needed workers, out at Twelve Mile Corner. They got these new machines to pasteurize milk; guess they need some helpers to do the pasteurizing."

"Hmm," answered Mary as she helped to put the groceries away and rearranged some that Frank had placed improperly. Mary responded, "I don't know much about this pasteurized system. I heard it's okay and the milk is good to drink; maybe, even safer to drink than the raw milk we've been drinking."

"Well Mom, I was thinking it might be better if I got a job. I could ask about this one that I heard about. It's great you giving me a room here and all, but they would also have a place for me to stay. I could help you out with some money. I'm pretty grown up now, Mom. I think I could work like Lou and Millard are doing." He was sorry he mentioned Millard's name because he knew his mom worried about Millard and now she might not be quick to let him go off on his own.

Mary knew that the city was not a good place for her son to be running around. She was also a little suspicious. She knew she had some missing money in her gas bill saving jar, and she also suspected that Frank had been smoking, a new habit that she did not approve of. She heard him a few times talk about Nick and some of his friends, but she never met them. It was odd too that Frank didn't seem eager that she should meet them. She hesitated. She thought for several minutes and it was quiet in the kitchen. "Yes," she said, "I will drive you out to the country and you can go to the dairy farms and ask for work. You call me if you need me."

The first dairy farm, Frank went to, called Lake Farm Dairy, needed help. They hired Frank. He was assigned a bunk bed in a dry, warm place in the barn where he could sleep. They showed him an outhouse, by the barn, a water pump and a big tin tub for bathing. They told him meals would be served every day: in the morning at 7:00, then at noon, and then again at 6:00 in the evening. He was to work and follow their directions from 8:00 a.m., until 6:00 p.m. every day. That is exactly what Frank did. At the end of each week he was given his pay.

Frank's job was to help pasteurize the milk, which they did in the farm house kitchen. They had a pasteurized tub that was connected to a pump system that heated milk with steam. Cleanliness was their major concern. They warned Frank that government inspectors might come to dairy farms and check for cleanliness. They showed him techniques of how to keep the area especially clean.

Frank's main job was to take the heated milk to the milk house, cool it down and bottle it. This farm dairy had up to 125 cows. They were a hard working family that respected everyone that worked for them. They treated their employees like family members. At night there was singing, piano music and story telling. Frank had never experienced quality family time. He enjoyed this experience so he didn't mind the long work hours.

He stayed there working steady until he had his seventeenth birthday. The family had even celebrated with him with cake and ice cream. The year was 1928. Unfortunately, that same evening they announced that they would have to let most of their helpers go. They had purchased new milking machines. These amazing machines would do the milking job quicker than the usual time it took a crew of workers to complete the jobs. Frank was sad to leave this family, but he also was restless and wanted to get out, spend some of his hard earned money and see what was beyond Portland.

Chapter Nine

Portland, Oregon 1928 Seventeen Years Old

Frank headed down the dirt path, leaving Lake Farm Dairy. He carried all his few belongings in a pillow case. It was time for a new adventure of life. On this day, September 27, 1928, he was seventeen years old.

He walked down Stark Street. It was a gravel dirt road with few cars. He decided he would head for town and see his mom first. Maybe he would also see his brother, Lou, before he left Portland.

He looked down the rugged road. A car was cruising faster than normal and spreading dust in the air. Frank stuck his thumb out not really thinking the car would slow down or even stop. As he expected, the car didn't slow down, it continued its speed. Then a little past Frank, the driver slammed on the brakes, skidded on the dirt and stopped. The male driver partly stood in the seat position, looked over the top of the black 1924 Studebaker, and yelled, "Need a ride?"

That was exactly what Frank needed; without hesitating he said, "Sure, much obliged."

At first he didn't notice, but when he got close to the running board he realized this was a three seated roadster and a plump older lady was sitting in the middle of the front leather seat. Still there was room for one more person. He crowded in the seat near the door. The car was impressive. Frank had little experience riding in cars; he anticipated this to be a fun ride.

"I'm Frank." He introduced himself.

"Hello, Frank, I'm Matt and this here is Elsie. Where you're headed?"

54

"I'm going into town if you're going that direction?"

"Sure, man, we're going into town too."

Matt appeared much older than Frank. He was dressed rather poorly for someone that could afford a fancy car. Frank soon realized that Matt probably cared more for the car's appearance than his own looks. As the auto moved forward, Matt talked loudly nonstop. Elsie's body bounced with the car movement, and her head nodded up and down approving or verifying whatever Matt said.

A major problem was Matt not paying close attention to his driving. He glanced at Frank often and leaned forward to state his messages more clearly. His erratic steering was making Frank nervous. There were no marked lanes on this dusty road, but there were obviously two sides. The cars on the right went one direction and cars coming from the other direction kept to their side of the road; except for Matt's car which was going on both sides of the road.

"How do like this classy Studebaker? I just bought it a few weeks ago. It's called a light 6, it's got a plated radiator, genuine leather seats and spoke wheels. Did you notice the spoke wheels?"
He continued on, not waiting for any response from Frank.

"I never had such a nice auto before. These genuine leather seats - feel nice don't they? It's got a hand cranking start up. Even got windshield wipers and a side mirror - can you beat that?"

He looked down trying to figure out how to demonstrate his wipers, when Frank had to yell at him: "Pull to the right, man, that car has the right-of-way."

His movement was too late. The other car had to pull off into the ditch to avoid an accident. As if it was the other driver's fault, Matt pumped on his brass horn, a loud "Aoogha, aoogha!" Frank raised his eyebrows and shook his head in disbelief. Matt continued to drive fast. He did not watch what was coming or what was going, which included some horses and cows that were crossing the road. He drove like he had all the space to himself.

Frank began to realize that this guy not only was a non-stop talker he was also a drinker and somewhat drunk. With his right hand, Matt grabbed a beer bottle off the floor, took a long swig, as he held the steering wheel with only his left hand.

Matt's conversation changed. "We're going to see the USS Oregon Navy Ship. It's docked right here in Portland. It's like a museum now. I was on that ship a few years back. I went from Portland to the Philippines - met those Filipinos. Then we went to China and back again. We stayed on the ship days and nights out on the sea. I served my time. It was a sturdy tough ship. Now it's a museum. Can you beat that? I didn't work on no museum. We were at sea, man, at sea. No, blasted, hell hole museum - an honest to God battleship."

His voice soften and he sounded like he was about to cry. "Now I'll be a tourist, looking to see what changes they've made. Going to let Elsie see my ship." He turned to Elsie and gave her a kiss on the check. Once again, he almost missed another auto. He didn't notice this time either.

There was a moment of silence. Frank was curious and wanted to ask him about being on a ship to China. Maybe, he could get some details about what his brother Millard might be experiencing. Yet, Frank didn't think Matt would listen long enough for him to even ask a question.

Matt changed his soft tone to a booming, loud voice. "That big steel tank is still at sea, even if it is sitting down there on the dock." Then he was silent as if memories were flooding his mind.

In a quiet voice he mumbled, "It isn't happy sitting, it's a sea vessel!"

He held his bottle with one hand and started to wipe his eyes with the other. He had no hands on the steering wheel. The car started to swerve to the left. Before the car was nearly out of control; now it was definitely out of control.

Frank wanted to grab the wheel, but Elsie was in the way. Just as it seemed necessary to do so, Matt turned the wheel and came back into focus.

Elsie finally spoke up. "We need gas, darling. Let's stop at the station and get some gas." The gas station was within sight.

They were still a long ways from town. Frank decided he had experienced as much tension as he wanted for one day. This ride was nerve-racking. He decided that walking wasn't such a bad idea after all. When Matt pulled into the station, Frank quickly got out of the car. He handed Matt a fifty cent piece and said, "Thanks for the ride. I'm going to walk from here. I need some fresh air."

Then he left. He turned his head back and yelled, "Slow down, man!"

Frank did not put his thumb out as he walked toward town. One ride like that a day was enough. He wanted to live longer than his seventeen years. He thought of some lyrics and then started whistling the song, "What do you do with a Drunken Sailor, What do you do with a drunken sailor, What do you do with a drunken sailor, early in the morning?" He chuckled when he remembered one of the last song lines, "Put him in a long boat till he's sober, put him in a long boat till he's sober, put him in a long boat till he's sober early in the morning."

Frank arrived at his mother's house later than he had planned. It was not late, late, but it was dark; already past 7:30 p.m. He opened the unlocked door. Immediately the lights went on and off, and on again. Then the shouts and song began, "Surprise, Surprise! Happy

Birthday to you, Happy Birthday to you, Happy Birthday dear, Gilbert, Frank, Happy Birthday to you!"

His mom and brother, Lou, were there to greet him. First, they hid in the darkness, flashed the lights, and then sang the celebration song. All this planning and partying to welcome him home.

Chocolate cake was on the table, seventeen candles were quickly lit. Lou reached into the ice box and pulled out ice cream. Frank blew out the candles, almost forgetting to make a wish, but he quickly corrected his error and secretly thought a wish for himself.

Frank was pleased and felt so relaxed and happy. He did feel at home. "How did you know I was coming?"

"Well," his mother answered, "we've been expecting you all afternoon. Mrs. Balmer, from Lake Farm Dairy called. She thought you were hitchhiking."

"I was." answered Frank, as he laid his pillow case on the couch, "but that didn't work too well."

Lou came over and gave Frank a strong hug. "Next time brother, call me I'll come and get you. I've got a new Studebaker."

Frank raised his eyebrows in surprise. "You've got to be kidding." He was amazed that Lou had a car and flabbergasted it was a new Studebaker.

As he returned his brother's embrace, he said, "I rode in a new Studebaker, but that one won't last long if the same driver keeps it."

"That bad?" Lou asked.

"I'd say much worse than bad."

Mary hugged Frank and told him how glad she was to see him. "I left dinner on the stove for you. I cooked up a stew with meat, potatoes, and carrots. I also baked some biscuits!"

Frank looked inside the big kettle. "Great! I'll eat that once I eat my cake and ice cream; birthdays are always a good time to eat dessert first, and then chow down the main meal."

He was tired and hungry; however, he also felt energized seeing his mom and brother.

He quickly shoved his food down, and accepted extra servings. Then he answered their questions about his dairy life experiences. He hesitated to tell them about his future plans. "I want to follow the harvest, work on farm lands, and get work wherever I can."

Mary went into the kitchen to wash dishes and let the boys visit. She was not eager to hear about plans her son had about leaving. She wanted to only linger with the happy thought that two of her boys were home, sitting in her own living room.

"Be smart, Frank," Lou advised. "Come on down to Central Market. Hell, the Lord knows we need good workers. I know the boss will hire you."

Frank thought a moment. Then he asked, "Is that the same foreman that was there two years ago?"

"Yeah," answered Lou wondering what difference it would make. "Why?"

"You know he doesn't like me," replied Frank.

"No, I don't know. You're a great worker. When Mrs. Balmer called she praised your work up and down. She told mom all about your 'diligence and trustworthiness' as an employee on the dairy farm."

"True," Frank answered, "but remember when us kids went berry picking out by Steward's place?"

"Sure I remember," said Lou, thinking back to those earlier days. "I remember getting my baskets full of berries while you sat there with your bowl, and didn't you bring cream and sugar with you? You did, didn't you? You'd sit there eating all the berries you picked - even adding cream and sugar!"

Frank chuckled, "Yeah, well... not only do you and I remember, but also your boss Ben remembers - I'd bet on it."

Lou thought for a moment, "We were at Ben's place back then? Wow, I guess you're right?"

"Yeah," answered Frank. "I got a good scolding, and he told Mr. Steward. Then I had to go back and pick berries the next day with no pay and no berries to eat."

"I don't remember all that," said Lou. "But, I believe you. Ben lacked a sense of humor - still lacks a sense of humor, but despite all that he needs workers. If you want a job down at Central, you call me. Ben likes me, and he'll be glad to have two hard working brothers." Lou looked right into Frank's eyes and dearly repeated the word, "brother."

Frank sat quietly for a few moments, "I'll think about it, but first I want to try working on farm lands. I want to see what's beyond Portland."

"How are you going to get from farm to farm?" Lou dared to ask. Then before Frank could answer, Lou knew. He looked at his dear brother and sighed. Then Lou whispered, so Mary would not hear. "Don't ride the boxcars, Frank; it's dangerous and you could get arrested and end up working on a chain gang. That's if you're lucky. You could also be injured badly… or get killed. Come on down to the meat plant. I'll get you a job."

Frank wanted to please his brother, but first he had to get away. He wanted to leave town for a while. He had money in his pocket, and he had farmhand experience. For sure he wasn't going to hitchhike from state to state. The boxcars were the way to go.

Frank had been thinking and planning about this idea for months. He visualized himself riding and seeing the country-sides. He planned to leave the next day.

He walked into the kitchen and held his mother in a warm embrace. Then he placed extra cash into her apron pocket. It was more money than what he had previously, and secretly, taken from her. She was surprised and pleased. She remembered the reason why he felt he had to repay. She only smiled and kissed him on the check. "Take care, Frank, take care."

Tomorrow he would depart, but tonight he and Lou would take a ride in Lou's Studebaker. Frank trusted Lou's driving.

Chapter Ten

Portland, Oregon to Miles City, Montana
1928 Seventeen Years Old

Despite the warnings his brother had cautioned him about the night before, he had a plan. He washed up in the bathroom basin, got dressed and sorted through his pillow case bag. He took out unnecessary items, and then added a couple oranges, bananas, and a tin drinking cup. After eating one piece of toast, a bowl of mush, and drinking a cup of hot coffee, he headed out the door.

He walked down the streets and over the bridge to the Portland Railroad Station enjoying the cool morning air. He knew a train was leaving at 8:15 a.m. heading to Montana. It was a passenger train, but there were freight trains leaving too. Some of the boxcars were empty.

Two hobos climbed into one of the boxcars. Frank followed them. By the time Frank got to the car and looked inside, the two men were seated in one of the far dark corners of the car. He yelled back at them and asked, "This train gonna to leave pretty soon?"

"Yeah," one of the men answered.

Frank asked, "Where's it headed to?"

"Where do you want to go?"

Frank knew his answer; he had given it lots of thought. "I'd like to go to Montana."

"Get on board then, this car will end up in Montana."
Frank climbed into the car. Not far from the other two riders, he sat on the rigid wood floor. "Never ridden on a boxcar before have ya?"

Frank looked at the hobo that asked. The guy wore two pair of overalls, two shirts and a long coat even though the day was warm. His black boots had soles that were torn. A gray wool cap covered part of his left forehead. Beside him was a red kerchief bundle that hung on the end of a stick. He was unshaven, but no real beard. Frank figured he looked about forty years old.

"What makes you think this is my first time?" Frank finally responded to his question.

"Well, I could tell when you asked, 'where we're headed,' you need to learn on your own which cars go where and which ones will stand still; maybe for weeks at a time. Also you're too clean shaven to have been on the road. Looks like you've been eatin okay too. You're too young. You should be with your family."

Frank nodded and agreed. "You're right man, but I'm gonna try my hand at earning some money following the harvest."

The man sighed like he heard bad news. He saw something about Frank that indicated a determination and he heard in Frank's voice a firm declaration. He decided it was no use to talk any sense to this kid; let him live his distorted dream and see what real life is all about.

He scooted closer to Frank to give him a few words of advice.

"Okay boy, listen to me. I'm gonna give you a few free lessons about boxcar riding; listen so you don't have to learn the hard way." As he spoke the train started to move. The boxcar door stayed ajar. The rattling began and the swaying movement caused them to lean against the corner wall. The noise got louder, but the advising hobo raised his voice louder too.

"First of all, no matter how cold it gets don't try to start a fire inside a box car. It's been tired, let's just say, disaster number one. "If you see a family in the boxcars stay away from that car. We have a code, leave families alone.

"Stay out of refrigerated cars they're called Reefers. These cars have cage-like compartments; figure those are ice cars. In the winter there might be no ice and they might be heated; don't be fooled. It will be warm, but when the door opens you'll be dead. Those heaters put out carbon monoxide gas. No air in those cars. Never ride in one!"

He paused. Frank was quiet too. The word dead echoed through their minds. The danger of riding boxcars all of a sudden became real.

The hobo continued his lessons as Frank paid close attention. "We don't ride in mail trains. You see bags of U.S. Mail just keep walking by. You'll end up on a chain gang for sure if you get in one of those cars; same with silk trains."

Finally, Frank had a chance to ask a question. "What are silk trains?"

"Silk trains carry silk; maybe, millions of dollars worth of silk. They have the right of way over all trains even passenger trains. It's a federal offense to be on a silk train."

"How will I know a silk train from any other train?"

"Oh, you'll know. They are heavily guarded and they are flat bed cars. Each car will look like it is carrying a huge steel safe. They move fast and only stop when they reach their destination. Last of all, you're packin' too much. Get rid of stuff. Hell, I'm packing too much. I carry this bindle stick, but when jumping trains it's too much. We both need to take my advice."

Except for the chugging of the engine and the rhythm of the train wheels, all was quiet. The train moved faster. This was Frank's first train ride. He had been listening so carefully to this hobo's advice he barely had time to sense the experience of his journey.

The hobo stood up hanging onto the side of the car. "I'll tell ya when we're near Montana, then follow me. I'll show you how and when to jump off this here movin train."

Frank nodded his thanks. The hobo wandered back to his original corner. He took off his coat and cap and got into a resting position. He talked quietly to the other hobo. Frank had no idea what they were saying. Maybe, he was telling his friend what a fool this young kid is to think he can ride the trains and follow the harvest.

Frank repeated in his mind all that the hobo had told him. Then his attention turned to the view outside of the moving car. Green fields were flat across the land. They had already passed the rivers and some of the mountain scenery. Frank did not feel tired he wanted to stay awake. He realized this was his first time, leaving the only city that he had ever known. He was going to a state he thought he would like to see.

Montana was 548 miles from Portland. He figured it would take all day and maybe into the night to get there. He debated whether to eat his snacks or wait. He decided to wait. He wanted to see when the other two guys ate, and how they spaced out their time. This was like going to a new school. Looking at these two sleeping hobos, he smiled. They were like professors: professors of life.

*****

Frank realized his next lesson would be the technique of jumping off a moving train. He needed the exact moment, and the body readiness for a successful landing. Several times he thought the moment was right, but his two fellow hobos yelled, "No, wait!"

So he waited. Then the timing was perfect. The train had slowed; the track was near a wide field of tall grass. "Now! "The three guys jumped. Frank landed on his knees; not exactly how he imagined. He figured next time he'd do better and land on his feet. He checked his sore knees. They were okay. Thankfully, his pillowcase bag of belongings was still with him. He looked around to see the other two riders, but they were already off in the distance.

Frank was alone now to explore the state of Montana. At first he followed the tracks, but it seemed like he was getting further from any town area so he headed across the fields looking for a road. Finally, he came to a road with a sign: 5 miles to Miles City. That was odd because Frank had intended to be in Missoula, Montana. He knew he had slept a while, but he didn't realize that his hours of sleep took him up to 400 miles farther than he intended.

He shook his head in disbelief, but it didn't really matter. No one in Montana was meeting him, there was no place in Montana that he needed to be, and he had no time frame. He realized he was free to be in any town, any time he wanted to be there. Unfortunately, his stomach was giving him a time frame. It was demanding food soon. What food he had packed he had eaten hours ago; fortunately, he had money. All he had to do was find a restaurant.

As he walked, he figured five miles wasn't that far. Miles City would be his destination. At first, he felt fine, but the day was warm; he had two shirts on, and he was wearing two pair of pants. He stopped to take one shirt off. He wadded it into his pillowcase. Rolled up his sleeves, and lowered his cap over his forehead, to keep the sun from hurting his eyes. He continued his journey.

After an hour and an half of walking, and pausing to look around, he arrived in the small town. He was surprised to see several saddled horses tied to posts, and many horse and buggies along the roadside; yet there were only a few automobiles. He definitely was in a western town. The only place that looked like there might be food had a sign high on the front wooden frame, Stockman Bar. With the hope of a good meal, he went inside. Sure enough, there was a counter and bar stools, but also, posted on the wall, was a menu list of food items.

He ordered the roast beef dinner, a cup of coffee, and begged for a tall glass of water. He turned his bar stool. The man sitting next to him appeared to be a train engineer.

The guy looked back at Frank. "New in town?" he asked.

"Yeah." Frank answered. "Just got off the Pacific Northern."

"Well, so did I. How do you like our new passenger depot? It just opened up last year. Mighty fine building. We use to have only a shed standing there. Now, it's very impressive."

Frank just nodded; he didn't want to admit he jumped off the train miles before Miles City. He didn't even see the train depot. He had his pillowcase under the bar stool; maybe this engineer didn't realize that Frank had taken his first hobo ride into Montana.

"What's it like being an engineer?" Frank asked.

"Well, I love running trains back and forth. I travel east and west every day, except Sundays."

Frank always felt eager to learn more about any subject so when he got the chance he asked questions. "How do you keep these big steam locomotives moving?"

"Well, you see, I don't do it alone. I've got a helper: the fireman. He keeps stoking the fire to keep that furnace hot. The pressure gauge shows him when to add coal and when to add water; we have to keep the steam going."

"My job is to keep the right speed. I need to keep gentle pressure on the throttle as I change the speed. After a while one gets the right feel of it and it becomes natural. Knowing how to use the brake handle when it's time to brake is the other part of my responsibility. There are rules too; we have to blow the whistle: 2 longs, 1 short and 1 long whenever we come to an intersection or a bridge. Have to tell the world we're coming. Hopefully, if they're in the way, they move. If not, we blast that whistle as long and loud as we can. Trains are not easy to stop. It's all a matter of feeling: feeling the throttle, feeling the brake handle, feeling each train."

He took a long pause and started to eat the food that was placed in front of him. "Yeah," he repeated, "once you get the feel of it, there is no other job. You and the train are one. The train needs you, and you need the train."

Frank felt he could understand. He had only taken one long ride, but already he felt akin to the train. Right now he was a wanderer in Montana. His plan was to take another train ride to somewhere, but he wasn't sure where that somewhere was going to be.

The engineer stopped eating, "By the way, I'm Edward." Frank introduced himself to him and thanked him for the visit. Edward said he enjoyed their conversation too. Once Edward left, Frank asked the waiter where he could get a place to clean up. The waiter must have figured that Frank had jumped off the train because he told him the only free place was the hobo jungle: down near the railroad station at a place called Milwaukee Park.

Frank paid his bill and thanked the waiter. He headed to the hobo jungle. Even though he had heard of such places, he had no idea what to expect. Once he neared the end of town, there was only a dirt path to follow. After walking a ways, he was relieved to see two rivers joining together: seeing the water helped him to feel cooler.

Other than the rivers, the scenery consisted of dry grass and gray mountains off in the distance: much different than the familiar green forest trees in the Portland area. Every once in a while, he would see a cow or some horses behind fence areas. He also noticed the blue sky. The largest sight in Montana seemed to be the wide blue sky - definitely lots of sky.

He was close to the train depot, the new station that Edward had described. He did not notice any hobo jungle. He gazed around, moved his body in all directions to see if he was missing something. There was a wide field across the road from where he stood. He walked more toward the field. He saw some sparse trees and bushes growing along the river's edge. He realized that, maybe behind those trees, hobos had created a space for themselves. He started to walk that direction.

As he got closer, he could actually smell a pot of mulligan stew: the odor of beans and bacon. He wasn't hungry but he walked gingerly in that direction. Then he noticed the camping area. A fire pit was there with a blazing fire and a heavy iron pot hanging above the fire pit. A clothesline was tied to two trees and clothes were hanging on the string. Buckets were scattered around on the ground, some filled with water, and he noticed mirrors hanging on some trees. Yes, he could clean up here and rest. He needed to decide what he was going to do and where he might be headed next.

He was about to set his bag down when a bearded guy tapped him on the shoulder. "Lookin' for a place to stay for awhile?"

"Yeah," Frank answered back, "I kinda need to clean up."

"Well, you've come to the right place. See that giant bathtub out there?" He pointed to the river. "That's the Yellowstone River - hell we've got two rivers here. You go upstream a ways and you get to the Tongue River. No one seems to care which river you wash up in. So make yourself at home. Place your belongings anywhere you want. We don't steal from each other."

Frank believed him and set his bag down beside some brush. He looked through his pillowcase and found his bar of soap: no towel. He'd use his shirt for a towel. He was hot and sweaty. Not ready to strip and jump in the water, but he definitely would splash around and cool off. He brought his extra shirt along. He decided to wash one shirt and hang it on the clothes line. For basic survival he'd use this hobo jungle to his advantage.

After cleaning up, he sat on the ground and looked around. He noticed that some of the guys were much older, but there were a few young ones too. Frank was not the youngest guy around. Some were what Frank would call kids. It was September. He wondered why they were not in school, why they were wanderers and needed to stay in a hobo jungle.

Then some action caught his eye. Two guys were wearing boxing gloves and sparing with each other. Now Frank was interested. He walked closer to them. He watched their movements intently. Finally, one of the guys turned to Frank and asked, "Ever boxed before?"

"No," answered Frank, "but I want to learn how."

"Ok," said the biggest guy. He took the gloves off his opponent and threw them at Frank.

Frank didn't hesitate. He remembered that he had to learn. He may have to defend himself, but also he had to get revenge. Even though he was away from Mr. Steward, freely traveling on his own, he hadn't forgotten his pain.

He had just freshened himself from the cool water; now he would probably get sweaty again, but he was willing to try to box.

Frank put the gloves on and looked directly in the eyes of this large guy. The man stared back but then spoke softly.

"Ok, before we start, we're goin' warm up. It's called shadow boxing. We're not goin hit each other. We're goin swing our arms like we might hit each other, but really we're not even near one another."

70

The big guy moved back and demonstrated. He swung his arms toward Frank, but nowhere near him. Frank copied the motions.

"Good, okay, now do the same only while your feet jog in place. You know, run but don't go anywhere."

Once again he demonstrated the technique. Frank followed the example. After several minutes of this warm-up, the big guy gave the next direction,

"Okey dokey, now this time you jab at my gloves, only my gloves." He emphasized the word only and repeated his command, "only my gloves, not extra hard just give some jabs. When I move my gloves, you keep your eye on them and jab at the center."

As soon as he stopped talking, he started to jog quickly and move his hands in all directions. Frank jabbed at the center of his hands, not extra hard, but consistent with a steady rhythm. He was accurate and never missed the center of the gloves no matter how quickly the big guy moved.

"Yeah you got it. You're a natural. That's it for today. That's a beginning lesson in boxing. Next time we'll try sparring."

Frank was anxious to learn more. "Why not today?"

"No, Boy. You did well, but the feel of boxing takes time. You need to dwell on what you felt today. Next time you'll do more. You'll find more guys to box with - if not here in other hobo jungles. Us boxers like to keep up; we've got to travel to get from one match to another - so you'll learn. Don't worry, you'll get the hang of it; boxing will come easy for you."

Frank said, "Thanks" and gave up trying to convince him to let him try some more. He had another errand to do. Realizing he was packing too much, to easily travel on trains, he decided to send his mom some of his stuff. Keeping one change of clothes meant he would probably have to wear extra clothes. A toothbrush, soap and a razor blade that might be all he needed.

So he hiked back to town. He found the post office. He asked for a piece of paper, a pen and a box. He wrote his mom a note: *Dear Mom, I'm in Montana… Great place to be. Decided not to keep all this stuff. Please save it for me. Will let you know off and on how I'm doing. Don't worry. Love, Frank*

He sent his package and note off to Portland. Now with everything either in his pockets, or part of what he was wearing, he had nothing to hold. His hands were free.

*****

That night, Frank missed his pillowcase. At least, with his few belongings, it made for a good pillow. Now he was without much of anything. He felt his shirt on the line. It was dry; that was what he used for a pillow. He found his own space, away from the fire pit, and got comfortable on the ground. He covered his face with his cap for privacy and bug protection. He slept.

It was 7:00 am when he woke. The scent of food was inviting. Could that smell possibly be bacon and eggs? He walked toward the fire. Several men were gathered around eating.

The morning was cool. He put his extra shirt on over his other shirt, added his jacket and placed his cap on his head. This would be his attire no matter what the weather.

"Mind if I eat?" He asked no one in particular, just whoever appeared to be in charge of the meal.

Several guys answered at once. "Yeah, eat!" A couple guys added, "That's what it's here for, to eat." "Get it while it's hot" "You wait, and it's all gone."

Frank sat on a rock and started to eat with his fingers. "Hey," one guy yelled at him, "we've got forks man. Use a fork." He handed Frank a fork.

"Sometimes town people help us out. You know, give us food, things we need. That's how we get by, with a little help now and then. Where you headed next?"

Frank looked at the older guy sitting next to him. He, too, was wearing extra clothes for a summer day. He looked tan and healthy so wandering and staying at hobo jungles appeared to be okay - at least for him.

Before Frank could answer, the guy started to give Frank some directional guidelines. "This town has two railroads. You probably came on the Pacific Railroad, but here there is another railroad called the Milwaukee Railroad. It goes all the way to New York. When you get to the train station you will see two tracks. If you don't want to go too far take the track for the Northern Pacific, or if you want to go cross country take, what we call, the Milwaukee Road. How far are you thinkin'?"

Frank paused; he really was going minute by minute. He was not sure of his plans. "Well, I guess I need work. I'm willing to do any work. I was thinking if the farmers are harvesting, I'd work for them. Know of any places where I could get work?"

The man put his hand on his chin and thought a while. "I heard tell that if you want to follow the harvest, start in North Dakota, the next state over. I heard they need workers.

I'm hanging round here a little while longer, but if you want work, head east. Take the Northern Pacific, and stay awake. You'll be in North Dakota soon."

Frank thanked him and went back to get seconds. He realized he better eat well if he was going to start working. He liked his freedom, but he knew money would go quickly. He would take the advice and head to North Dakota.

After filling up on a satisfying breakfast, Frank walked toward the train depot. He was curious about these two railroad tracks. The engineer was right; even seeing the train depot from a distance, Frank realized it was a mighty fine brick train station. He also saw the two tracks - one going slightly to the right and the other headed slightly to the left. He saw a train with the words, "Northern Pacific." That was the track he wanted to be on.

He knew he could not catch a train right at the station: too many people around would notice that he was trying to ride free. He did not have a train ticket. So instead he walked up the dirt path next to the tracks.

This would be a first for him, but he would have to jump aboard as the train passed by. His previous "hobo professors" didn't teach him any instructions about jumping on moving trains. Now Frank wished he would have asked some pertinent questions. What tricks are there to getting on a moving train? What are the no- nos? Frank was wishing they were nearby to tell him the exact moment of when to run, when to grab, and what to grab. His mind was racing with questions as he walked down the dirt path.

Then he heard the sound of the train coming. It was moving slow. Frank stopped walking and focused his eyes to watch each car as it passed. First the engine, then the tender (water tank car), closed freight cars, then several box cars in a row with opened doors. Frank ran like the wind. He picked up speed and ran as he used to run with his friend Tommy when they raced each other across Mr. Steward's fields. He saw a ladder on the side of one freight car. He reached, he grabbed the rail and pulled his weight up; his feet landed hard on the floor of the boxcar.

Two hobos were in the car watching him. "Good jump man! Looks like you know what you're doing kid. Come sit a spell and enjoy the ride!"

Frank sat and made himself comfortable. No way was he going to tell these guys that this was his first jump onto a moving train. His heart beat extra fast, and he had to catch his breath before he could say a word. Finally, he took a long breath and then asked, "How far to Dickinson, North Dakota?"

"Not far." One of the men was quick to respond. "It's just over 100 miles. If you end up in Bismarck you've gone too far."

Chapter Eleven

Dickinson, North Dakota 1928
Seventeen Years Old

Suddenly, Frank realized he would have to jump off the train, decide on his own when to take the leap. For a long time, he stood and stared, at what appeared as, moving ground. The train slowed slightly when he saw a sign that stated "Dickinson" it was then he made his jump. He landed on two feet and amazed himself on how easy that felt. The feeling was like beginners luck, when a person plays a game for the first time, doesn't understand the rules, but wins.

Once the train had passed, he gazed across the fields at his surroundings. The area appeared vast, but sparse, like there was no need to make choices. He only noticed one farm house off in the distance. The rest of the land was bare. He could tell that there was a house, a barn and a large shed of some kind. Maybe, they needed a worker.

The day was warm, he was glad he was carrying nothing. Everything he owned he wore, or put in his deep overall pockets. He took off his jacket and threw it over his shoulders. He started his hike toward the farm.

His hiking distance was over a mile, before he arrived at the open gate. The gate had a name on the fence "Jennings." "I'll have to speak to a Mr. Jennings" he said out loud to no one but himself. He whistled as he walked up the long dirt path to the house. There were a couple guys off in the field - a long distance off. He wondered if he should plow through the field and talk with them or knock on the farm house door. He decided the door would be best. He was hot and thirsty. His main concern was a tall glass of water.

He rapped on the door. Dogs barked inside. Frank loved dogs so hearing dogs made him feel welcomed. A lady wearing a house dress, and an apron covered somewhat with spots of flour, answered the door. She looked to be in her early 30's. Frank noticed her nice complexion and tanned arms. Her dark hair was pinned on top of her head, the way his mom wore her hair. She had a friendly looking smile. "Yes?" she asked Frank, and then she hollered at the dogs, "Quiet! Enough!" Immediately the two collie dogs obeyed. They sat eyeing Frank.

Madam, I'm here to ask about work. Seeing if you need any help for the fall harvest."

"Did you just get off that train?"

"Yes, madam I did."

"Where are you from?"

"I'm from out west - Portland, Oregon."

"Well, that's a long ways. You must be hot, thirsty and hungry?"

"Well, yes, Madam."

"Come on in, we've got food and yes we need workers. The Lord Himself must have brought you."

Frank was much obliged, but he didn't think the Lord deserved the credit he felt he was doing pretty well on his own – getting' around okay and managing his life.

Mrs. Jennings, as Frank learned to call her, was gracious and showed him around the house. It was a large log house with a living room filled with several upholstered chairs and a brown felt davenport. There was a RCA radio cabinet in the corner. In the other corner was a wood stove. Next to the stove was a stack of wood. They walked down a narrow hallway. On the walls were black and white family photos. Flowered wallpaper as the background. The wooden ceiling boards were painted white.

There was a separate dining room with a long picnic wooden table with wooden benches on each side. Twenty people could easily eat at this long table. Mrs. Jennings was describing her rooms and her furniture. "We only have two sons, but we often have farm helpers and here's where we all eat. During harvest times, we serve two main meals breakfast and dinner. My oldest son, Jeremy and I serve lunches out in the fields when we have workers."

She pointed out the window to where the outhouse was, and beyond the bunk house, and the barn. After her brief tour she invited him to sit a spell, until her husband and her boys came back from the fields.

They returned to the kitchen area. From the water pump, she filled a pitcher of cold spring water. Frank could smell the hot biscuits, fresh from the oven. She served him a tall glass of water, put the pitcher, and the biscuits on the table. Moving aside, she went back to her kitchen duties.

As if she forgot something, she came back and handed Frank a newspaper. "Here" she said, "while you're waitin' you can catch up on the news of North Dakota. There's an article in there all about Lindbergh doing his solo flight last year, if you want to read about his venture."

Frank sat at the table, enjoying hot biscuits, and drinking a tall glass of water, as if he was the man of the house, rather than a possible hired hand. He glanced at the headline: "Dakota Press Paper published since 1789." He read about speed regulations needed for autoists driving through town. Laws were needed because autos were running "like blue streaks or turning corners on 2 wheels." Another in town problem was "kids running over lawns and young girls gathering other people's flowers."

Two other articles caught his attention. One was "Homesteading for five dollars per acre." He secretly wished he had the funds to invest in that offer. The other headline stated that Ford had sold over 300,000 autos and was giving refunds to buyers of this last year - refunds of forty dollars! Frank didn't qualify for that offer either. Sighing, he thought about owning land and having a car. He didn't feel sad though, because he was comfortable, and work was a definite possibility. At that moment, six crew workers came in the doorway, two young boys and Mr. Jennings. They all wore overalls and dark dusty boots. They were strong, young looking guys. The two sons were also wearing overalls and boots. They wore straw hats too that they took off as soon as they came inside. Mr. Jennings was taller than Frank, probably about 6'5". He appeared more muscular than Frank, obviously a strong worker.

They all seemed surprised to see Frank sitting at the table, but not too surprised, because hobos coming off the train and eating at the table was common nowadays.

Mr. Jennings shook Frank's hand and introduced himself. He too asked Frank if he wanted work. In more detail, he asked if he had ever worked with horses, or ever did any farm planting. Frank remembered about his adventure with Old Blue and how he had raced through the fields until Old Blue wouldn't let him ride anymore. And he thought about Mr. Steward plowing the fields and planting seeds and then how he and Tommy dug up the dirt to find Indian arrow heads. He decided that those experiences helped to qualify him for work. "Yes, sir," he answered, "I've had experience on the farm." Then he truthfully, told about his quality work on the dairy farm.

"Well, this ain't no dairy farm. This is wheat and vegetables, but if you're as good a worker, as you confess to be, then welcome. The boys will show you where the bunk house is. We always have room for one more worker.

"We're through for today. Dinner will be at 6:00. Boys, show Frank where he can bunk up and get settled." That was Frank's initiation to the Jennings farm house.

Frank had a chance to wash up and sit on his assigned bunk before dinner. At 6:00 p.m. a dinner bell rang. Frank was more than ready to chow down a meal. He was pleased to see the table spread: fried chicken, mashed potatoes, gravy, biscuits, and corn on the cob. All homemade vittles.

Mr. Jennings said a table prayer. "Thank you Lord for this healthy grub we're about to eat, for these workers, for my wife and my two sons, for Frank our newest worker. For all this we give thanks. Amen." Everyone at the table agreed, "Amen."

Suddenly, everyone quickly dug into the bowls and passed food plates. Frank actually visualized pigs hogging the trough. These men were rough and ready when it came to feasting. Only Mrs. Jennings ate in a slow and polite manner. At times, she corrected her son's table manners. Otherwise, little was said. Food consumption was more priority than conversation.

Everyone cleared and rinsed their plate using the water pump by the sink. Mrs. Jennings and her sons did the rest of the clean up. Frank wandered around the acreage before going back to the bunk house. He had some tobacco that was given to him at the hobo jungle, so he rolled a cigarette and smoked as he walked around.

He discovered Mr. Jennings owned nine horses and several pigs. He also had chickens and hens in a chicken coop. Beef cows were grazing in a fenced field. Some corn stalks were standing tall. He saw evidence of green pumpkins yet to ripen and some that were already reddish orange. Beans and peas were growing on sticks ready to pick. He estimated that Mr. Jennings owned about ten acres of land. There was plenty of work to do here. Frank was eager to start, but first he needed a restful night.

A rooster crowed at 5:30 a.m. The men all woke up, did a quick wash-up and shave. In the farm house, they gathered again at the long table for breakfast.

Once again, Mrs. Jennings was ready with scrambled eggs, toast, mush, milk and strong wake-up coffee. Frank ate as much as he felt he was allowed, knowing he would need strength for his work. Already the temperature was in the low 60's, it would probably be a hot afternoon.

While eating, Mr. Jennings introduced the workers to Frank. He called their names and then asked them to say something about themselves to Frank. "I'm Joe. I love horses and working with them. Mostly, I take care of the horses. I'm a full-time worker here."

"I'm Jack. I live in the town of Dickinson. I've got a wife and a small son, age two. I help Mr. Jennings during harvest times."

"I'm Arthur. This is my brother Raymond. We live in town and only help when Mr. Jennings needs help. He's a good man to work for."

The last two men were rather serious-looking and quiet. Mr. Jennings called them Diego and Antonio. He admitted they didn't speak much English. They were from New Mexico. They came up to North Dakota with a missionary. Mr. Jennings gave a smile and praised their work. "I've got a great team here. And my two sons work in the fields too. You will see. All great workers! Gracias, amigos! Let's get started." Several men shook Frank's hand and welcomed him to the farm as they stepped out in the cool morning air to start the day.

A horse-drawn wagon was outside to haul the men to the fields. One of the crew men, Joe, was holding the reins and leading the horses. They rode out to the fields. Joe yelled at Frank, "Here's your stop." Frank leaped off the wagon. Mr. Jennings was already standing in the field waiting for him. He came to Frank's side. "See these rows of hay out here?"

"Yeah!" Frank saw long rows of hay on the ground.

"Well, my son Jack is coming down here with a wagon pulled by two horses and with two pitch forks. You take one pitch fork and sweep the hay and pile it on the wagon. Got it?"

"Sure." Frank quietly answered.

"You've used a pitch fork before – right?"

"Sure." Frank responded more loudly and with resolution, thinking how hard can it be to pitch hay into a wagon?

"Well, Jack will be here in a few minutes."

Frank looked again at the long rows. He said out loud, yet somewhat to himself, "This is gonna take hours of work."

Mr. Jennings was already walking across the field, but he heard Frank's comment. "Hell," he yelled back, "it will take days of work."

Within minutes, Jack was there. He pulled the reins and stopped the horses. Dust was blowing in the air from the horses and the wagon wheels. He handed Frank a large pitch fork. It had several prongs and was wider and heavier than Frank had imagined.

Frank started to shovel up the hay. He tossed the hay onto the back of the wagon. He did it several times, scrape, lift, and toss. Twelve year old Jack jumped off the wagon seat. "Here, let me show you something." He grabbed the other pitch fork off the back of the wagon. He ran toward the hay row, took a huge scoop of hay and tossed it on the wagon.

Frank was amazed that the young lean kid gathered three times the amount of hay he had on his pitch fork. He did the same demonstration three times, each time with energy and strength. He stopped and climbed back on the wagon. "Do it like that," he yelled at Frank, "otherwise this job will take months!"

"Got it," said Frank. He only needed to be told once. His next pile of hay surpassed what Jack did. This job required muscle strength, but a twelve year old kid wasn't gonna to outdo him.

He worked fast and furious. Successfully, he threw piles of hay on the wagon. Jack made sure the hay went evenly across the wagon boards as the pile got higher. They were a good team.

At noon, Mrs. Jennings and her second son, thirteen-year-old Jeremy, came out in the fields on another horse-drawn wagon. They brought food and buckets of water with tin cups. Jack and Frank stopped working. Frank wiped the sweat from his hands and face. Mrs. Jennings offered trays of ham sandwiches, homemade potato salad, and watermelon.

While sitting in the fields under a shady lone tree, they enjoyed a cooling, nourishing break. After eating, it was back to pitching hay.

On this first day, Jack and Frank spoke little. As the week continued, they became a co-operative team, and conversation became comfortable. Jack wanted to know about Frank's childhood days. Frank only shared some good-time memories.

He told about fun times with his Indian friend, Brave Heart (Tommy.) He didn't tell about Old Blue getting tired and stubborn – only about the excitement of the long horseback ride through the fields and down the dirt paths.

He shared stories about his school experiences and about winning the spelling bee contest. Jack said his schooling only happened between harvest times. His said his classes would not begin until

November. He and his brother would then ride their horses four miles down the road to the one-room schoolhouse. If winter got too bad they would have to do home schooling. Their mom made sure they did their reading, 'riting and 'rithemetic during those winter days.

Frank listened as Jack explained how he didn't care much for school. He didn't think he needed it because his plan was only to work with his dad and stay on the farm.

Jack admitted Jeremy was different. Jeremy loved to read and write; that was what he liked. Jeremy didn't much relish farm work.

Days went by with the same chore of piling hay on the wagon, and then piling stacks of hay in the barn. Finally, there was enough hay stored to last for the winter feedings.

Frank knew the other workers were running plows and making furrows to plant wheat grains. That was Frank's next job. Every day was a hard, hot grueling workday, but Frank liked working the plow, holding the reins and leading the horses. Yet, at 4:30 quitting time, he was anxious to wash up in the cool water basins by the bunkhouse. He realized this refuge and work would only last till the end of October. Then the wheat would be planted. Mr. Jennings wouldn't need the same amount of workers.

The crew of seven would reduce down to three. Frank knew Diego, Antonio and Joe would remain as full time workers. The other men would return to their homes. Frank was the only hobo, and maybe the only hobo who had stayed for a whole month of work. Each man he had worked with, he respected. They were all great at their jobs.

Mr. Jennings was a fair boss too. Frank would be generously paid, but then he would have to move on. Till then, every day they worked in the fields. Only Sundays were days of rest.

At the end of October, Frank left the Jennings farm. As he got near the gate, he heard Jack yell his name. "Frank, Frank, wait I've got something to tell ya. Wait!"

Frank stopped walking and waited for Jack. Jack was out of breath and panted for a minute before he was able to speak. "I just want to tell you Frank… I just want to tell you," He paused to breathe some more and to get the proper words together. "I just want to tell you… you're… you're a good worker!"

Frank smiled remembering his first day there and how Jack showed him how to pitch hay. Frank looked directly into Jack's eyes. He put his hand out to shake Jack's hand like grown men do when making an agreement.

"Keep doing your school work and help your dad. I'm telling you, Jack, you're already a good farmer. You've proven that you can do a man's work."

They held their hands together and did a final hand shake. Frank walked through the gate. He turned and waved. Jack stood and watched Frank leave.

Chapter Twelve

Dickinson, North Dakota to Chicago, Illinois 1928 Seventeen Years Old

Heading back to the area where he had jumped off the train earlier, Frank could see the Dickinson sign. The train came and slowed down. That's when he jumped on, and grabbed a rail, that was part of an open door boxcar.

Startled, he saw this car had several hobos riding inside. He decided to ride on top of the car. There was a ladder. He leaned on the outside wall, grabbed a ladder rung and started to climb. A few other guys were on top.

The day was warm. Frank thought why not enjoy the view and the breeze from up here? He had money in his pocket. Mr. Jennings had paid him generously: five dollars over the promised pay. Riding inside a boxcar with lots of riders made Frank somewhat fearful. There might be an argument or fight among the men. Frank figured he was safer on top of the boxcar this round where there were fewer men. He found his space and sat down. He watched the scenery pass quickly like a fast motion movie.

The key to the safety of this ride was not to fall asleep. He needed to stay awake and decide where his next destination would be. He wished he had a map. He wasn't sure when or where he was going to jump off. Maybe he'd make the leap when other hobos jumped.

In reality, he wouldn't be making the decision. The yard bulls would make the decision.

The ride was smooth. The scary troubling part was riding through a dark, low tunnel. The smoke from the steam locomotive didn't blow the black ashes and hot cinders into the sky; instead, these particles of soot landed on top of the train. Frank had to cover his head with his jacket and bury his face close to his shirt to keep from getting the debris in his eyes and the burning cinders on his face.

So far, tunnels were the only concern Frank was experiencing. He felt okay being on top of the train. The view was great, like being at the theater with the widest screen anyone has ever seen. On this sunny day, the land was vast and open, the sky was bright blue. The train moved at a steady smooth pace.

Frank wasn't alone. There were a few other men riding on top, but the noise of the train didn't allow conversation. Frank didn't mind, he wanted to be alone in his thoughts. He was concentrating on where he was going to be next. Also, thinking about how to spend or save the money he was carrying.

He was careful with these first hobo earnings. He only placed 5 one dollar- bills in his pocket. The rest of his pay 3 more five-dollar bills, were hidden in his shoes. Soon that would prove to be a wise decision.

The train was roaring along and Frank was feeling relaxed when all of a sudden, everything changed. The train slowed and braked. They were far away from any train station. Frank couldn't figure out why they were stopping.

Several men rode on horses – right beside the train cars. Frank figured there must be about thirty men. It appeared like the train was going to be robbed. The men carried rifles and fired several shots in the air.

After slowing to a crawl, the train jerked and came to a complete stop. Frank watched from above. He saw all the hobos in the train car below him being ordered to get out. He laid flat. He figured he would not be noticed.   The other guys riding on the top did the same. At first it appeared that they might not be seen. Then one of the thirty men climbed up the same ladder that Frank had used. He pointed his rifle toward them, "Get down, one at a time!"

Frank was scared. This might mean jail and chain gang time like he had heard about. He figured there was no way to escape. He obeyed, as they all did. The Railroad Detectives ordered the hobos to line up against the train. With rifles pointed at the hobos, they asked each individual hobo how much money he had. If a hobo had any money, he was to hand it over to the detective and then move to one side.

Each hobo dug in their pockets or their bundle sticks and either paid what money they had, or they were told to step aside and form another line. Frank wasn't sure what the consequences would be. Not only did these yard bulls have horses and guns, they also had a horse-drawn flatbed wagon; a wagon that could carry a group of men off to jail.

Finally, they reached Frank and demanded that he empty his pockets. He did. He pulled out his knife, razor blade, handkerchief, toothbrush and a bar of soap and 5 one-dollar bills. The yard bull took his five dollars and told him to stand to the side. Frank felt a tinge of sadness to see his hard earned money go so quickly even before he had decided how to spend his earnings. He was relieved though knowing he had money in his boots.

The detectives were quick with their duties. The train workers wanted to keep moving. This was a major delay for their scheduling. Finally, each man had been checked. More men were broke than the amount of men that had surrendered money.

As Frank suspected, the men that had no money were told to board the wagon. Where they were headed, Frank could only surmise.

Then the yard bulls ordered the train to move, which it did. The paying hobos stood in the dust and moved back as they watched their transportation leave without them.

One yard bull, already on his horse, yelled at them. "It's against the law to ride these freight trains. Stay off the trains!" They rode off creating more dust.

"Whatcha gonna do now?" One young guy asked Frank.

"I'm gonna wait for the next train and hope it slows down enough that I can jump aboard."

The young kid knew the answer to that hope. "I know where it slows down. I've been on this ride before. It's not too far from here. There is an area that curves. If you follow me, I'll show ya."

"Sure," said Frank. He had no other options in mind.

So together they hiked up the fields following the track line. A few other guys headed the same direction, but many scattered. Frank wasn't sure to what or to where they were going next.

"My name's Russ. What's your name?" Frank looked at this tall, lean dark- haired boy.

"I'm Frank. How old are you?"

"I'm fifteen, but I know what I'm doing. I'm out looking for work so I can help my family." The kid kicked the dirt to prove his statement. "How old are you?"

"I'm seventeen," answered Frank.

"You look older."

"Yeah, I guess I do," Frank agreed. He probably did look older. At times he felt older, like he missed some years when he should have enjoyed being a teenager instead of working hard like a grown man.

They walked in silence for a while.

The kid spoke up, "You know those yard bulls back there?"

Frank answered, "Yeah?" He questioned why he was asked. He didn't really "know" them, but he'd always remember the experience he had with them.

"Well," continued Russ, "they were mild compared to the ones in Pasco, Washington."

Frank was curious, "How so?"

"Well, my first train ride was in Washington. I heard about a yard bull called Pasco Pete. I was told don't mess with Pasco Pete. I was in Yakima and heading to Walla Walla. I rode a train through Pasco, pushing my luck. I was on top of the train: the same situation as on this last ride. The yard bulls came. They shouted for all the men to get off the train. One boxcar was loaded with guys, like here. Only this time there were only six yard bulls - yard bulls against 30 or more hobos. One young kid got so scared he stayed in the corner of the boxcar. Pasco Pete yelled at him, "Get out here, and get out here now!" Finally the kid moved. He moved slowly like he wasn't thinking, more like he was sleepwalking. When he got to the doorway, he jumped off the boxcar, dropped his bag and ran like the devil was chasing him. Pasco Pete didn't yell at him, just took his rifle and shot him in the back. He didn't have to shoot him. These Railroad detectives have only one duty to get the hobos off the trains. The kid was off the train so why shoot him? He was doing exactly what the yard bull wanted. He left the train."

Frank visualized this tragic story in his mind. He agreed no reason to shoot a kid. "What happened to you that day?" The kid bowed his head and didn't answer right away. Frank worried. The silence made him think he shouldn't have asked the question.

"I had two weeks in jail and worked on a chain gang."

Frank looked at Russ, this fifteen year old kid. Frank didn't have a younger brother, but he thought if he did he might look like Russ. No kid should be shot, and no kid should be slaving on a chain gang. He shook his head in disgust and sadness. He spit on the ground as if that gesture would take away the badness he felt. He vowed he'd stay away from Pasco, Washington.

*****

Russ was true to his word. They waited by the rails that curved around a rocky slope. When the train approached it did slow down. Russ and Frank watched the cars slowly go by. The engine, the tender and several boxcars passed. Russ yelled at Frank, "Next car we jump on!"

Russ was agile and quick. He grabbed the side ladder and climbed to the top. Frank followed. Frank felt they were still too close to the engine. The train picked up speed. The soot and hot cinders combined and appeared like white and black clouds drifting down upon them. From Frank's previous experience of being on top of a boxcar, he knew he needed to be further from the sooty smoke and the burning cinders.

He motioned to Russ that he wanted to move to the next boxcar. Russ nodded in agreement and jumped to the next car. Frank watched his technique and thought that looked easy. He followed Russ's example.

Russ walked to the end of the boxcar and made a second jump to the next boxcar. The train moved faster. Despite the speed, Frank also attempted the jump with confidence; however, this time the sole of his shoe caught on a piece of wood. Frank lost his balance and fell between the boxcars.

He landed onto the couplers (the narrow metal device that linked the cars together.) Though he landed on his feet, he fell to his knees and shook with fear. After several minutes of sheer panic and mumbling words, "Oh God, oh God," he realized he would have to climb back up to the top of the boxcar. He sighed and moaned. His legs ached from the fall.

Ladder bars were on the back of the boxcar. These were the same type of bars he used when he jumped on trains; however, those jumps were on slow moving trains. Now he was on a narrow coupler on a fast moving train. With effort, he stood upright. He leaned over the side and reached for the bar. Though he felt pain, he swung his body weight and placed his foot on the bottom ladder rung.

Upward he climbed. His feet slipped several times. The boxcar swayed as the train accelerated. He could barely think. All the while, he pretended he was on a mountain, without a rope. His purpose was to hang on to save his life, and to keep climbing. How he did it… he wasn't even sure. He made it only out of fearful necessity and determination.

When Frank got close to the top, Russ reached out his hand and helped him. "Man, where you've been?"

Frank panted and paused before he could answer. Finally he yelled, "Kinda' missed that last jump. I'll tell you one thing, when I get to Chicago, I'm gonna' buy me a new pair of boots!"

They both made themselves comfortable and sat in the middle of the boxcar roof. There were ridges there. These wooden ridges gave them a semi-safe feeling that they had some support, something to grab onto if necessary.

This ride had proven less than safe and certainly not as pleasant as Frank's first experience riding on top. Now he felt anxious. He knew he was definitely heading to Chicago. As always, they would have to jump off before they arrived at the train yard. He knew little about Chicago. He figured it would be an all-night ride. He wasn't exactly sure because he had already ridden part of the distance from North Dakota. The unknown troubled him. Also now he felt the pains of hunger. This whole last month he had eaten well, three meals a day, now he hadn't eaten since breakfast.

The sky was partially dark. The train kept a steady speed between 40 to 45 miles per hour. Russ and Frank took turns snoozing. One of them had to consistently stay awake. There was the constant fear of rolling off the top of a train, especially if you fell asleep. Even though Frank had just met Russ, he felt Russ was a responsible kid: one that he could trust. Frank slept first.

He dreamt he was falling. In his dream he wasn't falling between train cars instead he was floating in a downward lazy motion over a water fall. He woke up, startled. The moon gave some light. Way ahead was the dim distant light of the train's head light. He shook his head and tried to come to his senses.

"You okay?" Russ yelled.

"Yeah," Frank stretched out his legs. "How long did I sleep?"

"You've been sleeping for two hours."

"Have you been sitting there for two hours?" Frank realized how ridiculous the question was; at this speed there was no place for Russ to go, and thankfully it appeared that he had stayed awake.

"Yep, just sittin' here thinking I'm cold and I need a cigarette."

Frank agreed about being cold; however, he was somewhat surprised Russ smoked at his young age.

Russ answered with an added explanation, like he could read Frank's thoughts. "Yeah, I've been smoking since I was thirteen. My dad bought me the cigarettes."

"You have some now?"

Russ reached into his deep overall pocket. He pulled out a Camel cigarette and put it in the corner of his mouth. It was too windy on the train to light a cigarette: that would come later.

"Tell you what man, "if we both land on our feet when we jump off this train, I'll give you one of my cigarettes.

"That's a deal," agreed Frank.

Russ made himself comfortable. He lowered himself on the train's hard boarded roof. He took off his extra shirt, rolled it up for a pillow, and covered himself with his jacket tucked around him. He kept his cigarette dangling out of the side of his mouth, using it like a child would suck on his thumb. He curled up to rest. Frank noticed Russ quickly fell asleep. The steady rhythmic "clickety-clack, clickety-clack" of the train going across flat land seemed to be like a lullaby to a tired guy. Now it was Frank's turn to sit up straight and pay attention, despite the cold breeze and the rocking of the train.

He gazed at the moon. Lonely feelings overcame him as a heavy uncomfortable coat. He wished he was at his mom's home, with her and his brothers in one place. When Russ mentioned his dad, it made Frank think about his father, a man he barely remembered. His mom told him his dad went back to his homeland, Florida. Was his dad staring at the same moon? Did his father remember the wife and sons that he left?

Frank remembered the last day he saw his dad. He wanted to always keep that memory: a time when they laughed and played a silly hide and seek game. Did his father have the same memories? He sighed.

Hours went by. Finally, as the sun began to rise, the train slowed. Frank nudged Russ. "We got to go." Russ woke up and checked the surroundings. He grabbed his jacket, put it on and sat upright. Immediately he was alert.

They watched the landscape. This area did not look like North Dakota. Instead of wide open fields, they saw many scattered farm houses. Dirt roads were visible and went in different directions. It was still too early though to see people. Even the farmers would still be asleep. The train slowed and got quieter. They were near one of the busiest and newest railroad stations in America.

They had to jump soon or they would definitely be caught. Russ led the way again. He climbed down the side ladder, watched the ground and then jumped. He fell, lunged forward, and rolled on the grass. Frank followed seconds after Russ made his leap. It wasn't a perfect landing for either one of them. They both tumbled and rolled. After several minutes of feeling for broken bones, and brushing themselves off from the grass and dirt, they stood up. They looked at each other, satisfied for how they fared. Even though they didn't exactly land on their feet, Russ handed one of his cigarettes to Frank and lit the end.

Frank inhaled slowly. "This tastes like tar."

"Gosh," said Russ as he took a long puff, "it's Turkish tobacco, so they say."

"I don't know about that," said Frank. He was use to rolling his own smokes, and this was his first taste of any store bought cigarette. He wasn't pleased, but he smoked the whole cigarette anyway. He figured it might ease his hunger pains.

"I'll treat you to a meal," Frank offered.

"Sounds good." Russ was anxious to share his idea with Frank as to where he was headed next. "I decided last night to backtrack: I'm headin' for Minnesota. I got some family there, and I'm gonna' look them up."

"That sounds like a grand idea." Frank was glad to hear that Russ had a survival plan. "You know anything about Chicago?"

"Yep," answered Russ. "I know a café, not far from the train station, that serves breakfast."

"Let's head there. You know what… my mom told me I have relatives in Long Island, New York. I got an uncle and grandparents named Benjamin. Maybe, I'll go see…"

"Good luck," said Russ

"Good luck to you" said Frank. They kept hiking, with breakfast in mind.

Chapter Thirteen

Chicago, Illinois 1928 Seventeen Years Old

They arrived at the Stone Wall Café. The place was small and crowded. Frank figured the waiter knew that he and Russ were hobos that just jumped off the train; however, no one commented negatively about them instead, they were treated like welcomed customers.

After giving them several minutes of reading the menu, the waiter asked, "What will it be gentlemen?"

"Pancakes, ham and biscuits," Russ answered. Frank wanted to try the gravy and biscuits, and heck, because he had money, he added steak to the order. They were thirsty and drank several glasses of water and then relaxed with hot coffee.

Their hunger caused them to eat quickly, but they slowed down enough to praise the food. Russ paused and told Frank, "These biscuits taste like the ones mom made, only she filled them with jelly and put melted butter on top."

Frank chewed his steak that was surprisingly tender and tasty. He asked the waiter, "What kind of sauce do you put on this steak?" "Tell you man, Pete our chef, is one of the best. His steaks are mighty popular. He adds Worcestershire Sauce on all the meats. People seem to like it." Frank nodded, and kept eating.

When their plates were empty, Frank paid for both meals, a total of $1.50. He asked the waiter the directions to a hobo camp, guessing that every town had one, so this town must, and he was right. The waiter walked outside the restaurant to point the exact way.

Russ and Frank looked at each other. "Still headed to Minnesota?"

"Yep" answered Russ. "You still headed to New York?"

"Not yet, I want to check out Chicago. It looks like there's plenty to see around here."

They tightly gripped their hands in a gentleman hand shake, as if giving strength to one another. They waved to each other as Frank went one direction and Russ headed back to the train tracks.

When Frank got to the camp, he was surprised to see between thirty to forty men, camping in this campsite. He also noticed, back in the trees, rows of tents. A big, heavyset man that went by the name of "Beef" greeted him. "Hey, man, you look rather tired, need a place to stay?"

"Yeah," answered Frank. "I'm hoping to wash up and sleep."

"Well, you've come to the right place. Got to tell ya,' this campsite is different than any other hobo camp. We're part of the tourist union. Can you believe it? Us hobos are unionized. So there is a slight cost – if you can afford it." Beef looked at Frank as if he assumed that Frank had no to little money. His boots were worn with holes, his face was dirty from train soot, and even his shirt needed mending.

Frank was amazed. He heard about unions but never figured it involved hobo jungles. "This camp is really unionized?"

"Yep! Actually, hoboes have been unionized since 1889. After the Civil War, the men came home and didn't have jobs. They took their hoes and found work on their own: where the name 'hoboes' comes from. This camp has been part of the union since 1905."

"Interesting, what's the going rate for a night or two at a hobo camp?"

"Probably less than you figured," replied Beef. "We all have to pay a yearly due. It's good for any hobo camp you go to. The yearly due is one nickel. You got a nickel to spare?"

Frank reached into his overall pocket. He had loose change. He handed Beef his coin.

"Welcome, sign here!" Beef handed him a thick piece of cardboard where signatures were listed. "If you go to any other union camps, just tell them you paid Beef your yearly due. Add your name on the list and how long you figure you will stay?"

Frank hadn't given his future much thought, but with pencil in hand he wrote: FRANK - 3 nights. He assumed that if he stayed that long he could see some of Chicago.

"Oh yes," Beef added, "the union has a list of 15 rules, but I'll summarize them and make it simple: clean up after yourself and no fightin'."

The camp was near the railroad station and on the shores of Lake Michigan. The lake was where the men washed. They had buckets that the men could use, soap was provided, clotheslines to hang clothes, and two outhouses.

Frank spent the evening washing up and resting. He had a tent and a cot all to himself. It was before dark that he fell asleep. Finally, around 9:30 a.m. the smell of frying bacon stirred his senses. He had to focus, where was he? Then came the vivid memories of his last harrowing train experiences. Sighing he remembered losing his footing and falling between the train cars. To escape the memory of those fearful moments, he shook his head and ruffled his hair. Time for some needed breakfast and a cup of coffee.

He had slept in his overalls. Everything else, he had been wearing, he had washed, and those clothes were hanging on the clothes line.

When he first arrived at the hobo camp, he tried to wash off the soot and cinder stains on his hands and face, but even with the provided soap, he still had dark spots on his skin. His hair felt cleaner after a good washing, but he feared his skin might never come clean.

He stepped outside the tent to the cool morning air, and checked to see if his clothes were at least semi-dry. Grabbing them off the line, he returned to his cot space, got dressed and headed to the campfire where breakfast was being served.

"Morning, man" Beef was sitting on the ground drinking coffee from a tin mug. "You slept so long we thought you might have died in there."

"Nope," answered Frank. "I was just dead tired, but I feel much better this morning." As he filled a plate of food and sipped coffee, he added, "Much appreciate this breakfast! Someone knows how to make good coffee."

"Yep," responded Beef, "it's old Herb over there. He's the only one that can make it decent. He's been here over a week. We might convince him to stay just to keep making coffee for us."

"What about you?" Frank asked, "How long have you been here?"

"I'm on the move, but for now I've got a job here in Chicago, so guess I'll hang around a little longer."

"What's the job?"

"They've still got wooden sidewalks, and this town wants them paved. So I'm part of the paving crew. I've been working nine hours every day starting at noon and working till 9:00 p.m. Good pay. If it keeps up, I won't be riding the rails from place to place. I might settle right here, but I'm not sure. Chicago's a busy place, maybe too busy for my likin'."

"Tell me, Beef…" Frank hesitated thinking why this guy might be going by the name "Beef." He decided not to ask. Beef was a big, muscular man with dark tanned skin. His name fit the picture. Frank continued his main question, "What should I see in Chicago?"

Beef took some time to think through his reply. Frank sat on the log and ate his breakfast.

"Okay," Beef was ready with a list in his mind of what sights Frank should see. "Ride the L train. It goes over the whole town. I'm talking over – not on ground rails, but rails that are built twenty-five feet above the ground on viaducts. It's a great view of the city! It's an electric powered train, smooth ride, not like the rails you've been riding."

"Looks like you need new clothes; go to Sears. You can't miss Sears; it's a fourteen story building. Use to be a catalog store only, but now it's all retail. You can get whatever you need."

"My main advice, stay away from any speakeasy. They get raided now and then. They serve liquor despite prohibition: not the safest places to hang out."

All of these suggestions sounded exciting to Frank. He decided to follow Beef's ideas, except his advice about not going to a speakeasy. He was curious.

Frank walked into town. He was amazed how busy and large Chicago appeared. He knew the downtown area of Portland. It too was a busy city, but Chicago was at least three times the size and much more progressive.

Automobiles moved at 5 to 10 mph close together crowding the roads. The curb spaces were filled with parked autos. Street cars ran on the tracks down the middle of the street. A mass of people criss-crossed the roads along with a few horse and buggy carriages. It looked like chaos and sounded noisy with horns blaring, as if honking sounds would clear the avenues. Frank was thankful he wasn't driving. He wasn't sure if he was safe to cross a street on foot, let alone if he had to maneuver an automobile through this maze.

He was shocked at the amount of tall buildings. In Portland there was the Meier & Frank building fifteen stories high; yet here there were several buildings higher that reached to the sky. He spotted the Sears building and counted the stories, it was fourteen stories tall. He was excited seeing the building he was about to enter. Near the main entrance there was an acre of land designated for automobiles only. The lot accommodated many autos. They were all parked haphazardly. He wondered how they parked there without mishaps.

As soon as he entered the building, he noticed an escalator that he could take from floor to floor. As he gazed around at all the merchandise, he wished he had more funds. His belongings now only consisted of what he could wear or carry in his pockets. Yet, he longed to buy more. He saw many items he felt he needed: tin cups used for drinking, sharper small knives, tobaccos of all brands, overalls with deep pockets, warm woolen shirts, and many boots and shoes. Frank felt overwhelmed with the choices.

Not only did Sears carry small miscellaneous items and clothing of all sorts. Sears also had household merchandise like: refrigerators that produced ice cubes, gas stoves rather than just wood burning stoves, Hoover rug sweepers, washing machines, auto parts, tires, horns, and floor mats. Frank was amazed. If he had a home and an automobile he would do all his shopping in this store. He thought of his mother and how much fun she might have, if she had the opportunity, to explore and chose new household items. If he had lots of money, he would buy her whatever she wanted.

He needed boots. It was a time-consuming venture; he had to find the right boots, chose new undergarments and a warm shirt. After two hours, he finished his shopping, threw away some of his torn clothes and worn-out footwear and left Sears wearing his new shirt and boots. He felt richer, even though he had less money.

He looked up and saw the electric train cross over the Chicago viaduct. He decided taking a ride on the L train was a must. He walked up the stairs to the platform and paid his nickel. He actually sat on a seat, so different than his rides in the boxcars, or on the train car roofs. This was a peaceful smooth easy ride: not nerve-racking at all. Frank enjoyed the comfort, but admitted to himself that he felt no exciting rush as he did when jumping on a moving train.

On this trip he looked down and saw the shops, stores and the busy crowded streets of Chicago. He noticed a theater and the posted sign, "The Jazz Singer with Al Jolson." He took a round trip as the train went through downtown and returned back to the same platform from where he started. He walked a short distance, to the theater. He had a pocket full of change and decided the movie house would be his next stop.

Frank had heard Al Jolson sing on the radio. He liked his singing. Though he figured this movie would be a silent movie because all the movies that he had seen were silent, he still thought the entertainment would be interesting. He paid his dime to the ticket lady. The theater was beautiful inside with a plush red carpet, tall ivory statues, and decorative paintings in the lobby. Frank handed the usher his ticket. Silent cartoons were playing. It would be several minutes before the main feature would start.

Frank laughed and enjoyed a Mickey Mouse cartoon. Then the black and white movie started. Surprisingly, it started with the sound of orchestra music. This was the first time that Frank had ever heard sound on a film. A few other folks in the audience were surprised too; there was an audible gasp of surprise as the music played.

When the characters began their speaking, it was without sound, and the subtitles were written in bold letters on the screen. Immediately, the story was tense. The story started with Al as a young boy. This boy desired to be a professional singer. His father, a strong Orthodox Jew, wanted his boy to sing, but only for the Jewish ceremonies, not for entertainment elsewhere.

The conflict got tense when his son performed in a public saloon/ dance hall. Suddenly, there is sound! The audience could hear the young boy sing! As the film progressed, Al ran away from home. Frank related to the theme. He too was away from home: not for the same reasons, but he certainly felt for Al's character.

Every song Al sang, Frank enjoyed. He related to how much Al loved his mother and emotionally sang to her. Frank left the theater teary-eyed, thinking about how far he was away from his mother and brothers.

These films offered a continuous showing; people came in and out of the theater at their leisure. As Frank left the theater, he noticed all the street signs and landmarks so he could find his way back to the hobo jungle later. Now he was hungry. After spending $3.50 on his boots and clothes, he still had some money left. Next he wanted to see what a speakeasy was like.

Some guys about Frank's age were standing against a wall smoking. He went over and started up a conversation about his first observations of the fast-moving city. He praised the town and told the guys how lucky they were to live in Chicago. One guy offered Frank a smoke and continued chatting with him. Several of them had their own stories of living in Chicago. All their lives they had seen the town bloom and recover from when the town burned almost completely: back in 1871. Now it was one of the busiest cities in America. They told him Sears wasn't the tallest building. A guy named Joe walked out toward the street and pointed toward Lake Michigan. "Look upward," he said, "you'll see the Tribune Tower – thirty-six floors toward the sky."

Frank was impressed. "So that's where the Chicago Tribune prints their papers."

"Not only do the newsmen work there, they also have the WGN Radio Station recording out of that building. They probably have antennas up on the roof."

Then Frank asked his next question. "Where is the nearest speakeasy?"

The guys were silent. Then they snickered. Then they laughed. Frank patiently waited for his answer. Finally, Joe told him, "You won't get in, but I can tell you where it is and how to get there."

"Okay," Frank was ready to listen.

"The name is 'The Green Mill.' Head down North Broadway Street and you won't miss it. Look for a wooden building with a canopy cover over the doorway, and the door is green. But I'll warn you – you probably won't get in. You have to know the right people and wear the right clothes to get in there."

The other guys started to laugh again as they walked away. Frank didn't care about their sneers. With his new boots he felt confident. He was a decent young guy and maybe appeared richer than he was. He certainly would not admit he was staying in a hobo jungle.

Frank was about half a block away when Joe shouted more information, "Tell you, man, you have to know the right people. Obviously, you don't know them or you wouldn't be asking where the heck the place is."

"It's okay," Frank yelled back "I'll take my chances." He remembered what some guys said at the hobo jungle. "If you go to a speakeasy, you'll be lucky to get out with all your limbs; there could be fights or raids. Sometimes the police invade these places just to show they mean business about prohibition, or just to take all the liquor for themselves."

He definitely had been warned. Still, he wanted to see for himself. He was hungry too. Food and drink sounded inviting, and if he could have dinner with a gal, that would be even better.

He found the place. A small sign hung above the narrow door: The Green Mill. He tried to open the only door, as if to enter any public restaurant. It was locked. He knocked. He heard a rough voice. "Yeah, who is it?"

"I'm Frank. I'd like to come in and order dinner."

"Frank, I don't know you. Who sent you?"

Frank thought about the answer: "no one. I don't know any name to give. I just want to visit this speakeasy, hear the music and maybe meet a gal." Now he had told the whole truth.

"Well," yelled the voice behind the door, "you're in the wrong place. Get lost!"

Frank stepped back from the door. The guy's voice gave no hope of a second try. He started to walk away when a flapper gal walked near him. She had short dark hair and wore the skimpiest skirt that Frank had ever seen a gal wear, knee length. She could barely walk on her high heel shoes. Her bright red lipstick smile matched her bright red feathered hat. She had a top on that was frilly on the sleeves, but tight everywhere else. She was cute. Frank liked her looks, especially when she smiled.

"Are you trying to get in The Green Mill?"

"Sure," said Frank. "They have a sign. I assume they want customers."

"You're right honey; they want customers, but only certain ones. They like them to be rich, famous, and know someone.

"Now lucky you, I'm Daisy, and now you know someone special." She reached her hand to Frank's and shook his hand. It was like they were old time friends.

"You let me do the talking." She continued. "Remember you know me and you know me well. I'm Daisy Livingston. Got it?"

"Got it," said Frank. He liked how this scenario was playing out.

She knocked on the door, as he had. The same guy answered in his same gruff voice. There was no window to see each other, only the bright green door.

"Hey Mack, it's me, Daisy, and I got a dear friend with me visiting from out of town."

"Yeah, what's his name?"

Daisy looked at Frank. Frank had yet to tell her his name. He whispered, "Frank."

"Frank – Franklin Roosevelt." She answered.

Mack laughed. "Sure, I'm sure you know Mr. Roosevelt. Are you with Theodore Roosevelt too? Don't be stupid, Daisy."

"Not the real Franklin Roosevelt, but my dear friend Frank."

"Let me hear Frank's voice." Frank tried to change his normal sounding voice. "Yeah, hello," he said.

"Tell me, Frank, how well do you know Daisy? Tell me her last name."

"It's Livingston, Daisy Livingston."

"Ok," Mack mumbled reluctantly. "Give the password, Daisy."

"Keg" she answered. "Keg of beer."

"You got it." Mack opened the door. As they entered the dark hallway Mack stared at Frank and Frank stared back. Mack was a large guy, full of muscle, not fat, just muscle. He was older and slightly bald; he had scars on his face – all signs of a rough life. With his obvious strength and attitude, whatever scars he received, his opponent probably was in much worse shape: if he was still alive.

Frank said nothing and followed Daisy down the dark hallway. Daisy whispered to him, "Mack always asks the same question, 'What is my last name?' If the guy knows the answer he figures I know the guy. Really, I only give my last name to guys I like. I like you, Frank."

Frank smiled. He liked how this evening was progressing. Daisy climbed up some stairs and then entered another door. It was like opening a curtain on a stage. It changed from a dark narrow hallway to a large open room with its own stage and jazz musicians playing upbeat music. The room was colorful with red flowered wall paper and dark red carpet. There were black round tables and velvet cushioned chairs, but also booths on the side of the wall. A few booths even had windows.

People were dressed in party clothes sitting at tables eating, drinking and smoking. A slight haze of smoke penetrated throughout the room. The music and chatter were loud. Daisy waltzed through the room smiling and laughing like she owned the place and was the hostess. She seemed to know everyone, calling many by their first name. She often pointed to Frank and said, "Meet Franklin Roosevelt." People would laugh and greet Frank. Often they even joked, "…heard you might head to the White House like your cousin did. "Ha! Ha!"

Frank didn't mind being teased. He didn't mind having a recognizable fake name. Finally, Daisy landed at a table with two empty chairs. "We'll stay here," she said. "Are you hungry and thirsty?"

"Yeah," answered Frank. Now he worried about what this would cost. He realized he was expected to pay and pay for 2 meals. "Don't worry," Daisy said, like she knew what he was concerned about. "I get free drinks here. Hey, Junior," she yelled at a waiter, "bring us 2 Gin Rickies."

Junior smiled and yelled back, "Coming right up."

Daisy looked at Frank. He appeared a little worried about the drinks she ordered. "Don't worry. These drinks have some bourbon, but also lime juice. Just pretend you're drinking lime juice." Quickly, she handed Frank the menu. Foods and prices were listed. "Pick out a meal, Frank. We can share the cost."

Frank relaxed and picked out a steak dinner. Daisy picked out a lighter, less expensive chicken meal with all the trimmings.

The drinks came in a tea kettle and had to be poured in tea cups. "We use these to appear like we are drinking tea." Daisy explained as she daintily picked up a tea cup and held out her small right hand finger as she had seen other tea drinkers do.

"Using tea cups…," she continued to explain, "helps the officers. They can honestly testify we only have tea parties. Makes sense, right?" Frank laughed and agreed.

Some folks were dancing. Daisy was ready to dance. "You dance, Frank?"

"No" answered Frank. "I've never danced."

"Well, 'never' can always be changed." She grabbed his hand and led him to the crowded dance floor. Luckily, the tune was somewhat slow. She placed Frank's hand around her waist and held his other hand. They waited. The next song started with the sound of three chimes. Then the singer began the lyrics, "It's three o'clock in the morning… We've danced the whole night thru…" Frank tried to relax and follow her lead, but it was hard. Even his new boots didn't seem to help. They felt heavy as he tried to move gracefully with her steps. She whispered the beat, "1, 2, 3, 1, 2, 3."As they swayed together, Frank began to relax. He heard clearly the words, "I could keep on dancing forever with you." When they stopped, Daisy smiled and seemed pleased with his effort. They returned to their table. Their meals were steaming. Frank wanted to gobble quickly. He was hungry, but he followed her slow pace and cut his meat into small pieces.

Daisy pointed to the empty booth where Al Capone would usually sit. Frank had heard about Al Capone. He heard that Al was notorious for raids, and often he and his pals caused havoc. She said he liked to sit in that booth because he could see out the windows and know if trouble was coming in. She talked about him like he was a hero. She bragged, "He helps the poor and does right for the town of Chicago."

She didn't seem to fear him as a person that could or would endanger anyone. She didn't seem concerned about any raids or misconduct at this speakeasy. She acted like she was in a safe haven. Obviously, she was popular and well-liked.

They were in the middle of their meal when Al Capone walked in with six other guys. They were all dressed in black suits, fedora black hats and matching black leather shoes. When they walked into the room, the band quit playing, and a few people gave up their nearby seats – some even left their meals on the tables. Once Al and his buddies got seated, the band started to play "Rhapsody in Blue." "His favorite song," Daisy quietly told Frank.

Frank immediately got a déjà vu feeling. He remembered when he was in Portland. His teenage friends were trouble makers following their leader Nick. They did whatever Nick said even if it meant going against the law. Frank did too, for a while, but he came to his senses after a narrow escape from the police. He escaped from their influence by leaving.

He looked at Al Capone (or 'Scar Face" as he heard some guys call him.) He watched as these men shadowed him like he was their king – "the king of the pack." Frank knew they would do as he said even if it cost them. He also recognized a bully when he saw one. Al was a bully, a mean bully acting like a likeable popular person: a man supposedly improving society. Frank didn't believe the charade that he was portraying or even the positive words Daisy said about him.

The ambience of the club changed. Now the music perked up again, back to the usual jazz, but it still felt different, less free than it seemed before. The drinking was noticeable; more tea cups were filled.

Frank realized that the previous warnings he heard about speakeasies, the fights, and raids might happen tonight. He visualized the night that he hid in the bushes, as the cops searched for him. He remembered his fear when the yard bulls had them line up against the train cars, and it was either hand them money or come with them.

Frank was low on money. Now, if need be, he might not be able to pay his way out of trouble. He finished his meal. He stared at Daisy as she continued to politely eat her meal. She was not a hard-hearted woman; she was a beautiful young lady. She could pass for a princess if she was in a different setting: a smiling, lovely princess.

Frank sighed, and asked, "Is there a back door out of here?"

"Yes," she answered, "but the night is young. No need to leave early."

Frank took money out of his pocket, and placed a dollar on the table to help with the food expense.

"Sorry, dear, but I feel there is a need to leave early. Can you point to where there's a back door?"

"Okay, your loss." She smiled and stood up.

"No," Frank motioned for her to sit down. "Just point the way."

She answered back, "No, I will lead the way." She took his hand and gently pushed through the crowd until they arrived at another door in the back of the room. Then they entered another room – it too had chairs and tables, but now the room was empty, semi-dark and quiet. At the end of the room was another door. Daisy opened that door.

The opening led to a hallway and also to a side stairway.

"We could have some quiet alone time if you like," Daisy suggested and pointed to the stairway.

Frank was tempted: so tempted. He could still hear the nearby crowd and the loud music. He knew temptation before. "Keep stealing until you're the 'King of the Pack.'" Frank knew trouble and could sense trouble. He thought of Daisy, she was pretty and kind, but the door with Al Capone and his comrades was too close. There was a way to escape, an outside door. Without forethought, Frank leaned close to Daisy and kissed her on the lips. While he did so, she placed a dollar bill in his overall pocket: without him noticing. He didn't say anymore, just walked toward the exit door.

He opened the door to the outside. The alley was dark and narrow; garbage cans were lined up against the walls of the building. He knew the direction where the train depot was and he knew the direction of Lake Michigan. That was where he headed.

Chapter Fourteen

Chicago to Iowa 1928 Seventeen Years Old

That night, Frank noticed the dollar bill in his overall pocket. He decided it must have come from Daisy; she was the only person close to him to place money in his pocket. It was the same amount he had laid on the table to cover their meal cost. He smiled thinking about Daisy. She was the first gal he had kissed. He was glad it was her; she was special.

Frank wanted to go to New York. The plan was to arrive there before winter set in, but when he got back to the hobo camp, he heard about a work opportunity. They needed harvesters in Iowa. They were still picking corn. He was told the work would last all month and he would be well paid.

He went to the Railroad Station and got their timetables. By reading the timetables he was able to figure out the distance and the time frames of all the moving trains from Chicago. The trip to Iowa was about 178 miles on the Wabash Railroad. He would have to jump off the train before he got to Blanchard, where the station was. The freight trains would head to their own freight yards.

When he arrived at the Chicago freight yard, trains were parked. Some had open doors, some were closed. He wandered around looking for hobos. Studying his timetable, he knew for sure which train was clear to leave and which one was headed for Iowa. He jumped inside an open boxcar. Several hobos were seated at one corner. "Going to Blanchard?" one guy asked.

"That's exactly where I'm headed."

"Well, you're in the right spot."

Frank sat down on the hard wooden floor and stretched his legs out in front of him. In a few minutes, the train started to move. He turned to the same guy that spoke to him. "You know much about harvesting corn?"

"Sure, it's easy, if you don't mind working all day and not stopping."

Frank shrugged his shoulders; he figured he could work all day.

The fellow hobo moved closer to Frank so he could be heard as the train made its own sounds. "Iowa is known as one of the 'Midwest Corn Belt' states.

They plant so much corn they can feed the animals and people all across America. I worked for one of the farmers last year. The old man farmer told me we had planted over 10,000 kernels of corn per acre; hell, the guy owned over ten acres of land. During harvest time we picked, by hand, every one of those corn stalks. It takes every person in Iowa to help with the picking, and they are happy if anyone else shows up. The farmers are glad to see us. They'll feed us and give us a place to sleep. At the end of the month, they'll pay you. They'll encourage you to come back next year. That's what I did last year and now I'll be back."

"You know which farm you're going to?"

"Yep, and if you want to follow me, I'll take you to the same place."

Frank eyed this guy carefully. This man was older than him, maybe in his thirties. His clothes appeared worn, but he appeared clean and shaven. His shoes were in good shape, like Frank's new boots. Frank had a good sense about him, like he was okay.

"Yeah, I'll go with you, if you think I can get a job too."

"No problem, just follow me when I jump. By the way, my name is Jeb."

Frank figured that probably wasn't his birth name, but he didn't care, Jeb was okay.

"I'm Frank." They shook hands.

"Enjoy the ride," said Jeb. "It won't be long and there will be no more sittin' time."

Frank wasn't sleepy. It was morning and he had a good night's sleep at the hobo jungle the night before. He felt wide awake, but he did enjoy sitting. He put his jacket up against his back and made himself as comfortable as he could. The door of the car was still ajar. He watched the movement of blurry scenery passing by, as if it was moving rather than the train. The beauty of Lake Michigan was the wide open fields of grain and grasses. The train picked up speed. It moved fast. Frank could only estimate a speed of at least 40 to 50 miles per hour. He felt his body rock back and forth to the rhythm of the jogging train movement.

He worried about jumping off this moving train. Hopefully, Jeb knew when and where to jump in a safe manner. Frank appreciated jumping with someone who had more experience than he had when it came to leaping off moving trains. The forethought always made his heart beat faster, and his hands got sweaty as he visualized his landing that may or may not be successful. He tried to focus on the positive, perceiving a perfect jump where he landed on two feet off a slow moving train.

His thoughts changed to thinking about his brothers and his mother. He vowed that when he got working at this next farm house, if they had a phone, he would call his mom. He would wait until he got paid, but he would call before he headed to New York. The thought made him smile and relax as the train moved down the tracks.

He dozed off for a while. Jeb nudged him and told him the train slowed and it was close to where they were going to jump. Frank looked at the open door. There was nothing to be seen, but empty fields. Hopefully, there would be a farm house near. He stood up and stretched. He felt stiff and sore. To get his muscles to work for him and not against him, he did a few jogging in place steps. Jeb was already standing by the open door. Frank got behind him. He wished the train was going slower than it was. Jeb seemed more confident than Frank was feeling.

Jeb yelled at him, "In the next 100 yards from here – we jump!" Frank thought that Jeb's statement was a poor example of information; he had no idea how to determine how far or close 100 yards were from this moving train. Instead of looking at the ground closely and deciding when to jump, as he would do if he was on his own, he watched Jeb and decided he would follow Jeb's lead and hope for the best.

"Now!" yelled Jeb. Jeb leaped off the train and landed upright away from the tracks. Frank was several seconds behind him, and he too took a leap that got him away from the tracks. Unfortunately, he didn't land on his feet, rather he landed on his knees, but he was alright. The grassy ground protected him like a cushion. He stood up and brushed himself off. Jeb stood and watched Frank brush off the dry grass. Sighing, he said, "Now we hike."

Frank asked, "How far do we hike?" He could not see any farm houses or corn stalks. He heard this was a 'Corn Belt State.' Where were they hiding the corn?

"Follow and you will see." Jeb started walking a fast pace.

The day was sunny, but cool. It felt good to hike and exercise. Frank was feeling somewhat hungry and thirsty, but still okay. He felt positive that soon he'd be at a farmhouse with food and water.

They walked about three miles and crossed a knoll. As they changed direction, Frank saw a large white farm house ahead with a large white barn. The scene was rather odd, Frank had the idea all barns were painted red, not this one. There were fields of corn stalks. From where they stood, they could not see the end of the corn stalks. Jeb was right, if this was the place they were going to, it appeared there was plenty of work to be done. "This is the place." Jeb announced.

Frank had lots of questions, but Jeb kept walking and so did Frank. They had taken off their jackets and walked slower now. They were not packing any water. Water was what they needed. Frank knew Iowa wasn't one of the largest states, but with the wide open fields it looked enormous. The farm house ahead appeared to be at least a mile distance. Frank thought we will be tired and sweaty before we even get there, as if we've already completed a day's work.

Finally, they were near the gate. The letters: "Mueller" were carved on the gate. "Let me do the talking," said Jeb. "This guy is friendly, but not the jovial easygoing'- glad-to-see-you- type."

Frank was okay with letting Jeb lead the way. Jeb untied the gate and opened it. They walked through and Jeb retied the gate. There were ducks and geese roaming on the dirt path to the house. As they walked around them, Jeb explained their presence to Frank. "Yeah, Mr. Mueller made a pond in his back yard; he even has a small fountain to circulate the water. Then he got himself some ducks and geese. They've multiplied since I was here last."

Frank was okay with any animals. He appreciated all animals, and having ducks and geese wander the path just seemed like a welcoming committee, greeting them.

They reached the large front porch. The covered area looked inviting with wicker chairs and a wooden swing seat. Jeb knocked on the door. Two dogs appeared from the side yard and started barking.

The geese and ducks made sounds and frantically rushed to the back yard.

They waited several minutes before a gray-haired man with worn trousers opened the door. "Well, I'll be dammed if it ain't Jeb Swenson! What the hell? Did you parachute out of the sky? No, let me guess – still ridin' the box cars! Well, don't just stand there like there's nothing to do. Come on in and bring your friend with ya'."

It wasn't until they were inside the living room that Jeb had a chance to answer and to introduce Frank. As they talked, Frank remembered that the day was a Sunday. There was no working on Sundays. It was why everything seemed quiet when they arrived and why the fields were empty of workers.

Mr. Mueller called for his wife to come join them in the living room. He kindly introduced his dear wife Julia. She seemed younger looking than Mr. Mueller. She had dark hair, piled into a bun. She was tall and strong looking. Her face was without blemish and she had a friendly smile. Mr. Mueller asked them to be seated. He explained to them all about the planting and harvesting of the corn stalks. He told them how every ear of corn had to be picked with a husking knife and a heavy glove - one ear of corn at a time.

Julia didn't interrupt Mr. Mueller. After greeting Frank and Jeb with a nod and a smile, she headed to the kitchen. When she returned, she brought a tray of ice tea and cornbread biscuits. They gobbled and drank quickly. Mr. Mueller continued his explanations about the work that needed to be done, and that they only had this month of November to get the work completed: no matter if the weather changed to cold or snow or whatever.

Mr. Mueller stood up and told them he would show them where they could clean up and rest. He told them to come to the kitchen at 6:00 p.m. for a light supper; they had missed the main Sunday meal. He said work would start early in the morning. Breakfast would be served at 6:00 a.m. He strongly suggested they didn't miss breakfast.

He led them to the big white barn. The barn had seven horses in stalls, hay stacked from floor to ceiling. A ladder went up to a second floor in the tall barn. They followed him up the ladder. There were twelve cots up there for sleeping, a pile of warm blankets and pillows. "I've only got five other workers right now so you guys will be a great help this month. They drove my Ford into town this afternoon. I figured what the heck; I didn't want to go anywhere."

They followed him down the ladder. He showed them the outhouse and water pumps he had behind the barn. There was one private shed where he pumped water in with a hose. This was a space to shower. The water would be cold, but at least it provided a place to clean up. He told them they could heat up water on the kitchen stove whenever they wanted warmer water. There was also a tin tub in the shower stall. A bath was actually possible. Frank thought that might be a good idea before dinner while the other guys were in town.

After Mr. Mueller showed them the barn area, Jeb went up the ladder and put a blanket on one of the end empty cots and took off his boots to relax. Frank picked up the large pail of water and went to the house to heat up some water. He figured at least four trips back and forth and he could have a hot bath. He had soap in his pocket. The goal of getting somewhat clean became a possibility.

Before six o'clock the other crew men came back. By then Frank had finished his bathing, emptied, and cleaned out the tub. He had also arranged bedding for himself on one of the empty cots. The five guys walked into the bunk house together. They didn't seem all that surprised to see two strangers. "Hey guys," yelled one of the first ones to climb the ladder, "we've got company!"

The second guy up asked, "Are you guys gonna' help with the corn pickin'? If yes, then welcome"

Jeb was quick to answer, "Yes, sir, we're here to work."

"Great we need four more hands." The guys took turns giving their names and a little bit about where they were from. Several lived in Iowa and came to work because they knew Mr. Mueller. They knew that he was a fair man who would give them a decent wage. The other two guys were somewhat vague about their past whereabouts or future plans. Obviously, they were traveling too, like Jeb and Frank. No one seemed to care if they were vague about their comings and goings. Instead, it was each man praising the other for being there and being willing to work.

The dinner bell rang at 6:00. The guys all went into the main house and into the big dining room. The table was set for ten people. Frank counted in his head: five workers, he and Jeb, Mr. Mueller and Julia his wife, and one extra chair. After everyone was seated a young boy about 15 or 16 walked into the room. He wasn't introduced. Soon Frank realized he was part of the family. He was Mr. and Mrs. Mueller's son.

Frank remembered his last farm experience where the son taught him how to bale hay. He got a premonition that this boy, named Ken, would probably be his teacher in how to harvest corn. He smiled thinking about it. Well, at least Ken wasn't that much younger than Frank.

Not surprisingly, the dinner consisted of cornbread, corn on the cob, steak and plenty of mashed potatoes. Everyone seemed hungry and satisfied. At this farm house when a man finished eating, he cleared his place and left out the back door. Frank was one of the last men to leave the table. He asked Julia if he could help with the cleanup. She laughed and said, "No, thanks, Ken and I will wash the dishes – we have it down to a system." Still Frank finished clearing what was on the table. Then he carried some firewood from the barn to the kitchen wood pile. Julia looked surprised that Frank did this chore without being asked. She was grateful and told Frank she appreciated his helpfulness. "Least I could do," was Frank's answer. Then he went behind the barn rolled a cigarette and smoked it till there was nothing left.

Early the next morning, Frank heard the other animals that he had not even seen the night before. He heard a rooster crow, cows mooing, chickens chattering and the geese squawking. He knew it was early, but he wasn't sure how early. A couple guys were up and dressed and already rolled up their bedding on their cots. Frank slept in his clothes, so getting dressed wasn't an effort at all. He put his boots on and went down the ladder to freshen up for the morning. Hopefully, a splash of cold water would wake him up.

Before he got to the table, he knew there would be corn biscuits, and he guessed that maybe there would even be a corn mush or at least mush with corn. Smiling, he thought they should have had popcorn last night. He was right about the corn biscuits and the mush with corn. Scrambled eggs were also served, with hot coffee and milk. Frank ate well and helped to clear the table afterwards.

When he got outside he saw three wagon carts with two horses haltered to each cart. Ken was on one wagon yelling for Frank to come join him. Jeb was on the same wagon. As soon as Frank climbed on the cart, Ken spoke, "We've got a plan. Jeb is goin' to lead the horses. You and I will pick the corn ears. Does that sound good?"

Frank figured it didn't matter whether he agreed or not; that was the plan. "Sure, sounds good." They headed to the corn fields.

The corn stalks stood tall. Frank felt he was in a maze that seemed endless. He could still see the sky, but with the corn stalks surrounding him that was all he could see. The path between the stalks was a narrow dirt path only allowing enough room for the wagon cart that the horses pulled. "Here is where we start," Ken directed. He jumped out of the wagon, and then reached back under the wooden bench where he was sitting. He pulled out two sharp husking knives and gloves – one pair for himself and one pair for Frank. Ken grabbed the corn ear. He demonstrated how to pick corn quickly. "Grasp the ear firmly, pull down, and use your knife to hack it off. Then throw it in the wagon. Got it?" Ken stood back and waited for Frank's answer.

"Yeah, I got it."

Ken demonstrated another example, "You can also twist and pull, but using the knife is the quickest method. Just make sure your other hand isn't in the way. These knifes are the sharpest knives around."

Frank reassured him that he no intention of cutting himself.

"Okay, then..." Ken continued. "You take the right side and I'll go along the left side. If we keep a steady pace, side by side, then Jeb can move the wagon along at a steady pace. After a while we'll change places. That way our muscles won't ache too much."

Once again, Frank realized this younger kid was a fast hard worker. Frank was slower. Trying to keep a steady pace with Ken was a challenge. After an hour of doing the same routine, Frank got the hang of it, and they began to work more in unison. They worked three hours before Jeb called a change of shift. He said he would pick on Frank's corn stalk side, and Frank could sit in the wagon and lead the horses. They continued for another three hours when they stopped to eat lunch. It was 1:00 p.m. and already they had worked six hours.

They went back to the farmhouse for lunch and a time to freshen up. Ken told them they would probably only work till 4:00 p.m. because the days were getting shorter and it would start to get dark earlier. Frank was glad to stop work and to eat a hearty lunch of ham and cheese sandwiches, homemade potato salad, and drink plenty of cold water and coffee.

All morning, while Frank and Ken picked the corn, there was little   conversation. Frank was too busy trying to keep pace with Ken. It was different when Ken and Jeb picked corn. Frank heard them talk up a blue streak about many different subjects. Ken asked Jeb lots of questions about riding the rails: where Jeb had been, did he miss his home, did he have a family, and what advice would he give about riding the rails? Jeb was okay about answering; he told Ken he had been clear across the United States from California to New York. Yes, he did miss his home in San Diego, California, where it was sunny and warm every day of the year. His family only consisted of his parents and they told him it was okay if he explored the states and worked where and when he could. His advice to riding the rails was "Don't!"

Ken asked, "Why?"

Jeb was silent for a while and then just repeated his advice, "Don't!"

Frank knew why. Jeb probably had more dangerous experiences than Frank. Frank would give Ken the same advice. There was a sense of wanderlust that made traveling fun and exciting, but the dangers were always present and fearful. Frank felt thankful that at the present moment he had a place to rest, food to eat and work to accomplish.

Finally the afternoon ended, and they did quit at 4:00 p.m. Dinner would be served at 6:00 pm. Farm life always had a definite schedule. Frank didn't quit working when he got back to the farm house. He went into the barn and helped to get the horses back in their stalls, drying them off with towels, brushing their manes, feeding them and giving them water. Mr. Mueller was in the barn and appreciated Frank's help. He had been noticing how helpful Frank was even the night before when Frank brought wood into the main house without being asked.

Mr. Mueller started a conversation with Frank. "Tell me, Frank about yourself, your family, and your whereabouts."

"Well, sir, my family is in Portland, Oregon – at least that is where my mother and one brother are. My other brother is somewhere on a ship between here and China or he's in China."

Mr. Mueller hesitated to ask but did anyway, "What about your father?"

Frank took a few minutes to answer. "My father left us when I was four years old… I don't know about my father."

Mr. Mueller sighed; he was sorry he had asked about Frank's father. Now he felt he could ask no more questions.

Frank was aware of the awkward silence. "It's okay. My mom is a good woman; she's a nurse caring for elderly people. She's a good worker and she loves us."

Mr. Mueller smiled, "Yes, I'm sure she is a good woman." He had more questions for Frank, but he would wait. He noticed that Frank was a good worker. He was aware that Frank was doing more than he was asked to do and he also noticed that Frank did what was needed to be done without being told. Mr. Mueller was thinking about a future plan for him, but he would wait and watch before he presented his idea to him.

The next days they repeated the routine work. Frank picked corn, helped with the horses, and he also unloaded the wagons. They stored the corn in sheds that they called cribs. The corn needed time to dry before it could be used.

The only relaxing time for the workers was during the evenings and on Sundays. Jeb became the evening's entertainment. The men discovered that Jeb's love was music. In his pocket he carried a harmonica. He'd play songs that the men sang along with like: "Oh Susanna," "Red, Red Robin Comes Bob-Bob-Bobbin Along," and "Bye, Bye, Blackbird."

He also played songs on that small harmonica that made the sounds of the trains and the rhythm of the train wheels moving down the tracks. The other guys often sang along with Jeb or clapped their hands in time with his music.

On Sundays some of the men walked 10 to 14 miles to go to their own homes and be with their families. A couple times Frank and some of the other men went into town. The closest town was 14 miles away. One afternoon they walked, but it was a cold morning and not a pleasant walk. Only once did they ride to town. Braddyville was small and darn-near empty. There was only a gas station, a post office and a café. Frank decided it wasn't worth the effort, especially if it meant walking.

Work days continued. Ken became more talkative with Frank. He shared his school experiences and his future plans. "My father thinks I will someday own and run this farm, but I have other plans."

Frank wasn't nosy and really thought this might not be his business, but he figured Ken needed to talk to someone. He realized that this family didn't seem to have any nearby relatives or even close friends. The area they lived in was sparsely populated. The farmers lived miles from each other, so there wasn't much chance of visits. Frank didn't stop Ken from sharing his thoughts. He listened.

As they picked the corn, Ken shared his ideas: "Dad wants me to be in charge of this farm next summer. He thinks I can give the orders to the workers and show them step by step what needs to be done around here. He also knows that I can sell the corn and take the cows to market. He's taught me all I need to know to run this farm, but..."

Frank continued his thought, "but you have other concerns?"

"Yes, I do!" Ken's voice showed a determined attitude. "I've been offered a paid for college education. Our principal has told me that they need scientists and I've excelled in all the science classes. This will be an opportunity for me to go to California and major in science. I have the papers in my room. This is what I want to do."

Frank was slow to speak up, making sure that Ken didn't have more to add to this newsy piece of information. "Does your father know about your plan?"

"I don't think so."

Frank's only advice was, "You need to talk to him."

Frank didn't say it out loud, but he nodded his head to show that he approved of Ken's idea. The opportunity of getting a free education was the highest gift that a young boy could receive. If he loved the field of science, then that is what he should pursue. Frank had no idea, but Ken's plan would open an opportunity for Frank. Soon he would have to make a decision for his future too.

It was days later when Mr. Mueller talked to Frank about Ken; they were in the barn together caring for the horses. Frank loved being around the horses so he helped whenever he could. He had even helped with the cattle. There was one cow that got an infection and was in pain. Mr. Mueller had decided to put her down. Frank thought he could help to save the animal. He begged for a few days time. Knowing something about infections, as his mom was studying to be a nurse, his first step was to wash his pocket knife with boiling water. Then he cut into the inflammation of the cow's hide and removed the infected pus. Next, he got hot towels and held the towels on the infected area. He held the towels there for a ½ hour during the early morning, later in the late afternoon, and then later during the early evening. Ken also held hot packs on the cow.

Not only did Ken assist Frank, he watched him. Frank talked slow and in a low voice; this had a calming affect on the cow, that he named "Betsy."

Three days later, Betsy acted normal. The animal appeared to be healthy and the infected area was almost unnoticeable. The cow returned to her usual eating schedule and made no signs of discomfort. Mr. Mueller was pleased and impressed with Frank's care and his recovered cow. The bovine would be spared.

Mr. Mueller was forking out hay to the horses, when he brought up the subject that he had been thinking about for weeks. "I suppose Ken told you that he plans to go to California?"

Frank was surprised that Mr. Mueller knew Ken's plans. Ken had indicated to Frank that his father didn't know. "Yes, he told me."

"Well, he really hasn't told me; however, I know because Mr. Irvine, his principal, called me. They offered him free college education at Stanford University. They want him to study medicine. His room and board, and all expenses, will be paid for. He can't turn down an opportunity like that."

Frank nodded in agreement.

"I knew years ago that he would not be a farmer. He always gets straight A's and he reads all the time. The school has been good. They supplied him with books and extra assignments, always challenging him to do better."

Frank remained silent, wondering why Mr. Mueller felt a need to discuss this subject with him.

"Frank, the reason I address this issue with you is because I've appreciated all the work you've done while here this month. I'm extremely thankful how you saved our cow. I'd like to make you an offer. Instead of leaving at the end of the month, if you like, stay on. I'll pay you every month. You could work here all winter. I'd like you to be a manager here all next summer. I'd even offer you part of the inheritance to this farm land. This land is rich land. The crops are good. I will write up the paperwork and make a contract between you and me. Think about it, Frank. Don't make a quick decision." He walked out of the barn.

Frank was surprised. He wasn't through wandering the states. He still yearned to see New York. He was anxious to leave. He looked at the barn, and the animals. He stepped outdoors and studied the land, as if he hadn't seen it before. What would it be like to be part owner of acreage? He figured that these corn fields were producing money. He knew all the uses of corn and how much it was in demand. It was like someone offering him a part of a gold mine. Yet he was going to say no and walk away.

That night Frank asked to use the phone. Mr. Mueller said, "Of course, make your phone call."

Frank called the operator. "I need to make a collect call to Mary Rose in Portland, Oregon: Atwater 2234."

"Who shall I say is calling?"

"My name is Frank Rose, Gilbert Frank Rose." He knew his mom would like to hear his complete name. He hoped his mom would accept the call. He heard the rings. It rang four times before he heard his mom's voice, "Hello." Amazingly, it sounded like she was in the next room rather than miles away.

"This is the operator you have collect call from Gilbert Frank Rose, will you accept the charges?"

"Yes, yes, I will accept the call. Are you alright?"
"Yes, mom I'm fine. I'm in Iowa, working on a farm, picking corn."

"I'm so happy to hear your voice and you called at a perfect time. I want you to come home, your brother Millard will be here in three weeks."

"He's coming home?"

"Yes, but he will only be here a short while. Then he plans to leave on another ship that's going to Australia. Come home Frank and see your brother."

His mom's pleads were heartbreaking to Frank. He knew she was near tears mixed with sadness that her boys were far away, but also with hope that maybe, just maybe, they would be home together.

Frank made a decision, and a plan, that even surprised him. "I'll come home Mom. I have another week here to finish my job, but I will head home. I want to see Millard. I'll be there in time."

He hung up the phone. Mr. Mueller could not help but hear the conversation. He and Frank looked at each other. Without using words he knew what Frank's decision would be. He would not accept Mr. Mueller's offer.

Frank walked over to Mr. Mueller and shook his hand and said one word, "thanks." He hoped that Mr. Mueller would understand all that Frank was thanking him for: the hospitality, the trustfulness, the generous offer.

Frank headed to his sleeping quarters. He felt emotional. He hadn't heard his mother's voice in months. Memories made him feel like a child again when she told him either extreme sad news or uplifting news. They seldom had time to just chit-chat about daily activities. Tonight he heard promising news. He would be able to see Millard again.

Chapter Fifteen

Iowa to Chicago 1928 Seventeen Years Old

At the end of the week, during the early morning hour, Frank left the Mueller farm. Mr. Mueller had paid him generously. Frank could have paid for a train ticket, but he was okay with riding the freight train out of Iowa, as he did when he arrived in Iowa. Also, he had to save his money. He had no idea how long his trip would take or how much expense he would be forced to pay.

First, he had to backtrack to Chicago because that was the only route the Wabash trains went out of Iowa. In his overall pockets he had food. Mrs. Mueller had given him chicken sandwiches and corn. She placed plenty of oatmeal cookies in a long sock. She swore cookies were nutritious for a traveling man. He even had a small thermos of water; all of these items were jammed into his pockets. He wasn't comfortable wearing all his clothes and stuffing his pockets, but he was thankful. There would be no worries about food, until he got to Chicago.

The night before, he and Ken had studied Ken's atlas. His first ride from Blanchard to Chicago was a 481 mile trip. He estimated he'd be on the train over seven hours. From there he would have to go through parts of Wisconsin, Minnesota, and North Dakota. The plan included a stop in Montana. This trip would be a total of 16 hours and 1,102 miles. Hopefully, he would not devour all his food before he arrived at his first destination.

He wasn't sure where the freight yards were. He and Jeb had jumped off the freight train before it stopped. Now he assumed he'd have to jump on the moving train as it left Blanchard. The weather was colder now than it was when he first came to Iowa, feeling like the high thirties. The crisp morning air felt okay. He looked at the land differently now than he did months ago. Now he knew a family here. He had experienced working the fields and he was offered opportunity. That gesture would not be forgotten. He felt a kinship to the area and a fondness for the vast corn fields and the flat land.

Train sounds were in the distance. He waited. The sounds grew louder, yet the train wasn't going too fast. He ran closer to the tracks. It was the right moment. He directed his eyes to the side of a car with ladder rails and a door that was ajar; he ran faster, took a leap, grabbed the ladder bar and jumped inside the open door. He felt successful, like it was a smooth transition. He knew "too much confidence" could be a downfall, but he also felt that maybe he was getting the hang of it. It was like a dancer learning the steps to a dance, being able to enjoy the music and the rhythm, while swaying on the dance floor.

The boxcar was empty. At first he was glad to be alone, but as the ride continued, he realized having someone to talk to would help pass the time. He ate a couple cookies, saving his sandwiches for later. He concentrated on the view. Seeing the land pass like a blur was interesting. The daylight changed from the early morning bright sunlight to shadows of the grassy knolls. Iowa had so much land and so few people. He promised himself, "Remember the peacefulness of Iowa."

After dozing for several hours, he woke startled, wondering where he was. Feeling stiff and uncomfortable, he laughed to himself, thinking sleeping in a boxcar wasn't like sleeping in a bed. The Mueller's had spoiled him with three meals a day and a place to sleep at night with blankets, mattress and a pillow. Now it was back to cat-naps, when he could, and a stiff wooden board to lean against, or only hard ground to sleep on. It was going to be a rough trip home.

Near the Chicago Station, the train slowed down. It was a miracle that he woke up just in time to jump off this train. Everything, he owned, was still in his pockets. He hadn't even eaten his sandwiches yet. The temperature felt colder, and there was a pushing wind, but there was no snow on the ground yet. He felt lucky as he jumped off the train.

About 2:30 p.m. he arrived into the downtown area of Chicago. He wanted to see Daisy one more time, but he knew that wasn't going to happen today. There was a cafeteria at Sears and a public restroom. It was there he planned to buy more to eat, finish his chicken sandwich, and use the wash room to freshen up. His other goal was to get his mother and his brother gifts.

He felt glad to be in Chicago. This was a busy, welcoming city with all kinds of conveniences, especially for someone that had money in their pockets. Frank had some money. If hanging around was an option, he would see more sights and spend some of his money, but that was not an option. No, it was a trip to Sears and then towards home.

He walked on the wooden sidewalks, dodging other pedestrians. His month in Iowa had hindered his memory of the busy and crowded streets of Chicago. All he heard in Iowa was the noise of squawking ducks, clacking hens, mooing cows and the neighing sounds of horses. Here was the noise of autos: their blasting horns, the chatter and movement of masses of people. Frank was as amazed at the sights now, as he was weeks ago.

When he got to Sears, he completed his goals. He ate his cold, somewhat soggy chicken sandwiches, he ordered a warm hamburger to add to his meal, and drank hot coffee. He took time to clean up. Then he went and bought his mother a hat. She always wore a hat when she went out: not a flowery furry one, rather a plain hat that covered her head and had a silver pin on the side. This gift was the perfect hat with one bright shiny blue sapphire stone on the corner brim. Also this present fit nicely in his oversized pocket. He was satisfied!

Chapter Sixteen

Chicago to Fargo, North Dakota

Frank needed a train that would follow the Mississippi River, head toward Minnesota, and then head to North Dakota. Most of this travel time would be dark and cold. At 4:30 p.m. he saw the slow Northern Pacific freight coming. He ran and grabbed the side rail of a car that had its door ajar. Once inside the car he discovered the train car was frigid and empty. At first he thought it was great that he was alone – no one to bother him. After riding for over an hour, and darkness settled in, he wished there was another person near. He realized, like he did on his last trip, that he wanted to talk to someone. The night was young: sleep wasn't yet an option.

Frank imagined what it would be like if he was on a passenger train. He'd be riding in a comfortable cushioned seat, looking at a magazine, maybe smoking a cigarette, or talking to a fellow passenger. He might be waited on by one of the train's stewards. Yes, it would be extremely different than sitting on the hard wooded floor, leaning against the side board of an empty boxcar. He breathed and took in a whiff of dust and dirt.

His imagination continued to picture himself in a passenger train: warm blankets wrapped over his legs and chest. Now he had to hold his arms tight against himself to keep from shivering.

Tonight, riding the rails didn't seem like fun at all. Frank was anxious for daylight to come. He hoped he would not see snow, and he actually prayed he would not freeze before he got to Portland.

His thoughts turned to the time when he would see Millard. He listed, in his mind, all the questions he would ask his brother. What was it like to be in another country? How different was it riding on a ship compared to riding on a freight train? Was it safer sailing on roaring waves or bouncing over steel rails? He figured riding the rails was safer.

But... he laughed to himself, boarding a ship would be safer than jumping on and off a moving train. Frank wasn't a swimmer. Going up a gangplank or working on a rocking ship deck, especially during a storm, could be more fearsome than what he was experiencing.

His thoughts were becoming more confusing. His mind was repeating words: "easier, safer, harder, and riskier." Most important to him, and the one thought that still penetrated his mind, was that he was headed home to see his brother. He dozed off.

He slept through Wisconsin and Minnesota. At sunrise he awoke and figured he must be in North Dakota. There was a dusting of snow on the ground. Despite the two layers of clothes, his heavy boots, and his new gloves, he was cold.

The train moved fast. He wasn't sure when or where it would slow down enough for him to jump off. He didn't see any cities or even small towns. There were intersections, but so far he hadn't seen any autos or people at these crossings. It was a continuous trip of whizzing down the straight track.

A hungry feeling was taking over Frank's thoughts. His legs were stiff. He stood up, as the locomotive continued to speed down the tracks. Frank realized it would be hard to walk around in this jerky swaying empty car. Despite how unsteady he felt, he walked in circles. After several circle movements, he began to feel dizzy, but at least his muscles worked and felt normal.

A blurry view was still evident through the narrow open doorway. The grassy flat land passed quickly. More time lapsed and still Frank did not see any houses or evidence of a town. Despite not seeing sighs of civilization, he was ready to jump as soon as the train slowed down. He had no map, or guidebook to tell him when that might be.

Tobacco was in his pocket. It was awkward to do so, but despite the movements and jerking sensations, he rolled a cigarette, lit a match off his shoe and smoked. It wasn't on par with eating breakfast, but breathing in and exhaling relaxed him enough that he felt okay about having to wait.

A couple hours went by when Frank became aware that the train slowed its pace. Looking out the door he noticed an intersection and buildings ahead! The view showed a possibility of a town and places to eat. It was time to leap. He continued to stare as the grassy field appeared to be moving. After a broad leap, he landed on two feet, a satisfying experience. Looking straight ahead he started his walk to town.

The sign, posted over the street, showed Frank that he was in Fargo. These streets were not as busy as Chicago, but there were people and storefronts. Another sign was visible: Tom's Café. Frank walked in the doorway and sat at the soda counter. Satisfying his hunger was his main concern. He ordered a large breakfast with ham, eggs, biscuits, gravy and a cup of coffee. When the meal came, he had to remind himself to slow down and enjoy the food.

"Where are you from, Buddy?" The waiter questioned Frank.

"Now I'm from Iowa, but I'm heading back to my hometown Portland."

"Kind of a bad time to be traveling; it's December and the winter is in full swing. Man, you need about three more layers of clothes, like the mountain climbers wear."

Frank had no comment. He knew he was going to have to endure the cold with what he was wearing.

The waiter sighed and walked off to continue his duties.

Frank left the diner with a full stomach, but also with a lonely feeling. He felt lost in Fargo. He didn't fit in. Definitely, he was a stranger just passing through.

The waiter was right, he wasn't dressed warm enough for this climate. He saw a storefront window displaying jackets. He entered the store and looked at the displays. He felt the lining and the fur around the hood of several jackets. The material was thick and felt warm to the touch.

Taking one off the hanger, he tried it on. The jacket was heavier than his, but not too bulky. The zipper felt much tighter than his jacket. The price was clearly marked: two dollars. That was expensive!

He walked to the counter. "Excuse me, sir, but I'd like very much to buy this warmer jacket; however, I'd like to make a deal with you. See my jacket is still in good repair. Do you think we could make a trade? Maybe, you could give me something for my jacket to lessen the price of this jacket. I see you do sell used jackets. You could get a good price for this one."

The owner looked at Frank and then took the worn jacket in his hands. He could have suggested this customer look at the used ones to get a lower price, but he figured this young man needed warmer attire. The one he wanted to buy might be a life saving jacket, keeping him from freezing to death.

The owner examined the used jacket carefully while Frank stood silent and waited for the final decision. "Tell you what, son I don't see any tears in yours and it is a good common size. I'll give you fifty cents for your jacket, so your new jacket will be $1.50."

"It's a deal" Frank answered with excitement. He reached deep into his overall pocket, pulled out a dollar and a fifty-cent piece. He felt warm, as he walked down the street, feeling hopeful that he would actually make it to Portland without freezing to death.

He wandered down the tracks a distance until he was a ways from town. Knowing where the next freight train would start to slow down, he sat on a rock and patiently waited.

Time passed, it was almost an hour before he heard a freight train. Smoke was bellowing out the top of the engine. The sounds from the wheels were almost deafening. Frank stood up and ran past the engine until he saw an open boxcar. Three cars passed with closed doors. He picked up speed and ran directly toward the open door boxcar. He leaped aboard!

Inside the car were four other men huddled close together, away from the car door. "Welcome aboard!" said one older looking guy.

Frank nodded in their direction. He was somewhat out of breath mostly because it was so cold. Breathing heavy was common for him when running and jumping on a train; this action always got his adrenalin going and made him breathless.

"Where are you headed kid?" Frank was feeling mature for his age, but he knew that in comparison to the other guys, he was a kid.

"My final destination is Portland, Oregon."

"Well, you've got a ways to go, so make yourself comfortable."

Frank felt obligated to be polite and to continue the conversation. "Where are you guys headed?"

The oldest man continued to be the main spokesperson. "Well, my name is Thomas and I'm headed to Montana. The rest of these guys…" he pointed to the other four fellows, "they say they're headed to Washington State."

This was Frank's chance to ask about the yard bulls. "I hear tell the yard bulls in Washington are mean, and it's not easy getting through Washington."

This prompted one of the guys to speak up. "Hell, you can say that again. I spent three months in jail because of the yard bulls in Washington. My plan is to jump off as soon as we cross the border. I'm headed to Seattle, but I'll hitchhike from wherever, before I meet another yard bull."

"Where did you get stopped before?" Frank needed to know because he figured he'd have to go through Washington too.

"I got stopped in Spokane. If you've got any money, save some: you might get the chance to pay them off. My mistake was I was plum broke. They don't appreciate or respect poor folks. No Siree."

Frank remembered his one encounter where the yard bulls checked to see who had money, Yeah, it made a difference.

"Thanks for the tip."

Sitting down near the guys, Frank felt somewhat welcomed after this brief conversation. He would wait before bringing up any other topics. It would be a long ride.

After several minutes of looking out the open door and only hearing the sound of the train wheels, and seeing nothing but grassy empty plains, he asked his next question.

"You guys ever see any roaming buffalo in these parts?"

Once again Thomas was quick to answer. "You mean bison? Guess you don't know much about your history young man. The buffalo, or really bison, quit roaming in our land back in 1889. Back then, the railroad company even supplied folks with rifles so they could just haphazardly shoot the bison. Yeah, passengers shot them as the trains sped by."

"Really," responded Frank. "Why would they do that?"
"Crazy, right? It was a sport, like a sports game. They shot those animals and just left them to die. They didn't do these vicious acts for any purpose of using the hides or the food – no, just a waste. Many Sioux Indians lived around here. They were heartsick to see dead animals that were killed in that manner, for no reason."

Frank nodded in agreement. He knew Indians would never waste an animal. They never killed unless they needed to. Killing for no reason was unexplainable to them. "Basically…" Thomas continued, "…the buffalo herds are gone."

Frank was sorry he had asked. "What can we see as we go through North Dakota?'

The young guy spoke again. "In the morning light we will probably go through the badlands; there are only steep Rocky Mountains and rivers. Let me warn you; don't jump off in the badlands. You won't have any towns around, and no one will find you, if anyone tries to find you."

"Thanks," Frank answered with a discouraging tone. North Dakota didn't sound at all inviting, though he had been here before in Dickinson. The plan was to ride as far as Montana. He'd get off there and try to find Miles City again. The plan was to stop for one night at the hobo jungle for rest and a meal. That was his goal, but there would be a slight change. He would get a meal, but not at the hobo jungle.

Chapter Seventeen

North Dakota to Miles City, Montana

Frank, Millard and Lou were rolling down a grassy hillside. "I can roll faster than you guys," yelled Millard.

"Quit bragging you know I'm the fastest!" yelled Lou. Frank kept tumbling down the hillside. He knew he was the fastest. Then he saw a drop off. He was going to fall and die!

Thomas yelled, "Move, move away from the door." Suddenly, Frank woke up from his deep troubling sleep. He sat straight up and quickly realized he was near the open freight car door.

While the train moved extremely fast, he had slid toward the open gap of the doorway. The car tipped back and forth. He used his body strength and rolled away from the doorway.

His fellow hobos were sliding in the car too. "Thomas," he yelled, "what's going on?"

"I'm not sure," Thomas hollered back as he slid from side to side of the boxcar. The entire car shook. "We picked up speed, as soon as we crossed into Montana. We must be going about 90 miles per hour!"

Frank braced himself against the wall, feeling somewhat able to stay in one position. "Why would an engineer run a train this fast?"

Thomas didn't hesitate; he answered, "This isn't the first time I've been on a raging speeding train."

"This happened to you before?" Frank surprised himself that he was even asking such a question.

"Yeah, back in July 1922 in New Jersey."

The other hobos were paying attention now too. They also had been sliding and were trying their best to stay in one position as the train continued to shift back and forth, like a fishing boat at sea in rough waters.

Thomas continued, "I was on a freight train at Winslow Junction…" he chuckled, "you would think the name Winslow would prompt an engineer to slow down; no this freight train sped up. It was said the train was going 90 miles per hour over an open switch. The train derailed. Basically, it crashed!"

That was not the story ending they wanted to hear.

"Well, you made it," yelled Frank.

"Yeah, I did…, but seven folks didn't."

"You mean seven folks died?"

"That's what I mean."

No one asked any more questions. From the open car door they could see their surroundings. They were on a cliff, above a river's edge. If the train derailed now, it would fall over the rocks and drop a distance into a raging river.

The train car kept rolling back and forth. There were times when each one of them slid from one side to another side of the car. It would have been a humorous scene if they felt safe; instead, it was like a rollercoaster ride without the rollercoaster attendant supervising.

They were not sure if the engineer was awake and in charge-or if anyone was in control.

One hobo kid, who looked younger than Frank, started to pray out loud, "Hail Mary Mother full of grace, hear our prayers in this time of need…" The other guys listened in respect. This was no time to argue about one's religion or to not respect one's faith.

Thoughts were in agreement; they didn't want to die! Frank wanted the engineer to slow down the train so he could jump off, which was exactly what he planned to do.

The fast ride was continuous for at least a ½ hour. Finally, it did slow down to a more normal speed and then, just minutes later, to a near stopping speed. Frank knew, from the familiar scenery, that he was close to Miles City. "I don't know about you guys, but I'm departing."

Thomas advised him to wait a little longer till they got closer to town.

"Nope!" said Frank "Here's where I'm leaving." He gave a wave and wished them luck. Then he leaped off the train.

His jump was not a graceful leap. He ended up doing a roll on the snowy grass. It was similar to his nightmare, but now he was mildly wet and definitely cold.

He looked at his surroundings. He knew he was near Miles City, where he had been before. It was there that he had met his engineer friend. If he saw the same fellow again he would ask why a freight train would go 90 miles per hour.

He started his hike into town. On the way he tried to remember the name of his friend. Then it came to him, "Edward." Maybe, he could have another visit with Edward. He walked more swiftly. The town looked the same. Stockman Bar was open. Once again he sat at the bar on a bar stool. He took off his heavy jacket and placed it on the stool next to him. He looked at the wall menu and selected his breakfast meal.

That's when Edward walked in the doorway. He saw Frank and sat on the other bar stool. "Amazing," Edward greeted him, "I never thought I'd see you again."

"You almost didn't," answered Frank.

Edward looked at him, Frank seemed healthy enough. "Have you had some rough times?"

Frank spoke slowly, "I'd say the last few hours were rather rough. I want to ask you your opinion?"

"Sure." said Edward. "Ask away."

"Why would an engineer run a freight train up to 90 miles per hour?"Edward started to chuckle, "You must have jumped off that last freight train."

"Yeah, that's right." Frank didn't care anymore if Edward knew he was a hobo. It was okay being a hobo: there was no shame. Since he last met Edward, he had worked in Iowa and had even been offered permanent farm labor. He felt comfortable talking to Edward and respected his opinion.

Frank looked at Edward and asked, "How did you figure I jumped off the last freight train?"

"Oh, an educated guess: Old Leonard runs that track. Every once in a while he goes a little crazy especially near the water cliff." Frank agreed, "That's exactly where it all got crazy."

Edward continued, "Consider the thought that you are lucky to be alive. Leonard only thinks about his freight; after the cars are empty then he runs the train as fast as he wants. He never even considers that his freight cars might be carrying human beings. Yeah, consider yourself lucky."

Frank ordered his food and relaxed. He did feel lucky. Edward ordered food and started to eat too. "Hey, you got a place to stay tonight?"

"Yeah," answered Frank, "I'll be at the hobo jungle tonight."

"Come to my place around 5:00 p.m. and have dinner with us. It's close to the hobo jungle area. Helen, my wife, is a great cook." Edward wrote out the address and the directions.

"Much obliged," said Frank. He was pleased to be invited to a home.

When he arrived at the hobo jungle he was surprised to see that it was different than before. There were some wooden sheds with cots. Last time he was here, he slept on the ground and bathed in the river. Now they had shower stalls and indoor sheds with cots to sleep on. He cleaned up, even washed some of his clothing and got ready for his dinner meal.

Early that evening, Edward greeted him at the door. "Welcome Frank, come in."

Edward eyed him like he approved how clean and nice Frank looked. He noticed Frank's new jacket, and decent boots. Frank didn't appear like a hobo at all.

They walked toward the kitchen. Edward introduced Frank, as his friend, to his wife, Helen and to their collie dog, Lady. Frank bent down to pet the dog. Helen greeted Frank with a friendly smile as she continued her cooking chores. She had a big pot of stew steaming on the wood-burning stove. She was heavyset, with a clear complexion and a pleasant looking face.

Edward led Frank to the living room. The sitting area looked inviting with a blazing fire going in the fireplace and music playing on the phonograph.

"Mighty nice place," Frank commented.

"Thanks," answered Edward, "we like living here in Montana. We love the beautiful summer, and well, you know we can get miserable winters, but all in all, we like it here."

Helen called them to the table. She said a table blessing of thankfulness for the food. They passed the serving dishes and ate a full course dinner. Frank was hungry and really enjoyed this home cooked meal.

Helen started to eat and then looked toward Frank and asked, "How did you and Edward meet?"

Edward quickly answered, "He just got off the train this afternoon."

She looked back at Edward. "Oh," she responded, "the same train you came in on." It wasn't a question, it was a statement; so neither Frank nor Edward gave any more information.

Frank spoke next, "I came from Iowa, but got on the train in North Dakota. I'm heading to my home town in Portland, Oregon."

"Oh, Portland, I've been there; great shopping in Portland. I love Lipman & Wolfe and Meier & Franks. I wish we had some department stores like those around here." She continued on about her fun shopping adventures.

After dinner Edward invited Frank to stay and play Pinochle. The three of them cleared the dishes and then sat in the living room and played cards. Frank quickly caught on to how the game was played. He enjoyed card games.

After several rounds of Pinochle, Helen served them chocolate cake for dessert. They were eating at the card table, when Helen brought up the subject of hobos riding the freight trains.

Obviously, from the conversation, she had no idea that Frank was a hobo. She had assumed that he came into town on a passenger train. Still neither Frank nor Edward changed her assumption.

Helen stated, "Seems to be lots more men riding the freight trains. Often they come out this way and ask for work. You probably heard the hobo jungle isn't far from here."

Frank nodded in agreement, but did not add to her statements.

"Well, the other day some neighbor ladies and I had a discussion about the issue. We decided that if these hobos want food and expect us to fix them something to eat, then first they better be willing to do some chores for us; that seems reasonable. Don't you think?"

She waited for Edward and/or Frank to reply.

Frank and Edward looked at each other. It was as if they could read each other's mind. It wasn't the time to inform Helen that she had just fed and entertained a hobo in her home. They did not want to mention that this hobo had not done any chores; he had been an invited guest.

Finally, after a pause of silence, Edward spoke, "That might be okay, but sometimes these men come so hungry, they need to be fed before they can do any work."

Then Edward quoted two scripture verses from memory: "For I was hungered and ye gave me meat; I was thirsty, and ye gave me drink; I was a stranger and ye took me in.

"Be not forgetful to entertain strangers for thereby some have entertained angels unawares."

Helen was at a loss for any more words. She smiled, shrugged her shoulders, picked up the messy dishes and went back to the kitchen. Frank and Edward chuckled. Edward looked toward the kitchen, and quietly said, "Best she doesn't know your situation." He looked away and said out loud his thoughts, "It's always best to befriend everyone. Help those in need."

Frank knew he wasn't the Messiah nor was he an "unawares angel," but was blessed because Edward and Helen welcomed him into their home. He and Edward were still laughing about their secret when Helen came back into the living room. She wondered what they were laughing at, but decided not to ask. Men often talked and laughed concerning subjects that they didn't share with the women folks.

Frank stood and grabbed his jacket that was hung on a wooden hook by the doorway. "Thanks for the delicious dinner and your gracious hospitality. It was a pleasure to meet both of you." He shook Edward's hand and walked out the door.

Edward stepped out of the doorway and added a last statement: "Take care man, and be careful!"

Frank headed back to the hobo jungle.

Chapter Eighteen

Miles City, Montana to Butte, Montana

After a good night's sleep, Frank awoke early, ready to travel. As he stepped out of the cabin shelter, where he had slept, he could smell bacon cooking over the burning fire. Throwing on his extra shirt, over the clothes he was already wearing, he zipped up in his jacket and put on his boots. The morning was cold. No snow yet, but he could smell the moist air and knew snow was coming.

Heading toward the fire, he greeted three men that were already eating breakfast and drinking coffee. Hobos usually ate breakfast quietly as they contemplated their day. Schedules were never too clear unless they already had an assigned job. Frank didn't have a job, rather he had a destination, and he wanted to leave early.

Several times he said thanks to the men that had prepared the morning fire and the breakfast meal. After he ate, he was well satisfied and ready to depart. He knew the path the departing freight trains used. His hope was that "Crazy Leonard", the speeding engineer, would be off work sleeping, or at some other faraway place.

Many people were near the train depot, and Frank feared he might be caught if he was close to the railroad tracks, so he watched for a coming train from a nearby hillside. He surmised that when he heard or saw the train approach he could run down the grassy knoll, jump over the fence rail (that was at the end of the hillside), and then leap onto the train.

The train came and Frank carried out his plan. He ran down the hill, leaped over the rail, and jumped onto the freight car that he thought was the tender (the coal car behind the engine.) Instead, he landed on the back part of the engine cab.

Matt the Engineer, and Ken the Fireman yelled at him and motioned for him to climb right up and into the cab. Frank was sure he'd be asked to jump off the moving train or be arrested and given over to authorities when they reached the next town. Instead, they were congratulating him. "We didn't think you could do it," commented Matt.

.."Yeah," answered Ken, "I bet Matt, a twenty-five cent piece that you would not make that jump."

Matt replied, "I trusted that you could. You ran so fast and the way you leaped over the fence rail, it was like a small mound rather than a five foot fence."

Ken added the last part of what they witnessed, "Then you jumped on board: no hesitation, just a quick hop! We were picking up speed. Hell, if you would have waited even a few seconds you would not have made it, by then we'd be going too fast."

They both nodded in agreement, "a great jump!" Matt offered him a small space on the wooden bench. "Sit down, make yourself comfortable, and ride up here for a while."

Frank was relieved to meet Matt and Ken. When he first realized he was not on the tender, but the engine, he feared he'd meet "Crazy Leonard," That was an engineer he did not want to meet. His other thought was he'd have to leap off the train while it was picking up speed. He never imagined that he'd have a chance to ride with the engineer and the fireman in the cab!

Frank watched as Ken shoveled coal into the blazing firebox. He could smell the black tar coal as it hit the flames, but the odor didn't bother him. Ken showed him the water-tube boiler gauge. He explained that he had to watch the pressure gauge so the boiler in front didn't explode. That was a new concern that Frank had not thought about before this ride. Matt pulled the whistle cord with its short and long toots as they passed intersections. From the cab, the whistle sounded like a pipe organ repeating chords.

Matt also demonstrated how touchy the throttle was to hold, to keep the engine running and how it was used to change the speeds as they approached an intersection. The boiler ahead of them blocked their view. Their vision was limited to the side windows and a narrow window that viewed the track ahead of the engine. Frank realized how hard it would be to see if anything, animal or person, was on the tracks. He had seen the tracks from the top of train cars, and he realized that though the cab was comfortable, their view was restricted.

Matt told him how necessary it was to blast the whistle sounds every time they passed near an intersection. Ken agreed, "The train takes too long to stop if anything is in the way."

The view, that Frank could see, he enjoyed. Montana was beautiful country with pleasant grassy plains: only now not all green, but semi white and brown with a glaze of snow. In the distance, he viewed mountains. These peaks appeared light blue against the wide open sky.

The conversation was lively. They talked about when they first became train men, and Frank shared with them his goal to get home and see his brother. Frank felt semi-warm and comfortable even though the back of the cab was open and air was constantly blowing.

When they got near Billings, Matt gave him instructions: "Crawl out over the coals on the tender car and stay low! We don't want you to be seen as we pass through the Billings Station. We will be going fast. Don't worry we won't be stopping, just passing through." Frank did as he was advised. He knew that other hobos had ridden on the tender cars so he figured it would not be a problem. "We are close now," yelled Ken. Frank walked over the train couplings that held the cars together. He climbed the rail of the tender car and sank down over the coals. With his black jacket and black boots he felt he blended in with the dark hard coals. He was not at ease, but he figured he could cope for a while. Then they went through a dark, narrow tunnel. For several minutes all Frank could see was blackness. He was thankful he was in a coal bin rather than on top of the train with smoke blowing in his face. At least, in the bin, he had no fear of bumping his head on the cement ceiling of the tunnel.

The train slowed down and Frank stayed hidden. No sooner than they had passed through the town area, when he heard Ken yell at him to return to the cab. Matt and Ken had food laid out for their lunch. Frank was surprised to see cut sandwiches, bananas, oranges and cups of coffee. Ken pointed to the food, "Just help yourself and eat. We have plenty." Frank felt like he was royalty, getting a free pass, and luxury treatment.

Over the chugging noise of the train, Matt yelled, "We have to stop in Butte, Montana. You'll have to jump off before we arrive in Butte; we will let you know exactly when. Frank relaxed and didn't worry about his coming up stop. He knew that he was in good hands and for a while he would let these kind men do the thinking. He offered to help shovel the coal, but Ken was a heavy-set, strong man and didn't seem to mind the work. He just smiled and kept shoveling. Frank took a few deep breaths and leaned back to enjoy the ride.

As the train moved, Frank's body swayed with the train's motions. He felt relaxed and comfortable, when he heard Ken's voice. "We're close to where you'll have to jump off. We have to unload some freight, and change direction."

"No problem," said Frank. "I'm much obliged for your kindness and generosity. I'll remember you guys."

Ken answered, "Don't worry man just be safe. We're glad to hear that you're heading home. Watch out for the yard bulls." Then he repeated, "Be safe!"

Matt added a comment from remembering his first sight of Frank, "After watching you, we know hopping trains is your specialty!"

Frank was surprised at the compliment coming from a train engineer, no less. He waited for the signal. He was ready and waiting for Matt to nod at him when it was time to go. The train slowed down to a crawl. This speed was slower than Frank was used to whenever he jumped off moving trains. These train men seemed to be doing him an extra favor. Matt nodded and pointed toward the tracks and dirt. Frank was ready to leave. He was curious as to what Butte, Montana might have to offer. He gave a quick wave. While standing on the couplers ready to jump, he looked at the ground that appeared to be moving. He waited a few seconds calculating when to jump. He thought the landing would be easy there was snow on the ground. Even though the train had slowed down Frank did not land on his two feet. Somehow he landed on his knees. The snow was not soft rather hard and icy. His knees felt sore. He rubbed each knee and brushed off his pants. He figured if he started to walk he would feel okay.

He knew Butte was a mining town, but that was all he knew. Hopefully, there would be a place to spend the night. He started his walk to the sprawling buildings ahead. The town had a backdrop of blue tinged mountains in the distance.

Despite, the dusting of ground snow, the town had a look of grayness. The buildings were rough, wooden buildings. It was cold and crisp yet, the air did not smell fresh. There was a dusty smog that probably always existed from the mining industry. The first two story structure he came to had a sign on it, "Miner's Saloon." He decided that was the place to start.

He walked to the bar to place his order of food and drink. The bartender looked at him and then asked, "New in town?"

"Yes, sir" answered Frank.

He proudly stated, "I just hopped off that last freight train." He didn't add that the engineer and the fireman gave him permission to be on that freight train.

"Well, we have no hobo jungles here. You got any money for grub or are you just bumming and passing through?"

Frank had been feeling good about himself after the praise he had received and the unique train ride, but this guy's remarks were quick to knock down Frank's ego. He didn't care much though because he was hungry, he wanted food, and he had some money.

Frank looked directly at the bartender, "Don't worry man, I can pay for my meal. If there is a place to stay tonight I'd be much obliged."

The bartender stared back. He shrugged his shoulders as if he had decided Frank was an okay guy. He handed him a menu. "We have a row of flop houses at the end of the street. Just knock on the first door and ask for Misty. She'll give you a room for the night. Small but clean and it has running water you can clean up." Then he added, "Got cribs out back if you know what I mean."

Frank had heard about cribs where women stayed and waited for men, but he wasn't ready for companionship. He had a goal to keep his money and head to Portland.

"Thanks," said Frank. "I'll have the roast beef dinner with gravy, potatoes and cooked greens." He wasn't sure what "cooked greens," were but it sounded okay. He had dandelion greens at the hobo jungles. Often they were picked off the ground, cooked and eaten. He figured these greens, probably were real grown vegetables; it wasn't the season for dandelion weeds.

The bartender showed Frank two soda pop bottles. He quietly asked, "You want a beer or two?" Frank understood this was a way to sell liquor during prohibition.

"No, thanks, I'll have coffee with sugar and cream."

"Okay, man, suit yourself." The bartender headed back into the kitchen. Not only did he serve the food it appeared that he also cooked the food.

When Frank got his order and started to eat, a guy sat on the bar stool next to him. He looked at Frank and introduced himself, "Hey, buddy I'm Bruce, what's your name?"

"Just call me Frank," Frank mumbled as he continued eating.

"Well, Frank, what brings you to Butte?"

"Well, I came by train, but I'm headed home to Portland, Oregon."

"You don't say, Portland. Isn't that where it rains all the time?"

"Pretty much," answered Frank. "Tell, me Bruce, what do you do in Butte?"

"I'm a miner like all these other guys in here. I've only been doing it for six months."

"What do you mine for?"

"Well, years ago they were mining for silver and gold here, but now we mine for copper. There's a big need for copper. The government wants it as fast as we can bring it out of the ground. They use it for electrical wiring, phones, coins, automobiles, even pots and pans."

Frank turned away from his food plate and looked at this guy. His voice sounded old, but as Frank stared at him he realized he was young maybe about Frank's age. He was probably somewhere between 17 and 19. He had a short beard and his hair was so matted it was hard to tell what color it really was. Maybe it was what they called, dishwater blond, but it looked more like a dirty brown with only a few lighter streaks. He was muscular, but he wasn't heavy, he was thin. He had a semi smile that didn't match his sad looking eyes. His hands told the story of hard, dirty work. He had the appearance of a rough, tough character, though Frank suspected he had a kind caring side of him.

"Is your dad a miner too?"

Bruce didn't answer. There was awkward silence. Frank felt bad he had asked about Bruce's father. Frank didn't know the whereabouts of his own father. The only father figure he knew was Mr. Steward and that was not a father figure, as far as Frank was concerned. He decided not to wait for Bruce's answer.

"Hey, Bruce, tell me what's it like to live here in Butte."

"Well, it's like living in a pit, literally. I go to the mines every day. Every day I fear for my life. Back in 1917 they had a mine fire. One hundred and sixty-eight miners lost their lives." He stopped talking for a few minutes and looked away.

"My dad was one of those miners. I was eight years old then. I only have a few memories about my dad. The fire started when a cable fell and the foreman went down to check it out. He had a lamp, and an oily rag; the rag caught on fire on the cable's installation. Men were down 2000 feet. They poured water into the mine. That caused hot steam and men were burnt and trapped. Course some died because they lacked oxygen or because of the heavy smoke. We're not sure about dad. They never brought the bodies out of the mine. That mine is closed off now."

Before Frank could comment or show his empathy. Bruce continued.

"Then in 1920 the miners decided to go on strike. You know, get more pay, and safer conditions." Bruce talked more quietly. "But those company bosses didn't agree and shot down those miners – some right in the back. It was called the Anaconda Massacre. Did you hear about that?"

"No," said Frank. "I didn't hear that, but I've got an opinion. That wasn't right. Men have a right to speak up about safe work conditions."

Bruce nodded his head in agreement. He glanced toward the miners in the room, indicating that maybe they should change the subject.

"Let me tell you something else that happened in Butte. Last year someone famous came to town. Want to guess who?"

"No," answered Frank. He was trying to chew his food and he had no idea which famous person Bruce might be talking about.

"Well," said Bruce, "You've probably heard about Charles Lindberg flying over the Atlantic Ocean."

"Yeah," Frank answered.

"I heard tell he flew right through Hellgate Canyon in Missoula, Montana. That's what I heard. But, what I saw was he landed his plane right at our airfield here in Butte, Montana. Yes, sir, He landed his "Spirit of St. Louis" right here in Butte. I saw him in person! That happened on September 6, last year, 1927."

Frank could tell that Bruce cherished this history making event that he witnessed. Frank waited to make a comment.

Bruce added one more thought, "They call him 'Lucky Lindy' and indeed he is."

"You were lucky too. Lucky that you got to see the plane and Charles in person."

Bruce looked surprised. He felt really pleased that Frank had called him a lucky person. "Indeed I am." He nodded in agreement.

Bruce relished in that thought for a few moments. "Yeah, Charles spoke to the crowd of people right out here in the middle of the road. He told us there will be more flights comin' to our town. Butte will get mail by flight. Once a month a plane will fly in and deliver mail. Can you beat that? I might even order something out of a Sear's catalogue."

This idea opened an opportunity for Frank to tell Bruce all about his visit to Chicago. He shared what he saw and how he shopped in the Sears Department Store.

Bruce was delighted to hear Frank's stories about Chicago. As Frank finished his meal he was anxious to get to the Flop House and get cleaned up.

Bruce shook Frank's hand and said he enjoyed the conversation.

"Tell you what Frank, you want a job mining you just tell the foreman. His name is Joe. Say, Bruce sent you. You'd get a job. Not that I have much influence, but my dad was one of the best miners in town. All the fellow miners help me, and they would hire anyone I told them to out of respect for my dad. Don't take this offer lightly." He paused, "Hell, they call this town 'The Richest Hill on Earth.' "

"Thanks," said Frank. "I'm proud to have met you Bruce."

They shook hands and Frank walked out the door. He knew he would attempt almost any job, but not underground or even above ground mining.

The Flop House turned out to be more comfortable than expected. He was told he could heat up water in the main kitchen and carry those buckets of water to the bathroom tub down the hallway and take a bath. Frank made several water trips. Finally, he relaxed in a warm tub of water. The bed was comfortable. The night cost him a fifty-cent piece, but it was well worth it.

In the morning the saloon was closed, but there was a "Miner's Café." Every name in town seemed to have the name "miner" on it. There was even a school named, Miner's School. The café was near empty. This time no questions were asked. He ordered his breakfast and ate quietly.

After eating, he headed down the road. He planned to hop on a slow moving freight train near where he had jumped off the day before. He knew it would not be an easy ride, like his last one, but he had to keep moving to get to Portland.

It was still early so Frank wasn't too worried about anyone paying attention to him. He didn't try any long runs or fancy leaps; instead, he sat on the field, near the tracks, waiting for a slow moving train.

He planned for a careful jump and hoped for an open boxcar door. It wasn't what happened. Instead, he hopped on board too soon. Somehow he missed the one car that had an opened door. Instead he leaped onto the couplers between two cars. Now his only choice was riding below on the rods. He heard that sometimes hobos clung to the axle bracing rods below the train. He figured that would be too rough and dangerous, and he assumed extremely uncomfortable. The other choice was to ride on top of the car that he was bracing himself against. There was a ladder so he started the upward climb.

Chapter Nineteen

Butte, Montana to Spokane, Washington

No one else was riding on top of the car. He found a space on the curvature part of the roof. It was there he felt somewhat safe and steady. It was cold. He figured it was going to be a miserable ride. His consolation was that he was heading in the right direction and getting nearer home. He couldn't believe his change of luck. His last ride was in a cab, visiting with the engineer and the fireman. Now he was alone riding on top of a swaying car.

He had to stay alert for upcoming tunnels, keep himself bundled tightly to protect himself from freezing to death, and duck when the train slowed down so no yard bulls would see him.

It was a bumpy, noisy, smoky, uncomfortable ride. He rode this way for about an hour. All the while he thought about his future plans. He expected to jump off the train when he saw a sign saying he was near Spokane. His firm decision was to hitchhike into Spokane. As he contemplated his next moves, he almost missed seeing the approaching tunnel. He quickly unzipped his jacket and held it over his head. He ducked as low as he could against the train boards. The noise was deafening. The smoke suffocated his breathing.

Seconds went by, but they seemed like long minutes. His eyes were tightly closed. Keeping his eyes closed kept him from having flying soot debris floating into his eyes. Also, there was the possibility of hot flying cinders that could burn his eyes. Finally, he knew the train was back in the daylight. He glanced back. It was a long low tunnel. He felt dirty and sooty. Remembering his long hot bath of the night before, he wished he could soak in a tub again. He told himself it would happen when he got to his mother's place.

He stayed alert and waited for signs of Spokane. It was hard to keep track of the time. He figured he had been riding over an hour: maybe, two hours. From previously studying the time tables, he knew that Butte to Spokane was over a four hour trip.

A little ditty, to the rhythm of the train wheels, came to his mind. "Keep alert, keep alert, don't look down, look around, enjoy the ride, almost home, by and by." Singing and talking to himself wasn't one of his usual habits, but it was one way to help him to pay attention. With his jacket on and zipped tightly, he crossed his arms, leaned down to cuddle his body with as much warmth as he could. His eyes focused on seeing an intersection that might indicate he was near Spokane.

Finally, the bells clanged and the whistle blew its long and short sounds indicating an intersection was up ahead. The train slowed down. Frank looked up and saw the sign, "Spokane 5 miles ahead." He crawled to the end of the car. Then he lowered his body to climb down the ladder. He hung onto the ladder near the bottom rung. He looked at the fast moving ground. This is where he wanted to jump, but the train moved faster than he wanted. He gazed past the tracks. There was a field covered in snow. Hopefully, this time the snow was deep and soft, not icy like the last time he fell in snow. The time to jump was now. With one hand he let go of the ladder and with the other hand he pushed himself away from the train wall. His body flew in the air. He landed on his back in the soft snow.

He laid there several minutes. He waited for the train cars to whizz by. The train's movement caused a rush of wind and flying snow drifting around him. At last, it passed and the air was calm. The loud noise faded into the distance.

Touching his arms and legs, to make sure he had no broken bones, he decided he was okay. While brushing off the wet flakes, from his pants, he looked at his boots. They were covered in snow, but thankfully, his feet felt warm and dry. He kicked the snow away, only to place his boots in the deep snow again. He started his hike to town.

The shining sun and the white snow caused him to blink his eyes several times. He had to focus. He tried to see ahead. In the far distance the town was visible. The land was sprawled out underneath a line of mountain ranges. The city appeared larger than what he had anticipated.

After trudging through the snow for a short distance, he came to a gravel road. Tire tracks made a line on the snowy stretch. These tire marks were a sign of hope, an automobile might go by and he'd be able to catch a ride.

He walked over a mile when he heard the humming of an auto approaching. He stopped and stuck out his thumb signaling he needed a lift. The car slowed and stopped. An older man yelled out, "Need a ride?"

"Would be much obliged," Frank yelled back.

"I'm heading to town. Want to go that far?"

"Yes, sir, that would be extremely helpful."

Frank walked to the other side of the car, stomping the snow off his boots before climbing into the front seat of the Ford.

The man put the auto in gear and headed up the road. "My name is Luke," he said as he looked at Frank.

"Nice to meet you, I'm Frank."

Luke looked up and down at Frank. "Where are you headed?"

"Well, my long range plan is to be home in Portland. My immediate goal is to get some food, clean up and rest."

"I know a place, a decent place. My son works at the Davenport Hotel. It's the best place in town. You'd be amazed"

Frank wasn't sure how to respond to Luke's last remark. "I don't know if I can afford 'the best.'"

"Can you afford fifty-cents?"

Frank thought for a few minutes. He had spent that much in Butte, Montana, staying at the flop house. This Davenport Hotel sounded like a step above that, and if it was really for only fifty-cents, he could afford it. "Yes, I guess I can."

"Okay, then I will take you there. You will be flabbergasted. The rates are low now because tourists don't come up in the dead of winter."

Frank sat in wonder. First, Luke said he would be "amazed." Now he said he would be "flabbergasted." This place must be impressive!

Frank decided to change the subject, "What do you do in Spokane?"

"I'm a wheat farmer. You know much about farming?"

"Yeah, I do. I've worked on a dairy farm in Oregon, a wheat farm in North Dakota, and I picked corn in Iowa."

Luke raised his eyebrows, "I guess you do know something about farming."

They arrived in town. It was a busy city, similar in size to Portland. Frank was engrossed looking at the stores, "What is the population here?"

"Not sure what it is today. You know people get born and die every day, but back in 1910 they did a census. They said we had one hundred four thousand people in Spokane."

"Well, I'd say your city is beautiful: with the snow along the wide streets and wide sidewalks." Then Frank turned and noticed a river too. "And this river, running through town and the majestic mountains as a backdrop, it is impressive!"

Luke drove to Sprague Street. There was a tall five story brick building that took up the whole block. "Here's the hotel I was telling you about."

"Wow," said Frank. 'This looks like something I might see in Portland, Chicago or New York."

"Don't want to disappoint you, kid, but this year, 1928, Spokane is the largest city west of the Mississippi."

Frank was surprised. He knew about Seattle and Portland, but he was surprised about what he was learning about Spokane.

They got out the car and went up to the doorway of the hotel. The doors were glass revolving doors twirling in movement. Luke demonstrated how to walk into the door opening and push to get the doors to move, and then to move quickly out of the center as the doors kept moving. Luke laughed and agreed with Frank, it was a tricky maneuver as they went through the revolving doorway. They entered into a well lit lobby room. "Wait here," advised Luke.

He walked up to the main desk. Frank stood in place, gazing his eyes around this huge room that even included a balcony. A marble fireplace with logs crackling as they burned was nearby. The balcony had an opening where it appeared that there was a pipe organ and pipes were placed against the wall. Frank wondered if there was room, on that narrow balcony, for a person to actually play the pipe organ and how it would sound in this room with the high ceiling.

Suddenly Luke was back standing beside him. "This is my son James. James, this is Frank."

"Welcome to the Davenport Hotel. My hope is that this house may appeal to you as a home away from home." Frank knew this was a line that James probably had to say to each hotel guest, still he was flattered. He had never been in any place that was this impressive. Even the Sears store did not compare to this mansion. So being welcomed here as a guest was what he considered an honor.

James bowed toward Frank. Frank wasn't sure what the proper greeting should be, but he nodded toward James as a gesture of thanks.

"You have any luggage, sir?" Frank looked at James, who was ready to carry his luggage, if he had any. James was dressed in black pants with a red coat that even had tails hanging below his waist. He wore a black cap on his head.

Frank held out his hands and chuckled at James' question. "No, everything I own is in my pockets." He reached inside one pocket, "...including this hat I bought for my mother." He pulled the hat out of the crumpled paper bag.

"Very nice, sir." James was being professional and formal in his demeanor, even though his father was right beside him.

"If you will follow me, I will lead you to your room for the night."

Frank could not believe he was even inside this pristine hotel, let alone able to spend the night. The walls were of English walnut; beautiful dark wood carved with designs and scrolls. Hanging from the ceiling were crystal candle lit chandeliers: the kind of lighting that Frank had never seen before. Adding to the ambience, and to give the place the appearance of life, parrots were hanging from cages lower than the light fixtures.

"How do these parrots survive in their cages?" Frank asked.

"Oh," said James "we feed these birds every morning and evening." He pointed to the side wall; "we climb up to their cages on these moveable ladders." They stood listening to the chattering of the birds. Then Luke asked, "Can you show him the ballroom too?"

"Oh, yes," replied James, "an impressive space."

James opened the wide doors into the ballroom. The ornate arch walls carved in intricate designs made the room appear like a scene from a golden palace. Luke excitedly started to chat about the car show event that happened in 1915. "They brought autos in here, right into this ballroom. They even had arched tracks that reached to the ceiling. They drove those autos on the tracks up near the ceiling to be displayed. Yes sir, Ford put on an outstanding show!"

Frank tried to imagine this event as he looked around this huge room. Now it was empty except for tables and chairs off to the side. The walls were of marble and it had plenty of space for a large gathering of people. Frank believed that they could and did drive automobiles right into this room.

Next was the elevator ride to the fifth floor. James led the way to the room that Frank was to stay in. James unlocked the door. Frank reached into his pocket and gave him a quarter for his services. He knew that tipping was expected.

Surprisingly, James came all the way into the room and turned down the sheets on the bed, neatly folded them into a rolled up shape beneath the puffed up pillows.

Luke softly said, "He didn't learn that at home."

Next James showed Frank the closet that was complete with a white cotton robe and a clothes bag. James explained, "If you put your clothes in this bag tonight, before midnight, and place it outside your door in the hallway, a maid will come and pick the bag up. She will wash and iron your clothes and leave them in the doorway for you tomorrow morning."

Frank found this unbelievable, but certainly a welcoming gesture. He felt dirty from his last train ride and knew his clothes smelled sooty.

James continued, "We also have a restaurant downstairs where you can eat a decent meal."

Luke started to depart. They shook hands and said their good-byes.

After Luke left, Frank turned to James. "I'm so thankful your dad was gracious enough to bring me here. You know we just met this afternoon."

James nodded, "My dad is a good judge of character. He knows you're a good guy, that's why he suggested you come here for the night."

He walked toward the doorway, 'Enjoy the room, try the restaurant, you can pay at the desk in the lobby in the morning."

Frank took advantage of all the commodities. He had a wonderful evening eating the fine food in the restaurant. While there he talked to the waiter and heard the story of the beginning of this hotel. "Well… ,"said the tall lean waiter, as he leaned against the wall, as if he had no other obligations except to tell Frank the story of a man named Louis Davenport. "This is a story of a man with a dream, ambition and a hard work ethic. He first came to Spokane with only a $1.25 to his name and a waffle iron."

"That was all?" Frank asked.

"Yeah, that was it – no family – only him and his waffle iron. You see the waffle iron was his significant possession. He used it to start his restaurant where he served breakfast. Right here in this same room, he offered meals of waffles, sausage, eggs and orange juice. Then his dream went from serving guests in a restaurant to serving guests in a hotel. He convinced other investors to invest in his dream. It took years, but finally he was able to buy the entire block. The buildings, that were there, were torn down; however, his restaurant was saved. A man by the name of Kirtland Cutter also got involved. He was an architect."

Frank listened and was intrigued by the waiter's story. "If you want to build a dream, having an architect as a friend is a good start."

"Yeah," agreed the waiter. "His dream came true with a two-hundred million dollar hotel built right over his restaurant!" He shook his head, seemly still shocked from his own story. He went back to wiping off the table tops.

Before Frank left the restaurant, he asked the waiter about getting hot water to bathe in the porcelain tub in his room. "I will tell a servant and she will bring up several buckets of water for you."

"Oh, I could carry up the water." Frank replied.

"Don't worry, "answered the waiter, "the maids here have carts and it is no problem. On the carts they will have enough water to fill your tub."

So Frank went to his room and waited for the knock on his door. A young gal came with a cart and buckets. She poured the water in the tub. Once again Frank got a quarter out of his pocket and tipped here. His tips were adding up. He paid for his meal and tipped the waiter not only for serving him, but for his long story. No matter, now it was time to bathe and relax. He put on his robe. All his clothes were placed in the bag and then he put the bag out in the hallway. He was ready to relax in the warm tub. It would take extra washing to get the black soot out of his skin. At least he could try.

The next morning after breakfast, he paid for his room and his meals. He did not see James, but he left him a note thanking him for his marvelous service and for the opportunity of staying in this special hotel. He added it would be an experience that he would remember all his life.

He felt good. Wearing clean clothes made him feel like a million dollar man. Though now he was down to one dollar.

They had four choices of railroad lines: Great Northern, Northern Pacific, Union Pacific and Milwaukee Road. He was told, by the desk receptionist, that they all ran to Portland. All he had to do was take one that was headed southwest and remain on the train until Portland. She suggested it would probably be a seven hour or longer trip. The trip was over 350 miles. Frank walked out of the Davenport Hotel.

Chapter Twenty

Spokane, Washington to Portland, Oregon

Before Frank left town, he decided to wander the streets of Spokane. He realized that it would be a seven hour ride to Portland, if he was lucky enough to hop on a freight train that didn't stop. That meant he would need food and drink before he reached his destination.

His money was low. Staying at the Davenport Hotel was economical, but with tipping and paying for meals, he spent most of his hard earned money. Traveling from Iowa to Portland was costing him, even though his mode of travel was riding freight trains.

Spokane was a busy city. He saw a street car going down the middle of the main road. Autos, horses and buggies were parked along the curbs. People walked along the sidewalks leaving footprints in the snow. It was cold, but not miserable; temperatures slightly below freezing.

On the corner was a variety store. Not only did they have a soda fountain counter, an assortment of miscellaneous merchandise, they also had a grocery section. That's where Frank headed. In the store, he wandered down the narrow wooden floor aisles, and looked at the fruits and the vegetables. He felt a yearning for bananas, so he picked out three yellow bananas. He thought "protein." His mom often lectured him that a boy "needs protein." Also, he remembered how much he liked peanut butter. At another aisle he found a small jar of peanut butter. Noticing a pint size jar of apple juice he bought two of these and some tobacco, so he could smoke if he got the urge. All of these items came to the price of one dollar. It was his last amount of money.

He told himself it was okay; it was only a seven hour train ride home. He wasn't worried about the yard bulls. He heard they didn't like working on cold days, and they seldom worked the month of December. It was getting close to Christmas, another reason why hobos would not be riding and yard bulls would not care if they did. At least, that was Frank's reasoning. After paying for his items, and stuffing them in his deep pockets, he slowly captured his last view of the city and the Spokane River.

In the fields, he waited for an open freight boxcar. It had been about fifteen minutes when he heard the roaring engine and saw the black cloud of smoke. "Please let there be an open boxcar." There were two boxcars with open doors. He ran fast down the hill, and then ran beside the train tracks. Frank felt the wind, from the train, slapping his face. The dust and smoke blinded his eyes. The deafening blast of the engine made his ears ring. The first open door car arrived too quickly. He kept his pace and timed it perfectly. Grabbing the edge of the door, of the second car, he pulled himself into the open door.

He was safely inside the car when he heard, "Welcome aboard man."

The voice came from another hobo, sitting in the far corner of the boxcar. The man appeared slightly older than Frank; maybe in his late thirties. He was dressed in a black trench coat, and wore a stocking like cap over his ears. His boots were heavy black boots like Frank's boots.

Frank yelled at him, "Thanks for the welcome,"

"No problem, make yourself comfortable," he invited, as if he was in charge of this environment.

Frank tried to make himself comfortable. He wasn't ready for snacks, nor was he ready to sleep. It had been only a few moments when the other hobo came closer. At first, Frank was a little leery; usually hobos kept their distance, or if they came close, it was after eyeing each other for several minutes. Frank wasn't too worried though; he had no money for this hobo to steal, and since they had just met, there was no reason for any hard feelings.

"I'm Hank."

"Nice to meet ya. I'm Frank."

"Where you headed, Frank?"

"I'm aimin' to get home – to Portland. Oregon."

"Well, you're lucky. I'm headed all the way to California - Sacramento. I heard tell there is plenty of work in California. And I got a wife and kid in Sacramento."

Frank thought it best not to share too much information or to ask too many questions.

"What's waiting for you in Portland?"

"Well, that's my home. My mom and brothers are there waiting."

"Sounds inviting and encouraging."

"Yes, sir, it is." Frank was feeling comfortable now and sorry that he felt at all suspicious about Hank's presence.

"You know what, Frank, this could be a long ride. I got just the right way to past time, and it's here in my pocket."

Frank was curious. Hank pulled out a box of Bicycle Playing cards. Even though the train was rocking and they both were swaying back and forth with the train movements, Hank was able to shuffle, reshuffle and let his cards fold down like a card pro.

"Ever play poker?"

"No," answered Frank. "I've never had a deck of cards."

"Well, it's easy. Course, usually it involves betting. You know you take some money and bet that you will win the hand. If you do, you get the money that was bet against you. If you don't win, the other player gets the money."

Frank was ready to protest and explain why he couldn't bet any money, but before Frank had a chance to comment, Hank stopped shuffling and explained. "We won't bet anything, we'll just play. There are several poker games. I'll teach you a few between here and Portland."

Frank leaned forward. He was eager to learn. This card game sounded like an ideal way to pass traveling time.

Hank explained all the card terms: full house, straight flush, five draw poker, and the royal flush, which he said were high cards in the order of the same suit. He estimated that the chance of this happening was one in 650,000 deals. Frank liked high odds. He figured it was possible.

Hank dealt out five cards to Frank and five cards to himself. He braced the deck of cards with his foot so a sudden movement would not cause the cards to go flying across the boxcar floor. Then he taught Frank Five Card Stud.

Frank became absorbed in the game. He completely forgot where he was, or that only minutes ago, Hank was a complete stranger. Hank praised Frank for handling the cards like an expert, for quickly learning the calls, and for sitting there often with a "poker face" not revealing what he held so tight in his hands. If there had been bets involved, Frank would have won. Instead, he received words of praise: "Nice going, good game, that's the way to play poker."

They were near Tacoma. Frank had yet to eat his snacks, though he did drink his apple juice drinks as they played. All of a sudden, the train slowed down to a crawl. Hank stashed his cards in his pocket. He looked concerned. "This stop could mean trouble: this isn't a normal stop. There is no depot or a freight yard here, no reason to slow down unless..." He paused and looked out the open doorway. "Yard bulls!" he said to Frank.

Frank froze. He knew it was too late to jump off the train. There was no place to hide. He waited for Hank to come up with a brilliant escape plan. Instead, Hank said, "We'll have to face them, and face the consequences."

"What do you think will happen?" Frank was still hoping for some solution.

"I'd say we're in trouble. We may end up in the pokie or on the chain gang."

"Great," said Frank sarcastically. With a jerk the train stopped. Hank and Frank stood like statues waiting for the inevitable. Surprisingly, it looked like there were only two yard bulls, not a gang of them, as it was the last time Frank faced yard bulls.

"Get off the car!" yelled one of the men.

Hank and Frank obeyed and jumped off the car.

"Any other guys in this car?" asked one of the guards as he looked inside. The other yard bull held his rifle pointed right at Frank. Then he turned it at Hank.

"I suppose you guys know riding freights are illegal?"

"Yes sir," answered Frank.

He stepped closer to Frank and looked him in the eyes. "So tell me, young man, why are you in a freight car?"

"I'm headed to Portland. It's my home and I want to see my mother and my brother. My brother just came home from being on a cargo ship that went to China. It's been four years since I've seen him." "I...," he paused, "I just want to see my brother."

The yard bull didn't say anything. He just stared at Frank. He had a look of empathy like he believed Frank's story. Then he walked toward Hank. The other officer turned his rifle toward Hank. "What's your story?"

Hank cleared his throat and said, "I got a wife and one kid waiting for me in Sacramento. A friend told me I could get work if I headed back home. A carpenter's job is waiting for me."

"You've ever done carpentering work before?"

"Yes sir, I built the house my wife and kid live in."

"Why did you leave?" Even Frank was curious. It was cold standing by the outside of the train. He was uncomfortable and scared.

"I left to do mining out in Spokane because they needed miners."

"You got any money, from your mining."

"Yes sir, I do."

"How much you got?"

Suddenly, Frank's worries overtook his mind. He remembered last time when yard bulls took money from those that had it, and then sent them on their way; however, if they didn't have any they were hauled off to who knows where.

Hank didn't hesitate. He took out his wallet and showed the yard bull his dollar bills.

For some unknown reason, this yard bull appeared to believe their stories, and he didn't seem to care about Hank's money.

"You know what?" He walked around them, eyeing them again. "It's days before Christmas. I'm gonna let you guys finish your ride. This here freight will go all the way to Portland. You get off before Portland. It will cross the Columbia River." He looked at Frank. "You know where that is?"

Frank answered, "Yes, sir, I know."

When you get to the river, the train will slow down. As soon as it crosses over the Columbia River Railroad Bridge, you jump off. Got it? Don't get caught again. There will be no mercy. You see your mother and brother."

Then he looked at Hank, "You see your wife and take care of your son. No more traveling. Now my partner and I are walking away as if we never saw you guys. Get back on the same empty car."

The officer holding the rifle relaxed. He lowered the gun. He too seemed satisfied with the final verdict. Frank and Hank climbed aboard the train car. They both looked and felt like they had seen ghosts. Hank asked first, "Is it true seeing your mother and brother?"

"Yes," answered Frank, "it is all true. What about you? You got a wife and son?" "I do, and yes, I'm a carpenter. This is one yard bull that did the right thing. He let us hobos head home."

*****

The card playing ceased. There was silence. Frank took his pocket knife, peeled his banana, and smeared peanut butter on each side. He offered a banana to Hank. Hank said, "No thanks," as he pulled out his own wrapped peanut butter sandwich from his pocket. They both ate. It was quiet. It was peaceful. The stillness seemed to promote thankful thoughts.

The train started to move. It wasn't long when they reached the Columbia River and crossed the railroad bridge. Slowing down, the train almost stopped. "Here is where we leap," said Frank. Hank had been dozing, but he immediately appeared alert. They both looked out the door that was ajar. They watched the ground move beneath them and they jumped, one at a time. This time they both ended upright. They shook hands and parted ways.

Hank headed the opposite direction. Frank feared Hank would get on another train. He kept watching him as Hank walked along the tracks. Frank felt sad seeing him go, but Hank was smart and Frank trusted that Hank would make it home to his waiting family.

He yelled at Hank, "How are you gonna make it to California?"

Hank turned and yelled back, "I'm gonna hitchhike. I'll walk into town and find someone that is headed south. Don't worry man, I've hitchhiked before. It's another way to travel."

Frank smiled, remembering one of his fearful rides. He said quietly to himself, "Good luck, man."

Looking around the river front, Frank remembered when he almost got caught for trying to steal fishing rods, over a year ago. This memory he wanted to forget. He knew his way to his mom's place. He decided to just start walking.

There was no snow on the ground, which made for easy walking, but it was cold. The streets were quiet, not completely dark yet. He had heard people say this was the "magic hour;" the hour before complete darkness.

The evening felt magical. He was back in Portland. Soon he'd be seeing his mother and brother. He couldn't wait. Walking the streets at a faster pace, he headed directly to his mom's house.

Finally, he reached his mother's porch. He lightly tapped on the door, but he didn't wait for anyone to open it; he opened the unlocked door. As the door moved, he saw his mom wearing an apron, her long hair in a bun. She was a distance away in the kitchen, busy by the wood stove. Millard was sitting on the sofa reading the newspaper. "I'm home!" Frank announced.

Chapter Twenty-One

Portland, Oregon Family Visit & Work

Quickly, to slow the heat in the stove, Mary separated the logs. She wiped her hands on her apron and hurried into the living room. Millard dropped the paper to the floor, and yelled out, "Gilbert Franklin!" He ran to embrace his brother.

They stood in a hug position for several seconds, before letting go. They stared at one another, longing to capture all they had missed from not being together for four years. Mary stood back cherishing these moments of seeing her sons together and in her home.

Finally, the boys let go of one another. Frank walked over to his mom and whisked her off her feet, twirled her around, kissed her on the cheek, and then gently put her back on her feet. "I'm so happy to be home!" As the hugs were released, they all laughed for the sheer joy of seeing one another.

"Sit down, Frank, and tell us all about your trip here."

"Not yet. First, Mom, I want to hear how your life has been. What have you been doing? How are you feeling?"

Then he turned to Millard. "I need to hear your stories. What was it like traveling from Portland to China? They must have fed you well, you look heavier."

Millard laughed, "And you, brother, must have worked harder than what you were fed because you grew taller and thinner."

"Well," interjected Mary, "I have enough food to nourish you both. So clean up and let's eat before we share our stories."

"Oh, I almost forgot, I've got presents."

"Presents?" Mary and Millard asked, at the same time.

"Yeah, presents." Frank reached deep into his pockets. He pulled out the hat, with the sapphire stone, that he had carried for miles. He pushed it up, into shape, and handed the soft head covering to her. She placed it on right over her hair bun. Then she waltzed around the room with her new bonnet. "I love it" she exclaimed. "It is exactly what I would have picked out, if I would have had the chance.

Frank reached deeper into his pocket. He pulled out the new pocket knife and handed it to Millard. Hugs were exchanged again. Surprisingly, Millard had a gift to share too. He reached into his pocket and pulled out an Asian map. He handed it to Frank. "Here, dear brother, you can spend time looking at this map, and see all the places that I've been," He also handed him back the pouch of marbles and the arrow heads, that Frank had given him. "Keep these items. They meant the world to me, as I traveled the seas. I held these at night and prayed for you and wished you safety…prayed for myself a few times too."

Frank was moved emotionally by Millard's words. He didn't want his older brother to notice how sensitive he felt. He hugged his brother again. Then he moved away, and headed down the hallway to wash up. "Let's eat," he yelled.

*****

After the meal, Millard and Frank sat on the davenport, relaxing and chatting. Millard was quick to share his story of adventure. "Remember the early morning I left Steward's place?"

"Sure," answered Frank. "Your departure left me with a heartache. I felt sad for weeks."

"I know. I'm sorry about that little brother." He patted Frank on his knee. He was quiet, as if silent memories flooded his mind. "That same morning the West Humsea Ship left the Portland dock and I left too."

"That was the name of the ship?"

"Yeah, they had lots of ships with the first name Hum – one was even called Humbug and one was called Humhaw."

"Interesting. What was on the ship?"

"Let me tell you Frank, this ship was huge. It was slightly longer than a football field; about half the size of Mr. Steward's front lawn up to his porch. It could carry up to 2,000 tons of cargo. We carried tons of lumber."

He tried to imagine Millard on this giant ship during the same time that he was traveling on a train car. It was so different. Millard out on the ocean waves, while Frank was on the railroad tracks.

"How long were you at sea before your first stop?"

"Our first trip was day and night for four days. Our first stop was in Manila. You know where that is?"

Frank thought for a moment. He did study geography at school. "It's a city in the Philippines. You went all the way to the Philippines?"

"That's right brother, the Philippines was our first stop. I was so glad to get off the ship. We had a couple nights that were rough at sea; a great deal of rocking and rolling. The fog and the wind were extreme. Waves sprayed over the deck and left a flood of water. I wasn't sure I was going to make my first trip, let alone any future voyages.

I must say though, I had confidence in the captain and in the ship. I kept telling myself they would not let all that lumber get lost at sea, surely I'd be saved too."

"What was it like to be in Manila?"

"A foreign country is just that, it's foreign, strange and different. The city was busy, busier than Portland. People were rushing through the streets. No lane barriers, no traffic lights, just helter-skelter up and down the roads."

"Are we talking about automobiles?"

"Heavens no, I think I only saw two automobiles while I was in Manila. They use horse drawn carts and what they call, karitons which are carts pulled by carabao."

"Carabao?"

"Yeah, they are like water buffalo. I hear they are native and are only in the Philippines. They are heavy animals, larger than cows. They help with the plowing and pull the carts in town. The people walk or ride bikes and are always carrying their wares on long sticks over their shoulders, on their heads, or in big woven baskets."

"Tell you something else, Frank, the gals are pretty, thin and tan, just downright pretty. They smile. Everyone dresses up, like it is Sunday. Even the men wore white suit jackets and white pants as if they were headed to church."

"The days were horribly hot and the sun overly bright. The whole time I was there, I was sweating, and trying to appear formal in my jeans and heavy shirt. Mostly, I felt like I didn't fit in. I lingered under shady trees just biding my time. We were only there two days. On the third day, we set sail for Shanghai Port."

Frank was excited hearing Millard's tales. He felt at peace knowing that he was at his mother's home, sitting beside his brother. Months had gone by when he longed for this moment: a moment of being beside his older brother again.

Millard continued, "This next trip was longer and rougher than the trip to the Philippines. We were on the ship for six days, six rough days. The weather took a turn for the worst. Most of the men were getting seasick. During one of those storms I was ordered to work in the Engine Room; they needed help. One of the mates just yelled, "Hey kid, head to the Engine Room they need another body down there.""

"For some reason, I wasn't feeling seasick. I was doing okay. Several men that were working in the Engine Room were too sick to do their jobs. Down there I met a Spanish guy named Jose. He was the leader down there. He always yelled directions to everyone about what to do, how to keep the ship afloat and how to keep the steam engine running.

"During the storms, we just kept working for long hours. I know one day I worked all day, ate once, and then worked all night. Finally, the sea calmed down."

"Were you ever so scared that you thought the ship might sink?"

"I was terrified more than once, but the worst time was when we had to tow a schooner boat during a storm. That vessel got a leak. They were sending out an SOS signal."

"The ship got a leak?"

"Yeah, you'd be surprised, it happens more frequently than you would think. It happened when we were near Honolulu, but let me tell you about Shanghai first.

"Shanghai is a busier city than Manila. The streets are crowded with carts. These carts are not pulled by animals, rather pulled by men. Sometimes, people are passengers in the carts; other times men drag heavy loads in long carts, like lumber logs. Some of these logs were ones we had delivered. They loaded these logs on long carts and then these men (sometimes only six or eight men) pulled these longs logs on the carts through town."

Frank tried to visualize this scene. "That sounds cruel to expect men to pull logs that trucks should be carrying."

"You're right; it was painful to watch. These men appear physically weak and not tall in stature, but strong in determination. They leaned way low and struggled to pull the weight. I wanted to help: use my strength to assist. We were told, by the captain's orders to 'observe' but not to intervene in any way with these Chinese workers. He said, 'It would look suspicious.' According to him, they don't understand us or our culture. The barrier of language makes it impossible to explain our actions. The opposite is true too, we don't understand them either. It is a different world."

"From Shanghai, we headed up the East China Sea to Tokyo, Japan. In the town area we saw many children with their parents. They appeared to be happy and obedient. Groups of children were happily running around, while the small ones were being carried."

"Many of the areas are beautiful with gardens and rice farms off in the distance. They too, had carts pulled by a horse or by people."

"Was the weather warm there too?"

"Yes, it was. Many people carried umbrellas to protect themselves from the sun. Women fanned themselves with beautiful handmade fans. I bought one for Mom; you'll have to ask her to show it to you. The men and the women wore gowns called kimonos.

"There were temples there too, where they worship. When they go inside the temples, they take off their shoes. Shoes were laid on the ground in a heap. Most of the people wear white socks and walk in their socks if they go inside any place: though some children go barefoot.

"Oh yes, I saw something interesting done with our logs. They had a huge swing log held on chains fastened to these log poles. It was a giant swing. Men climbed up on the log, laughed, and just swung back and forth.

"Our next destination was Honolulu, Hawaii. In 1926 Honolulu built this Aloha Tower with an elevator. I rode the elevator up to the tenth floor, and saw a sweeping wide view of the seaport. The port is busy with cargo ships, fishing boats, and huge cruise ships. These cruise ships carry rich people that are just traveling around the world.

"The streets were busy with lots of automobiles and horse drawn carts. Beautiful gals were there greeting the ships."

"Sounds like you're missing having a girlfriend."

"You're right, brother, been at sea too long.

"Let me tell ya,' these gals in Hawaii are something else. When the cruise ships arrive these young gals line up in grass skirts, halter tops and bare feet; they dance and sing and hand out leis to the visitors."

"Leis?"

"Yeah, they are real fresh flowered necklaces. That I guess they've made. Course, they aren't free, free. The people receive the necklaces as gifts, but many other women are nearby selling all kinds of Hawaiian merchandise. They sell handmade jewelry, straw hats, Hawaiian style clothing, and woven baskets. People are quick to buy and spend their money.

"When we were on our way to Honolulu, we had our most scary storm situation. I don't know what the storm was officially called, a cyclone, typhoon, or a hurricane, but the winds were howling, the pouring rain splashing over the ship. Stuck working steadily in the engine room, I had no idea what it looked like at sea. I only knew what it felt like. At times we were sliding across the floor. Often we had to hold onto the walls or the equipment. I thought it was my end time. Brother, I was praying.

"I heard more details later. We actually had to tow the schooner (a three mast sailing vessel.) According to the captain, we saved some lives, our own lives, but also those men that were on the schooner.

I'll tell you Frank … I don't fear life much any more. I survived!"

"Mom said you might go next to Australia, is that true?"

"Hell, no! I've got a land job lined up. I know now I want to do mechanical work. I'm good at working with machines. There's this shop over by the Burnside Bridge; they make all kinds of stuff – automobile parts, appliances, all kinds of gadgets to fix things. I'm excited about working there. The head guy told me, just show up the first of the week and start working."

Frank was surprised. Millard was going to stay in Portland. He went on to tell Frank about where he found a room to rent, even had his own bathroom. "Not much of a kitchen," he admitted, "but it would do."

The plan was to see their brother, Lou, tomorrow. It would be a chance to ride in Lou's Studebaker and see Millard's place. Frank felt at ease. His visit with his brother was a cure for any past homesickness he felt. He knew he would sleep peacefully tonight in his mom's house.

185

After Christmas, Frank seriously thought about getting a job. For Christmas his mother gave him a bike – an English Racer bike. The name of the bike fit Frank's personality, "a wander bike." Frank loved the name. It made him feel happy to ride the bike every day. Such a fancy bike seemed like an unbelievable gift. She also gave him a rain jacket that really did keep him dry: like an overcoat meant to be worn over his heavier warmer jacket. It appeared that he had no excuse now not to try and seek employment.

The business name that his mom had given him was still in his pocket. He told her he would seek this manager and see about this job first, even though it was a long ways to the Swift Meat Packing Company. The company was in Northeast Portland, near Vancouver. Mary's house was in Southeast Portland, but riding across town did not seem daunting to Frank. He had been eating well, sleeping on schedule; he felt fine.

Early one Monday, while his mom was at her job, he got on his bike and headed toward North Portland. He had to ask one or two people on the way exactly where this meat market was located. It seemed that everyone he talked to was familiar with this plant. They said it included several buildings. There was the main meatpacking building, and acres of land where they had stockyards and kept animals. Before he even got there, he found out that this company hired many workers, and the meat from this company was shipped by rail to other parts of America.

He talked to one guy at great length and found out that Mr. Swift died in 1903; however, years earlier he had hired an engineer to help him figure out how to pack meat and transport it cross-country without it getting spoiled. An engineer came up with the design of the refrigerated railcars, called reefers. Frank knew about these cars. He was told not to ride in one – for a man they were like a death trap. He also found out Swift's full name was Gustavus Franklin Swift. Frank felt that, at least name wise, he had something in common with this meatpacking entrepreneur.

Finally, he arrived at the main office. He went to the front desk and asked to speak to a Mr. Miller (the name on the card his mother had given him). The secretary asked his name and he gave his formal name, Gilbert Franklin Rose. In a few short moments he was called into an office room.

Mr. Miller looked to be about his mother's age. Frank wondered how he knew his mother. Mr. Miller shook Frank's hand and asked him to be seated. Frank sat down on a wooden chair a few feet away from Mr. Miller's huge wooden paper cluttered desk. Mr. Miller leaned over the desk top and asked Frank what work experience Frank had. Frank listed dairy farming and his other farm work.

"Have you ever worked on an assembly line?" Mr. Miller asked.

Frank wasn't even sure what an assembly line was. "No sir."

"Well, if you've worked with other farm hands then, in a way, you probably have worked on assembly lines. It is like when workers join together to do one job. One worker does a part of the job, and then his work goes to another worker, and that worker finishes the job. For example, one person, here at this plant might bone the beef, and then the next person might package the meat and put it on a moving belt line so it can be transported to either the trucks or the train cars."

Frank listened, but he really didn't know anything about working in a meatpacking company. From his previous work experience, Frank figured he could easily learn to do the work because often he didn't know how to do a job, yet he still did okay.

Mr. Miller continued the interview, "I know your mother well. She worked as an in- home care nurse a couple years for my elderly aunt. Your mother is a good honest worker and she brags that you are a good worker and honest too. You agree with that statement?"

"Yes, sir," answered Frank "I agree."

"Well, then fill out this application form and you can start working this afternoon. Oh yes, the pay will be a dollar a day. Normal work days will be Monday through Friday, 8:30 a.m. till 3:00 p.m. Any questions?"

Frank had many questions, but he could not think of how to word a question when he didn't have any idea what he would be doing or even which one of these massive buildings he'd be working in.

Frank was told he could fill out the paperwork in the waiting room and give his papers to a Miss Spencer, the secretary. Shortly, a strong muscular man named Sam showed Frank all the ins and outs of working at this plant. One question Frank had to ask was where to leave his bike. Sam showed him a side of the building that was hidden from the road view and a safe place to leave his new bike. Then they went through a back door that led to a large locker room. Sam handed Frank a small key. "Don't lose this," he advised. There was a number on the key, 133. "This means you have locker number 133. They walked down a long row of lockers. Frank saw 133; he opened the door. Inside was a heavy leather fabric apron and overalls hanging on a hook.

Sam gave instructions, "You can leave your jacket and rain coat here. Put on this apron over your clothes and these rubber overalls over your pants. We have to wear these to protect our clothes and our bodies."

Frank did as he was told, but he wasn't too encouraged by these instructions. He wondered, how bad could it be working in a meat plant? There was a safety pin on the small key so he pinned the key to his apron. Sam led the way down several hallways to what they called the "hide shaking room." Sam opened the door. They walked into what felt like winter in North Dakota, extremely cold. Frank wished he had his warm jacket on instead of this heavy apron. There were hog hides hanging on high hooks: a long row of them. Men worked below them and took out white chunks of, what Sam called, rock salt. "That will be your job," he motioned to Frank. "These hides will be moving on these racks. As they move through, you have to make sure that no rock salt pieces are in the hide." Fan motors were running making it hard for Frank to hear every word Sam said. He noticed though how the racks moved and how long it took for the men to take the salty chucks out of the hides. Then the rack moved and more hides came in. Frank realized there was no downtime. For this job one had to move at a fast pace. He was ready. Sam asked Frank, "You want to try?"

Frank answered, "Sure."

They walked over sawdust and stood next to a hide. Sam did the first one. He scooped out handfuls of rock salt and threw it into a big bin. It took several scoops before the hide felt clean. Sam said it was important to use their bare hands so they could feel the smoothness of the hide to make sure no salt was still present. Frank only watched while Sam did several hides. Then Sam pointed to the next row and told Frank to try. Frank did the process just as Sam had shown him. Sam nodded approval. "Keep working for the next hour. I will be back and then I will show you the break room."

When Frank got to the break room, he spent several minutes washing his hands. Already, he could feel his hands stinging from the touch of the rough salt. There were snack bags available and water pitchers to drink from. Frank ate and drank. His break was only 15 minutes. He was told he could go back on his own to the hide shaking room and work until the 3 o'clock whistle blew. Then he was to go to his locker, leave his work clothes and take his locker key with him and return to work the next morning at 8:30 a.m.

Frank worked this job all through January and February. Not only was the job exhausting and repetitive, but riding his bike to work every early morning was hard too. Often he rode in the dark and in the rain. Usually riding home was easier as it was still daylight.

It was at the end of February, when Sam walked up to him, while Frank was working, and told him he was being promoted. Frank had no idea that promotion was even possible. Sam told him to follow him. They walked through the long hallways to another huge warehouse room. Before Sam opened the door, he told Frank that his wages would be higher. Instead of a dollar a day, he'd earn $1.50 each day. Then Sam opened the door. The area had a strong manure odor. They had cloth masks available if Frank wanted to wear one. Frank thought he would be okay without wearing a mask. He watched other workers do the job of shoveling fertilizer. Once again the room was an assembly type with a long conveyer belt. On the belt were bins. Frank was to shovel the fertilizer as fast as he could and fill the moving bins. It did not look like a hard job. Frank was glad to do something different. His hands were sore from handling the rock salt. At night his mother gave him lotion for his hands, but changing jobs would be the best solution. Plus, he was happy to get a salary raise. He started working and did fine. He only had to work a couple hours and the whistle blew. It was the next day he had problems.

He started off shoveling fertilizer early in the morning. He did okay until his lunch break. Then he went back. During his last three work hours, he started to cough and gag from the constant fumes of the fertilizer. There were no more break times. Continuing to work was his only option until he coughed uncontrollably and felt like he could not breathe. He left the room and walked out the back doorway. He sat outside on an empty ramp that usually was filled with packed crates ready to be loaded onto trucks. He sat there several minutes when Sam came out with a pitcher of water and a mug. "Here, drink up. Are you alright?"

Frank didn't hesitate. "I quit!"

Sam looked shocked. "Come on, Frank, you're a good worker. Don't feel bad about having a coughing fit in there. You're not the first man to leave that room."

"Man, I thought I was gonna die. I can't breathe that stuff. Sorry, even with the raise in salary, which I do appreciate, I've gotta quit." Sam wasn't going to give up. "Come back tomorrow. Stop in the office; there are other jobs here to consider. I'll get you work in another department, and I'll let you keep your salary raise."

So Frank clocked out, left early, and headed home. He had no idea what other job Sam had in mind. He figured it could not get worse. When Frank heard Sam's first sentence the next morning, he realized that yes, it could get worse. Sam walked into the office ready to show Frank what his next assignment would be. "Did you know, Frank, that right in this plant, we kill two million sheep a year?"

Frank didn't answer, but he thought of the answer. The answer was no, he did not know that. It really was the first time since he worked there, that he even heard the word "kill." All these dead animals he had been working with seemed more like hides, meat, not real animals that were alive: cattle, hogs and sheep. Frank loved animals, but he also knew that they were used for food: meat products, fish and game. He hadn't thought about sheep.

Sam opened another door, the sign on the door read "kill'em floor." In this room was another row of hooks hanging overhead, but on this rack sheep hung by their legs, upside down, still alive, making loud squealing sounds. Frank watched the workers. They had to take long, sharp knives and slit the throats of the live sheep. Blood poured out and sprayed into large troughs below. Frank was ready to walk out the door again and flatly state, I quit, but, he didn't. Sam showed him the heavy aprons that hung in the room, different ones than were in his locker. He showed him high boots he could wear and the rubber overalls. Frank put on the gear. He did as Sam told him and as the fellow workers demonstrated. This procedure he repeated for several weeks, until the end of March. His hands no longer hurt from the rock salt. Instead of gagging on the fertilizer odors, he could breathe, but mentally he felt pain. He knew his current job had to be done. People were surviving on the food that this company was producing. If he stopped working, someone else would do the job; the slaughter would still happen. He could only rationalize this job duty for so long. It was the end of March when he made his decision.

Frank had saved his hard-earned money and now he had a plan. He opted to tell Millard first. On his way home from work, that late Friday afternoon, he stopped at the shop where Millard worked. Millard was glad to see him. "Come on in, brother. I've got to show you what I'm making. It is a tool that can be extremely useful. It's a measuring tool with sliders on it. When used, the slider can be pressed against anything that needs measuring." He demonstrated, "See, it makes it easier to mark around the slider so an exact measurement can be made." Frank was impressed. After Millard demonstrated several of the tools he was working with, he told Frank he would buy him some food.

They went across the street to a small, quiet café. There they sat at the table while Frank told Millard his plan. Millard rolled his eyes and shook his head. He looked at his younger brother and worry flooded over him. Frank had a home to stay in and was making good money. He encouraged him to use his money and maybe find his own apartment to stay in. Frank shook his head. He was determined to follow his plan. Millard could not convince him otherwise.

At the time, March 1929, they didn't know that in less than seven months, the stock market would crash, that easy living was going to change to times of extreme depression, and jobs would be scarce. They didn't realize that there would not be a few hobos riding the rails; there would be thousands of hobos looking for work. Times would not be easy.

As Frank left the cafe, Millard just shook his head. Frank went home to tell his mom he planned to quit his job. He would give his two weeks notice, but by the third week of April his plan was to ride the rails to California.

End of Book I

Just Call Me Frank
Table of Contents Book II

Chapter Twenty-Two

Portland, Oregon to California April 1929
Seventeen Years Old

The early bright April morning sun woke Frank. He felt energized. After eating toast and drinking coffee, he started packing. Frank knew about packing lightly. He took his razor, a new bar of soap, a pocket knife, and a small tin cup. He placed these items deep into his overall pockets. He had debated about packing a lunch or not. When he awoke, the decision was made for him. His mom had packed a lunch in a brown paper sack. He gently placed the sack, his coins and dollars deep into his pockets. The extra dollar bills he placed in his shoes.

Even though the day was warm, he wore two shirts, heavy boots, and his warm jacket, because he knew the evening and the future days would be colder. Placing his gray tweed hat on his head, he walked out the door of his mother's place.

This time, he knew which tracks to go on, which freight train was heading to California, and the approximate time of departure. He had been studying schedules, and after work, he had talked to other hobos. This accumulation of information gave him a good sense of what to expect and how to plan.

Walking into town felt good. He felt at peace with the decision to leave Portland and to find work elsewhere. The idea of meeting new people and seeing new sights gave him a sense of enthusiasm. He wanted to be independent again and make his own decisions.

The last few days, he spent time reading about San Francisco. He was anxious to see the Fisherman's Wharf and ride the cable cars. He had read about long steep stairways that were built on the hilly streets; he wanted to climb those steps.

He arrived at the train rail yard and weaved his way over the tracks near where the boxcars were parked. Finding one empty car with an open door, he climbed aboard and moved into the back dark corner and sat down. According to the paper schedule, this train would leave shortly. He was surprised he had the car all to himself. Noticeably, there only a few hobos were hanging around the yard.

The ride would be 535 miles and could take up to 15 hours, hours that could include stops. The last few nights, he had spent time reading about what he might see along the way. Those listed main sights would be his land marks letting him know his location.

At least, that would work during the daylight. Some of his hours would be in complete darkness; hopefully, the hours when he might need to jump off into the unknown, would be daylight times. Before darkness, he would pay attention to his surroundings. Hopefully he would sleep during the night, and then wake up to early daylight.

The train moved slowly out of the rail yard. Frank heard the familiar sound of the chugging wheels and the roaring locomotive. He saw and smelled the heavy steaming smoke from the engine. He felt a wave of calmness flood over him. Surely, he surmised, riding the boxcars again was the right decision.

As the train left the rail yard, he watched the view. He was definitely leaving Portland. Realizing how strongly his brothers would miss him, and how his mother acted brave as she tried not to show her feelings, he suddenly felt sad and lonely.

The determination he felt only moments before seemed to disappear. But now the train was moving, heading to California. He would not turn back. As the engine picked up speed, he watched the scenery pass. The familiar sights disappeared, and the Willamette River was behind him. As the train kept a steady pace, the grassy fields zipped by, the tall fir trees zoomed in the distance; even the views of Mt. Hood and the Columbia River Gorge were finally part of the background.

Frank decided he would eat before complete darkness set in. He opened his lunch bag. Inside was a ham sandwich, ham from the meat company where he was working. A note from his mother was placed on top of the unwrapped sandwich: *My dear Frank. I will miss you as you seek other jobs and more adventure. I will pray for your safe return. You, Lou and Millard are my family. I love you all very much. Please return. I and your bike will be waiting. Love, Mom*

Frank paused. In his mind he could hear his mother's voice; he could see her happy smile. He remembered when they hugged each other when he returned home right before Christmas. "I will return Mom – don't worry. I'll be okay." He wished he would have said those words to her before he left.

He ate his sandwich. Then he made a pillow out of his jacket and laid down to sleep. His goal was to wake by dawn.

The early sunrise did wake Frank, but also he woke because the chugging train wheels had stopped. He heard voices outside the car. He tucked his lunch bag into his pocket. He grabbed his jacket and put it on. He still had his boots on. He stood up. Peeking out the door, it seemed the train was nowhere, not near a station, not near a rail yard, where they did loading and unloading, and they were not near a river or a town.

He had no idea where he was or how far he was from his destination. What was most concerning wasn't where he was, but the men walking along the tracks. Who were they? Could they be yard bulls checking out the cars? They were still off in the distance. If he timed it right he could probably sneak between the cars and escape across the field without them even noticing.

That was exactly what he did. He wandered across the fields, ducking behind trees and bushes whenever he felt the urge to do so. All this time, wondering where he was, how far was he from a main road, how far from a town? He wasn't even sure if he was still in Oregon or in California. The train off in the distance still did not move. It seemed to be stopped for no logical reason. Frank didn't dare go back. He disliked the idea of having to hitchhike, but he felt this might be his only option.

After passing a few bushes, he noticed the mountain off in the distance. The morning fog had covered part of the view, but finally it had lifted and he realized that he knew the name of this mountain. He had read about the view points between Portland and San Francisco; this was Mt. Shasta. Frank also remembered that there was a small town near Mt. Shasta, a town named Weed. His goals suddenly became clear: hike to Weed, get cleaned up and get some grub.

He hiked at least ten miles, before he saw the dusty dirt road that led into the main road of Weed. Carrying his jacket and one extra shirt, he felt hot, tired and dirty. Looking presentable wasn't possible, he'd have to go into town, find a place to eat, and meet someone who might be heading south.

When he arrived he only saw one place that might serve food. So he went into the small café. There was a bar, near the back, and tables in the front. He decided to sit at a table and hopefully get a good breakfast. Immediately, a male waiter came to his table and handed him a menu. "Good morning, sir, we have a motto here, kinda goes like our town's name: "Weed like to welcome you."

Frank was surprised with the greeting. "Well, thanks, I appreciate that welcome."

"The special this morning is grits and sausage, eggs on the side if you'd like."

"All that sounds good." Suddenly, Frank realized how hungry he felt.

"How do you like your eggs?"

"Sunny side up."

"Okay, you got 'em."

The waiter went back into the kitchen to fix the breakfast. He was the only worker. Frank was the only customer.

Frank sighed and waited for his food. He laid his jacket and extra shirt on the chair next to him. He wondered if there was a place to wash up. He stood up and yelled back into the kitchen. "Sir, is there a place I could wash my hands?"

The waiter/cook yelled back, "Sure, go out the door you came in, turn left, there is an outhouse there and a water pump behind the outhouse."

"Thanks," Frank said, and headed outside.

The meal tasted good. Frank felt satisfied, but with no other people around, he had his doubts about hitchhiking anywhere.

He finished his meal when the waiter sat on the chair next to him. "Hope you don't mind if we visit for a while. We get so few strangers in town; it is fun to find out where people come from and where they are headed."

Frank was glad to have a chat. He started his story of having work and family in Portland, Oregon, but wanting to come and see California.

"Hell, if you want work, you can stay right here in Weed. We have a lumber mill that always needs workers. You probably don't know this, but our town is named Weed because of Abner Weed. He's the guy that bought the only lumber mill around. He discovered that the winds from around Mt. Shasta helped to dry out the timber. Then he got the idea to run the lumber mill and buy 280 acres of land. The saw mill just keeps getting larger and more profitable. The place always needs more workers!"

Frank listened, but he wasn't interested in working in a lumber mill, at least not yet. "That's great, but I'm heading to San Francisco."

"San Francisco? So what's so special about that windy, always cold, hilly city that you want to go so far just to see it?"

"Oh, yeah, I want to see it, but I also want to work there. I'm thinking I might be able to get a job working at one of those gym places where they teach boxing and have boxing matches."

"You want to learn how to box?"

"Yeah, I do."

The waiter scratched his head and admitted, "I use to box. I was pretty good at it."

"With gloves and the whole bit?"

"Yeah, with gloves and the whole bit."

"You want to box professionally?"

"No," said Frank. "I just want to learn how to fight."

The waiter didn't answer for a couple minutes and just looked at Frank.

"Sounds like you have a target in mind. Like you know who you want to fight."

Frank immediately visualized mean Mr. Steward. Yes, he knew exactly who and why he wanted to learn how to box. He didn't answer the question.

"Let me tell you some things about boxing. It seems like you're carrying a grudge. Anger doesn't work well in boxing. You lose control when you fight in a state of anger. With boxing there are rules. With a bare fist fight there are no rules. You hit someone with a bare fist and they will hit back, anyway they can."

Frank remembered Mr. Steward's hook hand. If he struck Frank with his hook... well, Frank didn't want to think about it. All he knew was he wanted to be prepared to fight and learn some boxing skills. His goal seemed like the best option, if for no other reason than learning how to duck.

The waiter stood up and showed Frank a few boxing moves. He demonstrated how to keep his hands relaxed, even if he was wearing gloves, how to improve punching, ways to move the body quickly, and how to do a quick snapping jab!

Frank was impressed. Another customer walked in. The waiter quickly came back to his present reality. He took Frank's used plates off the table and headed back into the kitchen.

Frank enjoyed this free boxing lesson and the discussion, but he felt somewhat defeated. His immediate need and desire was to leave town and head down the road. He decided to pay his bill and walk around town to see if he could figure a way out of Weed. He left his money on the table and walked out.

*****

While wandering through the small town, Frank noticed tied up horses and a few automobiles. Finding a ride to San Francisco appeared dismal if not impossible. There was one mercantile store. Frank decided he needed some food to get him through the rest of the day whether he started hitchhiking or staying around.

As luck would have it, he met the right person. He was picking out some produce (apples and bananas) when he met lumberjack Jack who said his real name was John, but everyone called him Jack.

"You must be new in town; I've never seen you before." It was Jack's way of getting acquainted.

"Yes, I'm just passing through, heading to San Francisco."

"San Francisco, that's over 200 miles away! You've got a way of getting there or a plan of getting' there?"

"No, sir, I don't have neither."

"Well, my name is Jack. What's your name?"

Frank stopped sorting the fruit. He turned to shake hands with Jack. "My name is Frank, much obliged to meet ya."

Jack looked directly into Frank's eyes, like he was trying to figure out Frank's character. He seemed satisfied. "May I ask, how old you are?"

"I'm seventeen, sir."

Jack hesitated, still staring at Frank. Then he slowly stated, "You know what? This may be your lucky day. I've got a son, he's eighteen, and he's aiming to head to San Francisco. He has some wild idea he might find 'better work there' and make more money than workin' here in the lumber mill. Can you figure? Anyway, he's got this Ford auto, that he bought himself, and he's tending to head down south."

"You got any qualms against ridin' with him? Course, you don't know him, but he's an ok kid. Good worker too, just a guy that wants to wander instead of hanging around and making a good livin'... and inheriting a piece of land."

"I'd like to meet your son. I don't mind hitching a ride. I would even help with gas money. I left a job in Portland so I kinda know how he's feeling, wantin' to travel and all."

"Well, great. Here, I'll draw you a map, and you come over to our place tomorrow morning you two can meet. I think he plans on leaving tomorrow. I'd feel better if he weren't traveling solo. Never know what might go wrong between here and there. Oh, by the way. You got a driver's license?"

"No, sir, can't say that I have."

"Well, nothin' to learn how to drive. You could help with the drivin' – no matter if you got a license or not. No one around here cares much about that. No patrol along these back roads. Maybe, you could help with the driving."

"Here are the directions to my place." Frank looked at the piece of paper. It seemed clear and easy to read. "Okay, I'll see you all early tomorrow, and thanks for the offer." Frank, put the paper in his pocket and picked up his fruit.

"Well, I might not be there, but my wife and Nathan, my son, will be, so just rap on the front door." They shook hands again to settle the agreement.

Frank finished his shopping. He asked the clerk if there was a place he could spend the night. The clerk directed him to the only hotel in town, not on the main road, but hidden down an alley. That's where Frank headed.

Early the next morning, Frank followed Jack's directions. He hiked out to the farm house. He rapped on the front door. A woman answered. "You must be Frank," she quickly surmised.

"Yes, madam, I came to meet Nathan."

"Well, I'm Mrs. Miller. Jack told me about meeting you. I approve of this idea, riding with Nathan to San Francisco." She quieted her voice, "…as you probably guessed we are not happy about his plans to travel to the big city. Seems he is not in favor of our goals. We prefer to have him stay put, work at the lumber mill, and settle down right here in Weed. The mistake was he took all his earnings and bought himself an automobile. I guess once you purchase an auto you have to see how far it can go."

She moved across the living room and motioned for Frank to take a seat. "You know much about autos Frank?"

"No, madam, I've only ridden in them."

"Well, you and Nathan might learn a lot before you get to San Francisco. No repair shops between here and there." She sighed, "I guess you young ones will figure it out." She shook her head.

She yelled up the stairway for her son to get up and come downstairs. Nathan arrived looking as if he just got out of bed. He was tall, thin, with a thick head of blond ruffled hair. He had strong looking arms though, like his working days at the mill did create some firm muscles.

Mrs. Miller introduced Frank. "Son, this is Frank." She looked at Frank, "What is your last name?"

Frank stood up. "Frank Rose, madam."

"Hmm," she mumbled. "Well anyway, this is my son, Nathan. It's time you two got acquainted, especially if you plan to leave today."

Nathan reached over and shook Frank's hand. He still appeared to be sleepy and not energetic yet. Frank didn't know it, but Nathan was already packed and ready to leave; however, he didn't seem to be in any rush.

Frank eyed Nathan and wondered if they could get along or not. Maybe, he would have been wiser to just hop the next freight train out of town or take a chance hitchhiking. His thoughts were interrupted when Mrs. Miller told them she had breakfast ready for them in the kitchen.

They followed her through some wooden swinging doors and entered the dining area. The table was already set. Hot porridge and toast was ready. Then Mrs. Miller added fried eggs, and sausage. "Eat, eat," she encouraged them. She sat at the end of the table slowly taking a few bites, but mostly watched them as they quickly devoured the food and helped themselves to seconds. Mrs. Miller seemed pleased.

As soon as the eating time was completed, Nathan stood up and said he'd meet Frank outside shortly. Frank thanked Mrs. Miller and told her he'd wait outside. While waiting Frank rolled a cigarette, smoked and paced up and down the dirt driveway.

It wasn't long when Nathan appeared. He looked awake and eager to go. Nathan showed Frank all that he had packed the night before. He had a bag of clothes, even his favorite blanket, and pillow. He also showed Frank a California map, an extra tire, a can of oil, and an empty gallon jug for gasoline. All signs of extra preparedness, but also signs that Nathan might be a boy that would be homesick before he got fifty miles from town. Frank realized that he had no supplies to offer. All that Frank carried was in his pockets, nothing that would help them if they got stranded in some remote area.

Nathan opened the hood of the 1917 Ford Model T. He was excited to show Frank the mechanisms under the hood. Frank tried to figure out what each object was used for. Nathan eagerly started to name the engine parts. "Here is the crankshaft: it connects to the handle out here." He cranked the handle, and the engine started. While the motor was roaring, he pointed to the spark plugs, the coils to the spark plugs, the fuel tank, the carburetor, brake line, the water pump, and the radiator. He explained that the piston rings were inside the engine, and that the carburetor brought the gas to the motor. He seemed knowledgeable about his auto. At least, he could name the parts. Frank was impressed!

"I didn't buy this on time either. I paid for it with cash. I saved my money the whole time I worked at the lumber mill: two hundred and ninety bucks!"

The amount of money that Nathan saved was amazing. Frank had worked on jobs, but whenever he worked he had to spend money to get to the next job, or to get back home. Now he was going to do the same, spend money on traveling.

Nathan slammed down the hood. They climbed into the auto. "Any final good-byes?" Frank asked.

"Nope, I said them all. My friends think I've already left town."

Nathan was beginning to back out of the dirt driveway when his mom came running down the path. She carried with her a large tote bag of food and drinks.

Nathan reached out and gave her a hug through the top of the open door space and grabbed the huge bag. "Mom, we're not gonna' starve!" They laughed, waved, and threw hand kisses back and forth. Frank too yelled out, "Much obliged!"

It seemed like whenever Frank traveled, he used these words of gratitude often. Many strangers had been kind and generous to him. He wondered why he was having good experiences with strangers, compared to his youth when he had to live with mean Mr. Steward.

He also thought it was strange that Nathan wanted to leave Weed when he had loving, concerned parents, and a chance for a full-time career. Frank thought working in a lumber mill had to be easier than working at his last job: slaughtering sheep.

Nathan put his foot on the pedal and turned the steering wheel. They bounced on the seats. Nathan drove faster than Frank thought was wise. The dirt flew.

Nathan looked over at Frank; he raised his voice and asked, "You want to guess how fast this auto can go?" There was a speedometer. Frank looked at it. They were traveling 8 miles per hour which seemed fast enough.

Frank answered, "I guess it could go up to 10 or 15 miles per hour."

"Nope, Ford tested it and claims it can go up to 40 miles per hour! He actually won a race to prove his point."

"Well," said Frank cautiously, "let's just try to get there in one piece, not with parts strewed across California."

They went through the town of Weed: Nathan's final good-bye and the only way to Highway 99. He drove down Weed Boulevard, then to Edgewood Road, then to Steward Springs Road. "This will take us to Highway 99. Nathan seemed wide awake now. He was excited to leave Weed. "Every mile we take will be one mile closer to San Fran-cis-co!"

Chapter Twenty-Three

Weed to Shasta City

The speed limit was posted: 18 mph. Nathan kept a steady speed between 20 and 25 mph. Finally, Frank had a chance to ask his question. "What was it like working at the lumber mill?"

Nathan seemed okay answering, "Lumber is a good business. Everyone in this town is excited about the lumber mill. If you don't work there, they look at you like something is wrong with you. I love the trees. I feel sad every time a tree is chopped down, but I would never say that out loud, here in Weed. You ever hear of Frederick Weyerhaeuser?"

Frank had to admit he never heard of him.

"Well, he started his business in 1860 in Rock Island, Illinois. They cut so many trees back east, he moved out here - in the northwest - really in Washington and Oregon. He passed away in 1914. I hear tell that when he died he owned over two million acres of pine forests. Can you believe that? He owned the forests: forests of trees just to chop down."

Frank didn't know anything about the lumber business or the amount of trees that were being cut down, but he understood Nathan's passion. He had seen the landscapes from his train rides. He knew about the forests views, the beauty of the trees locked together especially across the Mt. Hood area in Oregon.

'Your love for the trees, is that why you quit working at the mill?"

"No, hell, I wanted to keep living. Working at the mill, or even in the woods, that's dangerous work. I saw so many injuries. The last one was a friend of mine."

Nathan quit speaking. Frank waited.

"He got caught in one of those band saws – huge saws that can cut up a Redwood Tree. Let's just say… he didn't survive." They rode in silence until Nathan added more comments about his frustration.

"I started work when I was fifteen. I've been working six days a week, ten hours every day. The mill only closes on Sundays. Everyone thinks Sundays are days of worship. Mom got annoyed with me. I was supposed to attend church on Sundays. I slept in every Sunday morning. I have nothing against God, mind you, I was just dead tired."

After hearing this story, Frank felt somewhat guilty for leaving his job at the meat plant. Yes, it was emotional, and rough work on the "kill'em" floor, but it wasn't as dangerous as the lumber mill.

They were quiet for a while. Frank enjoyed watching the scenery at a slower pace than his train rides. Nathan kept driving. Another hour went by when Nathan decided he was hungry. "Let's pull off here and have a picnic." Frank agreed.

Nathan veered the auto off to the left. They stopped the vehicle. There on a grassy plain they spread out Nathan's blanket, ate most of the food his mom had packed and they rested. It was after an hour of rest time when they noticed the change of weather.

The bright, sunny afternoon was hidden by dark, cumulus clouds. "Are we going to have a downpour?" Frank asked Nathan. He assumed Nathan would know something about California weather.

"We do get heavy rain storms every once in a while. They don't last, but still it can be a lot of rain."

"Well, maybe we should get back on the main road and away from these dirt roads."

"Good idea," Nathan agreed.

They packed up the extra food, the blanket, even what garbage they had accumulated. They tossed it all into the back seat. Then Nathan grabbed what looked like canvas pillow cases with snaps. "These are curtains; we need to snap them on the back doors to keep the rain out."

Frank quickly realized that the back seat was going to get drenched if they didn't cover the open spaces. Quickly, they started snapping on the curtains. It was an easy task, except they were trying to race against the wetness of the raindrops. As Frank finished the task, Nathan cranked up the Ford.

Once again, their bodies bounced on the seats as they drove over the dirt pits. The clouds turned darker and darker. All of a sudden, the rain poured. Luckily, they had a leather roof overhead. The road became a mass of soggy mud in minutes.

Frank was use to Portland showers, but this was a heavy, steady downpour. The auto wheels were spinning in the dirt and the water was rising. They had to stop.

After fifteen minutes, Frank asked Nathan why the rain was continuing. Nathan had no answer. It was forty-five minutes of total downpour rain before it even began to decrease. There were times of thunder sounds and visible lightning streaks. It was too early for darkness, but the daylight had turned to a dark gray hue. The tires were sinking into muddy holes.

Nathan and Frank had several sighs of despair and disbelief. Mostly they were quiet in their own thoughts of how this situation would get resolved. Finally, it was semi-still with only a drizzle of rain. Frank got out of the auto to inspect their plight.

"We need a shovel or something to dig with."

Nathan looked in his small tote bag. He knew he didn't have a shovel but maybe there would be something. Surprisingly, there was a small handled garden hoe in his bag. He didn't even know why because he never did any gardening, but his mom did. Maybe, for some unknown reason, she had used his tool bag. He handed the hoe to Frank.

Frank looked at it and didn't complain about its small size. He just started digging. He dug around each tire, removed scoops of water, and kicked mounds of dirt aside.

Finally, he advised Nathan to crank up the auto and try to move forward. The engine started. Frank felt like he needed more help, but he knew that Nathan needed to stay in the auto to keep it running. Frank yelled for him to just idle the engine while he dug out some more. This process was repeated several times: dig, rev the engine, dig, rev the engine, push, and dig some more. It was after several tries that the auto actually moved forward. As the auto moved, Frank ran, jumped on the side board, opened the door, and sat down. It struck him rather funny that he had to run to catch a vehicle instead of catching a train car. In his mind, it was easy and certainly less dangerous.

Nathan headed the auto into the field. He figured there would be less chance of the Ford sinking into the mud. He had to avoid rocks, trees, shrubs, and even dirt holes, but he made it, and they saw the paved road ahead. Even the highway had places of high water, but they didn't fear sink holes.

They were dirty, their clothes were wet, and their boots were muddy. They had no idea where they were. It wasn't complete darkness yet; once the rain stopped there was actual daylight. There were no other autos on the road, as if everyone knew about the storm coming, except for them.

Nathan pulled over on the side of the road. He stopped and unfolded the map. From what he could tell, they could be at Shasta City in a couple hours.

When they arrived at Shasta City they discovered there were campsites for overnight stops. For fifty cents they could stay for the night. There was no need to hurry to Redding, and it was still daylight. "What the heck," said Nathan "let's pay the fifty cents and get ourselves a tent with two cots."

The place reminded Frank of his last hobo camp, except this place wasn't for hobos; it was for traveling families. They were shown where there was a row of outhouses. Nathan placed his blanket on one cot. Frank did not have any bedding: he would make do with his jacket and his extra shirt.

They decided to hike into town, only blocks away, and get some supper. They walked into a place called Shasta Diner. A male waiter came straight to the booth where Nathan and Frank were seated. "What can I get for you guys?"

"Guess we need to see what you are offering," said Frank.

"The list is on the wall." The waiter pointed to a wall menu. Frank read the list out loud: "Steak Dinners, Hamburger Sandwiches, and Chicken Dinners, choices of Home-made fries or mashed potatoes and gravy. Drinks: coffee or tea."

The choices were basic and limited. "Guess I'll do the steak dinner with mashed potatoes." Nathan decided on the hamburger sandwich, and they both ordered coffee.

The restaurant was somewhat empty with only one other family sitting in the back corner booth. Then another gentleman walked in and took a table seat near their booth.

After he ordered, he leaned over and asked them if they were new residents in town or just passing through. Frank enjoyed talking with strangers so he was quick to reply. "Sir, we're just passing through. Can you tell us some interesting tidbits about Shasta?"

"Sure," the stranger moved his chair closer to their booth. "What do you want to know?"

"Oh, we'd like to hear about the history of this place and anything else of interest."

"Well…" the man thought for a few seconds before he started his tales.

"This place just recently got an official name of Mount Shasta City. The mountain is named Mount Shasta but our city had several names. The most popular one was Strawberry Valley. In 1924 the name officially became Shasta City."

"The mountain is what is most important in our town. Why, this is the fifth highest mountain in California."

Nathan agreed, "It is beautiful. The mountain view is why we decided to camp here for the night."

The gentleman continued, "There are stories about this mountain. It is unique, standing alone, not part of any mountain range. You guys believe in creatures from outer space?"

Frank had heard of unexplained night lights, but he didn't believe in such nonsense. He had yet to see any unusual sights in the night skies. Nathan didn't answer, but Frank emphatically said, "No, sir!"

"Well, I do! So do many old folks around these parts because we've seen different kinds of lights and moving shadows around this place. I've heard unusual sounds too. I've done lots of hiking around the mountain. I can't say I'm scared of it. I'm just curious because I know strange events happen. Not only can the weather change quickly, but also there are sights and sounds that cannot be explained. Some people claim the mountain has magical powers."

Frank didn't know what to say. It is hard to argue with one's testimony of what he has experienced.

"What have you seen?"

"I've seen lights in the dark sky that are not planes. They've circled around and around and then disappeared. I've seen large footprints in the snow, that don't match any animal prints I know of. Some of these prints I saw right near my own footprints, and I would swear I was the only live creature walking the path."

Nathan listened intently. He knew about the mountain because he could see it off in the distance from his home in Weed. He had not heard about these mountain tales. "Are there other stories about this mountain?"

"Yes, the natives around here believe there is an ancient living civilization existing under this mountain. You know it is a volcano that erupted back in 1789. They believe that somehow people survived, that life goes on despite this eruption".

The food order came to their table. The man moved his chair back to his table. Nathan appeared nervous from hearing these stories. Frank was just hungry and started to chow down his dinner.

The gentleman leaned back and stated, "Don't worry guys; I haven't heard any stories about any creature, or power hurting any passing traveler."

"Good," answered Frank. He cut his steak and started to chew.

As they hiked back to the campsite they viewed the mountain as the evening shadows started to cover the scene. "Still want to stay here tonight?"

Nathan stopped walking and spent a few seconds looking directly at the mountain. "Sure," he answered. "How often can a mountain erupt? I doubt it will happen tonight."

They continued their walk back to the campsite.

Frank and Nathan were awakened by the bright sunshine. Now they looked at the near-by snow-capped mountain as a mystery: more awesome than it had looked the day before. They agreed to grab some breakfast and then do some hiking before they left the area; however, while they were eating at the Café they heard about hiking trails ten miles down the road. Still fearing the stories they had heard the night before, they decided the trails away from the mountain might be more inviting and less intimidating. This meant going ten miles east of highway 99, away from their designated route.

Before they left town, they stopped at the Richfield gas station and filled up the 10 gallon tank. Then Nathan turned the crank and steered the Model T to Highway 89. He handed the written directions to Frank. Frank read the directions out loud: "Go about ten miles and follow a sign that will say McCloud, then look for a sign that says Fowler's Campground, turn into the campground. There will be signs that will point to the hiking trails that will go to the Lower Falls, Middle Falls and the Upper Falls."

"Sounds easy," said Frank.

What the map didn't say was that highway 89 was not a cement paved road, as was highway 99. Highway 89 was a winding, one lane, gravel, rocky road with elevation changes and barely room for oncoming automobiles to pass, let alone if a truck should come from the opposite direction.

Frank realized that Nathan was nervous driving on this stretch of roadway, so he stayed quiet and looked at the surrounding view. Mt. Shasta was behind them. Along the roadside was forest area. The sun rays penetrated through the pine branches. Every twisted turn was a new sight of beauty. They had even seen a few wandering deer along the roadside.

Finally, in less than an hour's drive time, they came to Fowler's Campsite. They drove on the gravel path, through the open wooden gates. It was a private campsite where people paid to spend the night; however, no one was at the main entrance, and they did not see any "Do Not Enter" signs. Nathan drove by other parked automobiles and past cabins that were designated for overnight lodgers. Then Frank noticed the signs to the hiking trails. "Here they are - park anywhere!"

"Okay," Nathan stopped the vehicle and parked next to another Model T Ford.

They each grabbed their jackets from the back seat. The Lower Falls Trail looked easy enough, and in the distance they could hear the water running like the sound of creek water going down stream.

The trail was narrow, dirty and rocky. It was less than one mile. Suddenly, there was the waterfall and a pool of water. There was a family with 3 young children splashing in the water. On the same path was the sign leading to the Middle Falls. "Let's keep going," suggested Frank.

They hiked to the next waterfall. These falls were more impressive. The span of water was wider, higher, and the pool below was deeper. There were no other people around this area. They were surrounded by a forest of trees, a few separate logs flat on the ground, and brush over parts of the path. They sat on one of the logs and discussed whether they should trudge forward to see the Upper Falls or if they should go back.

"It is so beautiful and relaxing here. I've never seen a waterfall before."

Nathan was surprised. "Haven't you been to Multnomah Falls in Oregon?"

"No," answered Frank. "I've heard about them, but no, I have yet to see them. I've been in the country, I've seen forests, but I haven't seen waterfalls. I haven't had much interest in water adventures. I have yet to learn how to swim. Not that one could swim in these falls. Really, I'm surprised how peaceful it is to watch these waters rage over the rocks and shower into the pools."

They were quiet for several minutes. Then Nathan stood up and read the nearby sign: "Upper Falls." The sign did not indicate how far up they would have to hike to see the last falls. The trail looked steep and narrow; not as easy as the last two trails. The path was more rocky than clear. This path might be a challenge.

Nathan reminded Frank that their main goal was to get to the next town, Redding, which was about seventy miles down the road, and to get there before dark. Still there was a sight to see ahead; maybe this was their only chance to see this water fall.

Frank decided, "Let's do it." They started the upward climb. Mostly they looked downward, watching where to place each foot.

"Do you think there might be bear around these parts?"

"I'm sure there are," answered Frank.
"What do we do if we see a bear?"

"Well, I heard it's best to make noise if you're hiking through the woods. You don't want to surprise a bear."

"Right!" Nathan started to whistle. At first he whistled a tune that Frank thought was rather catchy, but maybe one that Nathan made up. Then he whistled a tune Frank was familiar with, "Home, Home on the Range."

Frank started to hum along. Then he thought a few minutes and decided to add his own lyrics. He sang, "Home, home in the woods, where the deer and the bear might be seen." He looked around, and then added the rest of the chorus… "Where the creeks run free to the river below, and the thick tall trees shade the stream."

Nathan made a whistle sound showing he was impressed. Frank repeated the song once more and then Nathan sang along. Hopefully, the bears would want to keep their distance. The rushing water could be heard: louder than the Lower Falls. The trail made a slight turn, and there below them was a raging water falls. It was a tremendous sight. As the sun shone into the water mist, a rainbow appeared over the falls. They could feel the cool wet spray dampen their faces and jackets.

Frank and Nathan stood quietly. Frank wished he had a camera to capture this sight. The feeling was odd because he had seen many scenes on his train rides: rocky mountains in the distance, thick forest trees, long acres of grassy plains, but this was the first time he wanted to capture the scene on film. "You know, Nathan, this was worth the hike. Seeing this sight gives me energy. It's like hearing these waterfalls and seeing their power creates a power within me. The sight gives me a desire to see more: climb a mountain, take a boat ride, travel the land, and explore parts of the world I have yet to see."

Nathan agreed. He also wanted to get back to his automobile. "Let's get moving, and maybe we will get closer to accomplish our main goal of getting to San Francisco."

They started their hike down the trail. It was easier hiking downward, and now they knew the way so the distance seemed shorter. It was around 2:00 p.m. when they reached the parking lot. They decided to get something to eat in McCloud.

Chapter Twenty-Four

Mt. Shasta to McCloud, California

Nathan followed Highway 89. He saw the sign, 5 miles McCloud. In less than a ½ hour, they drove slowly through the main street of this western town. The surrounding views were great. Mt. Shasta still towered in the distance, and several scenic waterfalls were nearby.

The main street was busy with parked automobiles. Several buildings faced a boardwalk that included rails where folks could tie up their horse and buggies. Frank looked at the signs. There was one huge building with the name "Mercantile." The building was a combination store and hotel. There was a Meat Market, Café, and Soda Fountain. Down the road Frank could see other businesses too. He thought there might be a speakeasy at the end of the street. Frank was hungry and suggested that they eat at the Café.

A water pump was near the side of the doorway. They stopped to wash their hands, splashed water on their faces, and drank from the water pump by cupping their hands and slurping as many gulps of water as they needed. Letting the sun semi-dry them off, they wiped their hands on their pants and walked into the Café. They sat on wooden stools at the counter.

"My treat!"

"Why's that?" Nathan asked.

"I'll pay because you paid for the last gas fill-up."

"Okay," Nathan agreed. He studied the menu more intently. There was a list of choices: sandwiches and complete dinners. They were hungry. Nathan thought of his mother's cooking. "You know my mom fixed the best and the freshest chicken ever. I'm ordering a chicken dinner."

Frank thought of his mother and the meat that he brought home from the butcher shop. He ordered a pot roast dinner.

They had barely ordered their meal when a gentleman sat on the stool next to Frank. "You guys new to these parts?"

"Yeah," answered Frank. "We're on our way to San Francisco."

"Off the beaten path, I'd say. Shouldn't you be on Highway 99?"

"You're right. We should be. We stopped to see the Lower, Middle, and Upper Water Falls."

"Wise decision. Well, you've got only about three-hundred and twenty miles to get to San Francisco: eighty-six miles if you want to stop in Redding. We've got a nice town here if you want a place to hang your hat. Where are you guys from?"

"I'm from Portland and my friend here is from Weed."

"Weed? I know about Weed; it's a lumber town like here. You could get work in Weed."

"True," said Nathan. "I was working at the mill."

"Lumber is everything in these here parts. Why, McCloud Lumber Mill owns this town. Every building on this street is owned by 'Mother McCloud'; that's what we call our lumber mill. The mill buys the homes and all the stores. We've got steam heat, and we use it to heat every home. I'll tell you, if you own a house here and need a pipe fixed, like water or a heating pipe, 'Mother McCloud' will fix it. You get a job in this town and you'll be well takin' care of."

Nathan decided that explaining to this man why he didn't want to work at any lumber mill would be useless. Also, he decided not to share his dream of finding a whole new different career in San Francisco.

The meals came and all three men started to eat. Amazingly, the food was tasty. Frank and Nathan ate like it would be their last meal. They didn't know it, but there would be many hours before they would get a chance to eat again.

By the time they left the restaurant and headed toward Highway 99, it was after 5 o'clock. The ride was smooth. They were full of food and the auto was full of fuel. As they rode along Nathan remembered one comment that the gentleman had said in the restaurant.

"Didn't that guy say that it was eighty-six miles to Redding?"

"Yeah, that sounds about right."

"Well, at the rate we are going at 18 miles per hour, we won't get to Redding until dark, maybe around 8:30 p.m."

Frank shrugged his shoulders; he was use to traveling at night. He didn't think it mattered. "It's okay if it is dark. You got headlights on this thing?"

Nathan decided to tell Frank the truth. "Matter-of-fact, I do have headlights, but I haven't really driven much in the dark."

Now Frank wished that he knew how to drive because then he could do the driving. "Pull over," he said. "Now is as good of time, as any, for me to learn how to drive this carriage."

Nathan pulled off to the side of the road and put on the parking brake. The engine was still running; however, Nathan got out of the auto, and Frank got in the driver's seat. Nathan explained the clutch, and the three floor pedals. Then the directions came fast and confusing: release park brake, hand brake forward, push left pedal down, far right pedal is the brake, middle reverse, clutch, other pedal, give it the gas. The auto lurched forward and bumped over some dirt pits on the road. Frank barely had time to turn the wheel. He started off too fast. Nathan yelled, "Ease up on the gas pedal!"

It was a challenge. Frank wished he had paid more attention to Nathan's driving. He kept at it. Finally after several minutes of weaving and jerking movements, the Model T went smoothly down the road. Frank began to enjoy the ride. He kept the speed between eighteen and twenty-five miles per hour. Every time he reached twenty-five miles per hour, Nathan reminded him, "You're going too fast."

Frank had driven for over an hour when all of a sudden, the auto jerked and kept jerking. Frank could feel the steering wheel pull to one side. He held the wheel tightly while he tried to steer the auto in a straight path. Nathan shouted, "Pump the brakes, and turn off the road." Frank wasn't even sure what "pump the brakes meant." Nathan demonstrated with his foot on the passenger side of the auto. Frank started to copy his motions and was able to get the auto in control as he steered it to the side of the road. Nathan sighed, "I haven't had one yet, but I think we've got a flat tire! It might have happened when you first started driving. I thought then you drove over a couple pot holes as we left the side of the road."

"Shucks," said Frank. "A flat tire could have happened when we were driving on Highway 89 the whole road was full of holes and rocks."

"The flat tire didn't happen then; it just popped now!"

"True, the blowout could have happened then and there. It could have been a slow leak and now the air just blew out!"

"No, I'm sure it happened when you hit the road too fast and hard, when you first started driving!"

"If that was true, the tire would have leaked over an hour ago." There was silence as if they both realized the argument wasn't making any sense. Nathan went to the back of the auto and pulled up the latch, that held the spare tire, and then he lifted the tire to the ground. Next, he reached inside the auto to get out his tool box.

"You've changed a tire before?"

"No," answered Nathan.

"Have you seen anyone else change a tire before?"

"No," answered Nathan.

Frank sighed. They had gone at least twenty miles away from McCloud. During those twenty miles they only saw one or two other autos and no other towns or gas stations. "It can't be that hard," said Nathan. "I've got all-purpose tools. "See all these open shapes and sizes; this tool is suppose to be good for every bolt and screw on this auto. This other one is a crow-bar. Frank noticed each tool had the letters "FORD" marked on the silver coating. And to Frank's surprise, Nathan had a small jack.

Nathan went to the front of the auto. He put his jack under the side where the flat tire was and started to pump up the jack. It worked. The auto was raised off the ground, the flat tire hanging in the air. Then he took his other "all-purpose tool" and started to loosen the four bolts on each tire. Frank stood by, ready to help take the tire off and hand him the next tire. The bolts were on tighter than Nathan expected. Two came off but the last two were on extremely tight. Frank took over and jerked and twisted the tool using all the muscle he had. He was able to loosen both bolts. The tire and the rim fell to the ground. The wooden spokes stayed in place. Now all they had to do was repeat the process in reverse and get the good tire on the wheel. Fortunately, the rubber tubing was in the new tire.

Everything was ready to go. It was getting dark, but Nathan was well prepared for that too; he had a flashlight. They took turns working on the tire or holding the flashlight.

Finally, the work was finished. It was dark. Nathan wiped off his hands on his pants and told Frank he would drive. Frank didn't argue. "My dad and I have been this way before. I think there is a park alongside the road not far from here. We can rest there for the night."

Frank figured he could not convince Nathan to drive all the way to Redding in the dark. Frank was willing to drive again, but he realized Nathan was now overprotective of his auto. It was going to be a long night. Frank started thinking about food: dinner, late snacks and an early breakfast. Unfortunately, they had eaten all their previous snacks. Their next meal would have to wait till morning and about sixty more miles down the road.

The night was long and difficult. Nathan easily found the park. He remembered past times when his father had taken him there. It was a pleasant place with a creek running through a rocky area. A wooden bridge crossed over a narrow waterfall. Many tall trees surrounded the grassy fields. They were the only people there. Using their one and only flashlight, they leaned into the creek, splashed and slurped the refreshing water. The evening was cool, but not cold.

They parked the Model T a short ways from the creek so the noise of the rushing stream would not disturb their sleep. Many other sounds disturbed their rest including an owl that hooted during the night. The gentle wind swayed the tree tops, and there were other sounds, that they imagined or that were real: slight noises that sounded like feet slithering through the park, either from human or animal foot-steps.

They tried to make themselves comfortable. Frank took the back seat. He placed their belongings on the floor and stretched out on the seat. The position didn't work. His legs were too long. Nathan had his blanket and pillow and made a comfortable nest in the front seat.

They were both restless, and after an hour of tossing around with maybe only moments of shut eye, they decided to move the blanket outside on the grassy lawn.

That was where they both finally fell asleep: on the ground, under the glittering stars. Frank woke up first. It was early. The light from the early morning sun awakened him. His stomach growled from want of food. He walked to the creek to slurp more water which helped to satisfy the strong urge of hunger. Nathan was sound asleep. Frank decided to walk around for a bit, but if Nathan did not arise on his own, he would wake him up. He remembered when he first went to meet Nathan. Nathan was sleeping in late that day, even though it was their first travel day and it was near noon.

The park was beautiful with morning dew on the grass; yet, the air already felt warm. Frank realized he might like California. This area had less rain than Portland, and it had warm sunny days. "What's taking you so long to get started?" It was Nathan yelling, "It's time we hit the road!"

Frank walked back to the auto. Nathan had already packed their belongings neatly in the back seat, and he had cranked up the Ford. It was purring along, like a horse waiting for its rider to gallop off. Frank was glad to see that Nathan was ready to leave. Food, gasoline, and a spare tire was all they needed. Their hopes were to arrive in Redding before dark. They knew the distance to Redding; however, they were not sure what towns might be closer. Nathan asked Frank to read the map again to see if food and gas was near-by.

Frank studied the map. The only large-printed word that indicated what was ahead was the name "Redding." In small print was a place called Lakehead. It was on the way. Frank suggested they stop there. They got back on the main highway. The auto purred along at 20 mph. Nathan was anxious to get somewhere. He, too, was hungry. They drove for an hour when they saw a sign that said "Lakehead." Nathan slowed down. He drove by a gas station. He kept driving to see if there were any other stores, shops, or a café around. All they saw was the long stretch of road ahead, mountains in the distance, flat bare land and a sign "22 miles to Redding."

"What?" Nathan was frustrated. "I think the town of Lakehead consists of one gas station." He turned the auto and retraced the path back to the one gas station. "Let's hope this station can fix a spare tire."

Frank only had one thought on his mind, "I hope this place has something to eat or somebody knows where we can get some food." They each shouted their main concern. "Spare tire!" "Food!"

Nathan pulled into the gas station next to a pump. An elderly guy came limping slowly to their Model T. "I see you need a new spare tire."

Nathan was glad that he had noticed. "Yes, sir, I do, or I need to get this one fixed."

"Well, the rim looks okay, but the tire is no good. I could give you a new, inflated tire and put it on your rim, if you like."

"I would appreciate that. How much would it cost to get that done?"

"How much you got?"

Nathan hesitated to answer. All of a sudden he felt leery of this guy.

The old man started to laugh. "Just kidding. But it will cost you four bucks. I will take some time: about an hour to get the job done."

Nathan thought four dollars was a rather high price. He also thought the job should get done quicker than an hour. It didn't appear that there was anyone else around or any other duties for this man to do except to fix their tire.

"Take it or leave it."

"Guess I'll let you do it."

"Four bucks?"

"Yeah, four bucks."

Frank spoke up, "Are you the only one working here?"

"Yes, sir, I've been working here for a long time. I bought this place about fifteen years ago. Course, then nothing was here but the land."

"You get enough business here?"

"I get enough."

"Is there any nearby town?'

"Redding, up ahead, twenty-two miles up the road."

"Great, do you happen to have any food items for sale? We haven't eaten since yesterday."

"Well, not really. I have some candy bars and pop for sale."

Nathan and Frank looked at each other. "Fill it up, fix the tire and I guess we will buy some candy bars and pop."

Frank was upset that the candy bars were limited in choices and the guy insisted on selling them at twenty-five cents each when usually they would only cost five cents each. This short stop was costing them more than they expected: gas, candy bars, two root beers and a new spare tire. They agreed on evenly sharing the cost. After carefully counting out their coins and dollars, they left the money on the wooden counter and went outside.

The day felt warm. While they waited for the tire to be fixed, they sat in the shade, ate candy bars, and drank their pop. They were still hungry but agreed no more spending until they got to Redding where they could get a meal. It did take an hour of slow time, but finally the tire was finished.

As they drove off, finally leaving Lakehead, they heard the man holler: "Come back again."

Frank and Nathan laughed and then laughed some more. They repeated the words: "Come back again. How crazy does he think we are?"

"I would walk to Redding – all twenty-two miles before I would stop at his place again." Frank was still annoyed that the gentleman cheated them on the cost of the candy bars.

Frank was quiet. He had a worrisome question on his mind. He started to speak and then he hesitated... Yet, he needed to ask, "Any idea how much money you have left?"

"No," answered Nathan.

"Not that I want to pry in your personal business, but it is concerning. We've still got a ways to go."

"I know. About how much money do you have left?"

"Don't know. I will have to stop and count it."

"We'll figure it out when we get to Redding. Now let's just enjoy the view."

The auto moved smoothly over the cement road. Every once in a while they would see another auto. An hour ahead was a town that hopefully would satisfy their hunger needs.

Chapter Twenty-Five

Redding, California

The hour trip to Redding went smooth. "What do you think we will see in Redding?" Frank was curious and figured that Nathan might know something about the town beings he lived in California.

"Redding was a gold mining town. But I hear tell they are not mining for gold any longer. Now it is like a western, farming town."

"Why, do you think, they are not mining for gold anymore?"

"That's a good question. Maybe we will find out when we get there."

Nathan drove a little faster, up to 25 mph. He was anxious to stop driving and to eat.

They were surprised when they arrived in the downtown area of Redding. It was definitely a "western cowboy looking area." The town had plenty of places to eat and saloons were plentiful. Frank was hoping they had good food.

Autos were parked along the main street, but also horses, and some horse and carriages were tied to posts. Nathan wasn't too happy having to park his auto near the horses with horse dung on the ground, but he really had no choice.

They walked into a place called "Pete's Bar and Grill." At least, the name sounded like food would be a priority. They sat on the bar stools and looked at the wall for the menu list. Before ordering, they both checked their own pockets and figured out their money supply. Frank still had some money in his shoes, but he wasn't sure how much. That money was designated not to be spent, unless he really needed it. Hunger outweighed good common sense. Nathan and Frank ordered steak dinners that cost a dollar each. They could have gone for soup and sandwiches for less than a dollar, but they felt like they were deserving of steak.

After eating, Frank realized he might have to find work in this town before they continued their travels. Before he could think through that idea, he saw the Redding Theater sign. He had a strong urge to see a movie. "Tell you what, let's find a place where we can spend the night and then let's treat ourselves to a movie."

"Are you kidding? I don't think we can afford to go to a movie."

"Sure we can – even in Chicago the movie was only ten cents. Do you have a dime?"

Nathan checked his pockets. "Yeah, I have a dime, but this might be my breakfast in the morning."

"Don't worry, I think I can earn some money in this town before we leave."

"Really, how do you plan to do that?" Nathan looked around the town. It consisted mostly of saloons, one store that probably carried a supply of every needed item and food supplies, a bank, and a building that might be a post office. He didn't figure Frank could get a one day job in any of these places.

Frank guessed what Nathan was thinking. "I'm not lookin' for jobs here in town. I'll find work at people's farms or houses. Just wait. You will see."

Nathan shrugged his shoulders and looked around for a place that they could spend the night. He saw a sign that said "Redding Hotel." "Guess we need to check out that place."

They walked to the hotel. It was a tall brick building. It didn't look too bad. They walked inside. The lobby room looked clean. No-one was in the lobby. There was a bell on the desk. Frank rang the bell. A tall, thin man came to the desk. "Yes, gentlemen can I help you?"

"Yes, sir, we would like a place to stay tonight. Do you have any rooms?"

"That's what we're here for… sign here."

Frank signed his name FRANK on the top line. There were no other names on the paper. Frank wondered if they were the only night guests.

The tall man came out from behind the desk and led them down a long narrow, dark hallway. Then he used a key to unlock one of the doors. He opened the door. Inside was a large bed, a window, a basin and a bucket of water, soap and towels beside the basin. The man explained, "…the outhouse is out back, just go down the hallway and open the back door. That door is always unlocked."

Frank had yet to pay. "How much?"

"How long do you plan to stay?"

Frank and Nathan looked at each other. Frank thought about needing at least one day to work and earn some money. "We plan to stay for two nights."

"That will be 20 cents."

Frank reached into his pocket and paid the man twenty cents. Nathan seemed agreeable though he looked somewhat surprised that the decision was made so quickly.

Nathan and Frank looked around their room for the night. "What do we do now?"

"Why don't you rest awhile, and I'll go check out the job situation."

"You really plan to work?"

"Sure, it is the only way we will get to San Francisco."

"Okay," agreed Nathan. "First, I will count all my money. You count yours, and we will look at this situation in a realistic manner."

"Sounds good."

Nathan sat on the one chair in the room. Frank sat on the bed. Frank took off his shoes and surprised Nathan by pulling some dollars out of his shoe to add to his coin pile. Nathan took out his wallet from his pocket. Nathan was pleased to discover he had a total of eight dollars. He thought it was going to be less, but he also realized that if he had to change a tire again he was in trouble.

Frank counted his money: a total of ten dollars. He was realistic and knew that ten dollars, though it seemed like a lot, it would not go far.

"Be back soon," Frank left the hotel and went to look for work.

When he got outdoors, he wished he had asked to borrow Nathan's auto so he could drive around town and the surrounding area, but he didn't. Instead, he hiked around the place to see if anyone appeared to need an extra hand. There were some houses near town; a few could use some yard work. He walked up to one house. The grass was overgrown, but there was a white picket fence and a large inviting looking porch with a wooden cushioned swing hanging from the rafters. There was also a back side door. Frank decided that maybe he should knock on the back door, since he was not an invited guest.

He knocked several times. A woman wearing an apron, with gray hair pinned back and a smile answered the door. "May I help you?"

Frank was surprised that she was so friendly to a stranger. "Well, madam, I was really going to ask if I could help you. I happened to notice that your lawn needs mowing and I was wondering if you could use a handyman's help."

"So, you want some work?"

"Yes, madam, I am traveling through and honestly I need more funds. For a small fee I would be happy to do some chores for you."

"Sir, are you a good worker?"

"Yes, madam, I am."

"Well, you do seem like an honest young man. I've been praying for an honest man to come and do some work for me. I believe the Lord sent you."

Frank was surprised by that statement. It wasn't the first time someone had said that the "Lord sent him." He always felt that his ideas and whereabouts were strictly determined by his own intentions.

"Maybe so, madam, maybe so."

"Well, I need the lawn mowed. I also have a pile of wood that needs chopping."

She wiped her hands on her apron and walked out through the door. She led Frank to the backyard shed. There was a hand mower, an axe and a tall stack of un-chopped wood. "You mow the lawn, chop all this wood into piles that I can handle, and I will pay you."

"Sounds fair. Okay if I start now?"

"I always say, don't put off what needs to be done while the day is young."

Frank nodded in agreement, though he realized the day was not that young. He wished it was early morning rather than late afternoon. This was a two day job.

He rolled up his sleeves and grabbed the handle of the lawn mower and headed for the front yard. As he did so, he noticed there was a backyard too that needed the grass cut. He said out loud, "Well, so be it."

He worked three, warm sunny hours. Dusk was setting in. He knocked on the back door. The house-lady came to the door. She walked outdoors and looked at the lawn and saw the start of the wood chopping. She was pleased at how much Frank had accomplished.

"I'll come back tomorrow. I will finish the job."

"You need some pay today?"

"No, thank you. You can pay me tomorrow when the jobs are done."

"Okay, young man, see you tomorrow."

"It will be early."

"That's okay, the wood isn't going anyplace."

Frank smiled, and left to return to the hotel. He walked back and felt tired, but knew he still wanted to see a show before they left Redding. When he got back Nathan was worried. "Man, you were gone so long I thought you hopped a freight train and left town."

"No, I found work like I said I would."

"You got some pay?"

"Not yet, but I will get paid tomorrow when the job is done."

Frank went to the water bucket and started to wash up. "Get ready; we're going to the movies. Remember?"

They paid their dimes and went into the dark theater to watch two films. They were silent films, which Frank was use to, but he was also somewhat disappointed since he had seen a semi-sound film in Chicago. They laughed through the "Big Business" film with Laurel and Hardy trying their best to sell Christmas trees. Then they saw a couple short cartoons, and then the main feature, a film titled "Asphalt", a silent German made film with English subtitles. It was little confusing, but the plot was suspenseful. A girl got caught stealing a diamond. She tried to get out of her predicament by seducing the police officer. The film held their interest and for 85 minutes they were out of reality and into a plot of mystery. It was late when they left the theater, after midnight.

"I have to get up early."

"Why?" asked Nathan.

"I have to finish a job, remember."

"Yeah, you're right. We don't check out tomorrow. Guess I will have to roam around town. Maybe, I can learn some history while I'm there and find out why the gold rush ended."

It was early the next morning; Frank went to the corner store. It was closed. He was hoping to get some food for breakfast. Instead, he went straight to the lady's house. He knocked on the back door.

She was up, dressed and ready to greet him. "I made some biscuits and cooked some bacon. Would you like some?"

"Yes, madam, that would be most welcoming."

"Go to the front porch and enjoy my swing. I will bring you a plate of food. Would you like some coffee too?"

Frank was amazed. He expected to work and eat later. This offer of food and drink was a pleasant surprise. "Yes, if you have some."

"No problem, absolutely, no problem."

Frank sat on the lawn swing and swung gently back and forth. Mr. Steward had a lawn swing on his porch, but Frank was never allowed to swing on that seat. Now he realized how comfortable a lawn swing was. He wished he had been able to relax once in a while at the Stewards' place by just sitting on a lawn swing.

She arrived with the plate of food and the hot cup of coffee. Frank took his time to eat. As he finished the breakfast meal, he knocked on the door to return the empty dishes.

"Best I start working now."

"Yes, you go ahead. Knock on the back door when you are through and I will pay you. I'll probably be in the kitchen."

"Yes, madam, I will let you know when the job is done."

Frank went to the shed and started chopping wood.

He chopped wood for several hours and stacked it all in one tall neat pile. It really was the first time he had stacked wood, so several times he rearranged the pile so every piece would stay firm and not fall if another piece was moved.

At the end of the project, he felt satisfied with a job well-done. He knocked on her back door. She responded quickly and had an envelope that she handed to him.

"Do you want to see the pile of wood?"

"No, I will see it in due time. When I need a log, I'll go out to the shed and get it. I might not need it till winter. It actually can snow here during the winter – then yes, I will need wood to burn."

"Okay, then the job is done."

"Here is your pay. Thank you so much, you are a God-send!"

"Thank you! I much appreciate your kindness and generosity."

"You are welcome and you deserve every penny I gave you."

"Thanks!"

Frank waited till he was back at the hotel to open the envelope. He was more than pleased with the amount of money he was paid. He felt guilty for receiving two five-dollar bills. Surely, he shouldn't keep the total amount. There was a note. *Sir, please don't embarrass me by feeling a need to return any of this pay. The job was needed to be done. I have no way and no one to help on these chores. I truly appreciated your fine work. I could see your stack of wood from my kitchen window. I know you took care to do it right. I am pleased. Keep the money. You will probably need it for your travels. Thank you for working for me. Lillian.*

So her name is Lillian. What a kind, generous lady. Frank decided he would keep the money. He put one five-dollar bill in his pocket and the other five-dollar bill in his shoe. He sat on the side of the bed and quietly wondered about her kindness for several minutes. He felt blessed, often he met kind people. She was one of them.

Frank rested on the bed. Hours went by. When Nathan returned he talked about the days of the gold rush: "Okay, Frank this is what I learned about why there is no longer a mad search for gold in this town, compared to when men came in mass numbers for that one purpose. There were no property rights or rules about land protection, nor even rules about slavery. It was a time of madness in the search of gold. Gold was found, some got rich. Others came and went back home poor with no riches. They even did hydraulic drilling for this precious metal. Much of the land was destroyed. By 1850 there was less gold to be found. The surface gold where people panned for the gem seemed to disappear. Deep mining was the only possible way of finding gold. By 1859 logging became more popular than the search for gold. We know that. Logging is still the main job around these parts."

The word "logging" reminded Nathan why he was heading to San Francisco. He wanted a different job and a new place to live. "Let's go get something to eat."

"Great idea. I'll pay for dinner, but no steak. Let's go with sandwiches and soup. Tonight we will go to the store and get some food supplies. Tomorrow we will head down the road."

Nathan agreed. "Sounds, like a plan. Maybe, I'll even let you do some of the driving again."

Frank was surprised Nathan would make such an offer. "Really…?"

Chapter Twenty-Six

Redding to Sacramento, California

That evening Frank and Nathan agreed they would depart early the next morning. The hotel manager told them it was about one hundred and sixty miles to Sacramento. They figured that they could do that in one day, if they didn't make any stops.

The plan didn't exactly work. They slept longer than they had expected, waking up around 10:00 a.m. They slowly got ready. The first stop was the corner store. They bought a bag full of grocery items so they could eat on the way, rather than stopping at cafés to eat. When they finally got on the road, Nathan drove first and drove for forty miles. Frank enjoyed the view of the plentiful orchards of oranges and peaches, of open grassy fields, and farm acres with grazing cattle.

Nathan felt tired and hungry. He pulled the auto over by the side of the road and drove down a dusty path. He turned off the engine, pulled out his blanket, and laid it on the ground. That's where they would sit and have their picnic brunch. They dug through their food bag. Frank took out his pocket knife and spread peanut butter on a banana and on a slice of bread. They each drank their bottles of apple juice. They also had two bags of cookies, fresh apples and oranges. The day was warm and sunny.

"What do you plan to do when we get to San Francisco?"

Frank knew the answer. He had been thinking about the future possibilities for months. "I plan to find work. I'd like to find a job in a gym where they teach men how to box and do physical fitness exercises. I want to be stronger and be able to box… if I need to."

"Really, do you think you might need to fight someone?"

"I might."

Nathan decided not to question Frank's motives any more. He tried to visualize him in a different setting. Yes, Frank was strong looking. He had firm muscles and had the look of a hardy, healthy guy. He didn't see any anger in Frank's demeanor or reason to fear Frank. Yet, Frank probably could and would fight if he needed to.

Frank looked at Nathan, "What do want to do in San Francisco?"

"I, too, want to find work. I'm not sure what kind of work: anything other than logging. It's a busy city so maybe I'll become some type of business man. Who knows?"

Nathan gathered up his food scraps. He drank more of his apple juice and put his food items back in the bag. While standing up he told Frank, "Your turn to drive."

This time Frank turned the crank and started up the auto. He climbed up onto the seat. Before he moved the auto, he took time to look at the three pedals, reviewing in his mind which one did what. He slowly went over the dusty path until he got to the cement highway 99. Even then, he accelerated slowly. He was determined not to cause another flat tire incident.

Nathan seemed more relaxed this time too. He took time to enjoy the view. The road was open with only a few autos going one direction or another at the same time. It appeared there was nothing to worry about except trying to get to Sacramento before dark.

Frank drove for over an hour when all of a sudden the auto sputtered and then just stopped, right in the middle of the road. "What's wrong now?" Frank was frustrated that something went wrong while he was driving.

There was an auto coming up behind them. The driver just veered around them and kept putt-putting down the road. Frank and Nathan had to get out and push the Model T to the side of the road. "I think we forgot to buy more gas." Surprisingly, Nathan was not mad at Frank, just matter-of-fact about what "they" forgot to do.

Frank admitted, "It probably happened because I was so concerned about buying food this morning. I only mentioned the groceries and not the gasoline."

"No, it's my fault, it's my auto. Dad told me, "Son, be in charge of your own auto." Nathan sat on the grass and sighed.

Frank stood, ready to take some action, "I absolutely hate hitchhiking, but it is our only option. I haven't seen a gas station since we left Redding so I guess it will have to be hiking down the road and backtracking with the fuel."

Nathan stood, "No, I should do the hitchhiking: like I said it's my auto."

"That's exactly why you stay with the auto. I'll hitchhike. Don't worry, I will come back. Discouragingly he added, "No trains around to catch. I'll be back." Frank reached inside the front seat and got his cap. He reached behind the backseat and pulled out the gas can and started his walk down the road.

Nathan yelled after him. "We could just wait till someone goes by and flag them down."

"No, I'll either find a station, or a farmhouse where there might be gas, or catch a ride, if the driver knows where a station is."

Frank wasn't sure what the temperature was, but it was hot. His cap protected his face from the bright sun, but he could feel the sun rays heating his arms and back.

He walked several miles seeing nothing in sight. They had passed one town: Chico. Frank mumbled to himself, "Why didn't we stop in Chico?"

Frank heard an auto coming. He stuck out his thumb. The auto passed him leaving a cloud of dust that Frank had to brush away from his eyes and forehead. He started to cough but kept on walking. He looked away from the highway to see if there were any nearby farm houses.

Often people kept extra gasoline at their homes. Frank could buy some if they had any. He walked for over an hour. Finally he saw a sign.

There was a nearby town: Marysville. The name sounded promising. There was a sign that looked inviting too, "Gateway to the Gold Fields." Surely, they would have a gas station. Even if there was only one: that was all he needed.

By the time he saw the main street of Marysville, he was hot and tired. He figured he had walked at least ten miles. Marysville was a small town that looked inviting. At the end of the road was a gas station. He bypassed several stores, even a theater and went straight to the Shell Service Station. He walked into their small shop. "I need to buy some gas."

"Looks like you need more than gas." The man behind the counter grabbed a glass pitcher that he had behind the counter. He went outside and pumped a pitcher full of water. "Have a drink, sir, and then we can talk about gasoline."

Frank held the pitcher up to his mouth and drank the whole amount. "Want another pitcherful to pour over you?"

"Actually, that would be great."

The service manger went back outside filled the pitcher up with water again and brought it to Frank. Frank stepped outside. He stood on the dirty ground near the side of the front door of the service station. He was hot and sweaty. He poured the water over himself. This water bath helped him to feel alert. He knew his clothes would dry quickly. There was a slight breeze, but still the temperature was high.

"Now," said the service attendant, "Let's fill this can up with gas." Frank handed him the container that he had carried for miles. He sat on the step while the man filled it up. "That will be 25 cents." Frank reached in his pocket and gave the man two-bits.

"I'm curious. How far do you think you walked?'

"I think about ten miles."

"Where's your auto?"

Frank pointed, "About ten miles that direction."

"What's your final destination?"

"Well, we, my friend and I, we're heading to Sacramento."

"Well, that's about forty miles the opposite direction. I have to stay and watch the station, but I've got a son that could drive you back to where you left the auto."

"Really? How much will that cost?"

"Let's just say you buy him a gallon of gas."

"Sounds good to me," Frank handed him another quarter.

The man went and got his son. It took several minutes. Frank just sat on the step and waited. Finally, he heard the auto chugging toward the station. It was an older model than Nathan's, but it looked okay. The man filled it with gasoline. He introduced his son Tom to Frank. Frank climbed into the front seat with his gas can.

Off they went. Right away, Frank realized that this young boy drove too fast and wasn't too concern about driving safely. "How long have you been driving?"

"Oh, about two months. This isn't my auto. It's Dad's. How long have you been driving?"

Frank had to admit the truth. "Actually, I've only driven twice, but I think I've got the hang of it. Do you mind if I try and drive this auto?"

"I don't mind. I'm not sure if my dad would mind, but what the heck." Tom pulled off to the side of the road. He left the motor running as they exchanged seats. Frank felt relieved, though he had to ask the kid a few questions about the controls. It did feel different than Nathan's auto, yet Frank figured he could drive it straight down the road and not run into any other horse, cow, or auto that might be in their path. Tom seemed relaxed too. He leaned back and seemed to enjoy the ride. For the next ten miles he talked about his girlfriend Marybelle and his future plans of getting out of Marysville and finding work elsewhere. While he talked he waved his hands around and looked directly at Frank. It reminded Frank as to why he quickly asked to drive, rather than letting Tom drive down the road over the speed limit.

Frank tried to give him a few teachable moments. He demonstrated how to hold the steering wheel with a steady hand and to keep focused on the road. He told him that even though there was opportunity to weave from lane to lane, he needed to stay in one lane because if another auto came, either around him or from the other direction, he could be in the way. He felt Tom was listening. He hoped so because Tom would have to drive himself back to the station.

When they finally arrived, back to where Nathan was waiting, Frank paid Tom a dollar. "I really appreciate this ride back. Remember, Tom, stay in your lane, and watch the road."

"Jeepers, I will! I can't believe you paid me a dollar. I really appreciate this. I didn't even have to do all the driving. Thanks and take care."

Frank waved a good-bye. He, too, was thankful he didn't have to experience a scary ride. It seemed that hitchhiking wasn't the safest or best way to travel. He'd go by train again if he had a choice.

Nathan was happy to see him. He took the can and filled up the tank. Once again they headed down the road. Nathan was more than ready to drive. They were not going to make it to Sacramento before dark. It was either find a campsite to stop at or sleep on the ground somewhere.

Frank looked at the map. He discovered there was another town before Sacramento: Roseville. Rose matched his last name. This fact alone caught his interest. Darkness was beginning to set. It seemed logical to stop at a town for the night. Nathan agreed.

There was a sign right along Highway 99: "Roseville." The town looked interesting with several large buildings: a library, post office, hotels and the Southern Pacific Railroad Station. Frank heard the inviting sounds of the trains. It was like they were calling to him, "Come ride the rails…come." He knew he would be jumping on the trains again, but not tonight.

They stopped at one of the hotels and asked about getting a room. They were told the cost would be fifty cents. That was fine. They were tired and needed a place to stay.

The next morning, they walked through the town and saw the flowing creeks, one small creek named Linda, the gardens of roses, and the small town itself. Frank was impressed. Roseville seemed like a peaceful community. They found a café and ate a full breakfast. They were anxious to head down the road to Sacramento. The waiter at the café told them they could be in Sacramento within the hour. This time they remembered to gas up before they got back on the highway.

Nathan encouraged Frank to drive. "Why don't you drive into Sacramento?"

"Are you sure?"

"Yeah, I'm sure. You're a good driver. And this might be..." Nathan was going to say "your last chance to drive." He realized that once they arrived in Sacramento, they would probably get on a ferry and head to San Francisco. That might be when they would go their separate ways.

Frank took the wheel. The hour went quickly and then they saw the sign "Sacramento." They didn't have to look for the capitol building; the highway went by this main building as it weaved through town.

Nathan had a strong urge to see the sights. "Let's stop and see the capitol."

Frank agreed and parked the auto along the marked parking spaces on the road. Many steps led to the capitol building. They walked up this long stairway. The huge doors were open. They walked inside and noticed many visitors touring the enormous lobby. A group of five adults were listening to a young gal as she explained the details of the lobby's high decorative ceiling. She turned her attention to Frank and Nathan. "Welcome gentlemen, come join our group. We are just beginning our tour of this remarkable structure."

They saw no other choice. They stood by the other adults and listened to the presentation. "As I was saying, my name is Marie.   Welcome to Sacramento's Capitol." She continued, "This building was built to look like the Capitol in Washington D.C. It was completed in the year 1896. Like the building in D.C. the front of this building also has white tall pillars. This huge lobby is similar in style too. Notice the dome ceiling, the gold wallpaper, and the high archways down the hallways." She started to lead the group down the hall.

Marie appeared to be about the same age as Frank and Nathan. She had long, dark hair with slight curls bouncing on her back as she walked. Her long flowing skirt swayed as she moved. She often laughed a soft laugh and the tour group mimicked her laughter, as if her smile and laughter was contagious.

She led the group up a long flight of stairs. "This room here was the office of the governor back in 1906."

Nathan spoke up, "Who was the governor in 1906?"

She looked directly at Nathan. "I'm glad you asked. His name was George Pardee. He is often called, 'the earthquake governor' not because he caused earthquakes…" She smiled and chuckled. "Rather because in the year 1906 there was the devastating earthquake and fire that destroyed many of the buildings in San Francisco. After that earthquake, he ordered a state investigation and major study of earthquakes. Matter-of-fact, scientists are still working diligently to follow that order – trying to determine all the scientific facts about earthquakes."

Frank didn't want to think about San Francisco being a dangerous place to live because of earthquakes. The town was his next planned destination.

Marie led the group down more hallways, in and out of office rooms, and into a large room called the library room. Nathan asked more questions, "What is the dome size, the cost of the building materials, and the name of the wall paper designs?" Frank wondered if Nathan was asking questions because he really was curious about these details or did he just want to get Marie's attention?

After they toured the entire inside of the capitol building, she directed them to an open doorway which led to the garden area. "There are forty acres here. As you can see, there are many plants and trees, but still plenty of space for future gardens. These groves of trees are planted in memory of those who died during the Civil War."

She pointed to other plants. "Most of the plants here are native to California. Also, please feel free to browse around The Rose Garden."

The small group scattered and wandered around the plants. Frank headed down a pathway to see more plants. Marie and Nathan lingered behind the others. He stepped closer in her direction, "Excuse me. I'd like to introduce myself. My name is Nathan and I think you did a splendid job of giving this tour."

"Why, thank you, Nathan. I'm glad you were able to participate." Marie smiled.

There were several moments of silence. Nathan turned to look at the flowers. Marie started to leave and then turned back. "Do you live here in Sacramento or are you just passing through?"

Nathan moved closer to her, "Oh, I'm just passing through: on my way to San Francisco."

"Oh, I see. Well, I wish you a safe trip." She walked away.

Nathan walked toward Frank. Frank hadn't heard the conversation, but he saw them from a distance. He knew that Nathan had spoken to her. Frank wasn't sure; however, he thought that Nathan looked disappointed. "I think it's time to leave. Mighty interesting place, but we've seen all that we can see today."

"Sure," answered Nathan. They headed to the auto.

They got to the parked car when Nathan blurted out his idea, "I want to see if Marie will go out with me."

Frank was surprised, "What?"

"She's beautiful, don't you agree?"

"Yeah, she's a pretty gal, but you are heading to San Francisco and we could maybe catch a ferry today. There is no time to hang around and get to know Marie."

"Give me a chance. I've got an idea. If it doesn't work, I will be with you and try to catch a ferry."

"Okay." Frank took cigarette papers out of his pocket and rolled them around a pouch of tobacco. He lit the cigarette, and stood leaning against the auto, while Nathan ran back up the capitol stairs. Frank waited. He finished his cigarette. While walking up and down the sidewalk, he rolled another cigarette and then stood and smoked it till only a stub was left. He threw it on the ground and stepped on it with his foot. He leaned against Nathan's Ford. Then he sat in the car for awhile. Finally, he saw Nathan. Nathan ran down the long flight of steps.

He was panting, and nearly out of breath, when he finally told Frank, "She said 'yes' to dinner!"

Frank got out of the auto. "Really, so we're staying in town for dinner?"

"That's right." Nathan went to the front of the auto and cranked up the car. He went to the driver's side and climbed into the car waiting, for Frank, as if he had been the one waiting all this time. Frank got into the auto. He seemed puzzled about the whole plan. "We need to talk. So you are smitten by this Marie, but really you don't know anything about her."

The motor hummed and the car shook, ready to go, but Nathan did not step on the pedals. Instead he looked at Frank. "Yes, I do. I know she is beautiful, smart and has a job, so she must be reliable. Also, she has a nice smile and she said yes to my invitation to dinner. Oh, by the way, I said you would be there too. You know it is best if there is another person there so she is not worried about having dinner alone with a stranger."

"Now she should be concerned about having dinner alone with two strangers!"

Nathan put his hand on the throttle, "Let's drive around town and locate a nice place where we can eat. Matter-of-fact, I'm hungry. If the food is good, then that is where we will have dinner too."

Frank could sense their money departing right before his eyes. Less money and he still had to get to San Francisco. He smiled though, thinking about how excited Nathan appeared. Hopefully, the evening would go well.

They drove through town looking for the cafe that Marie suggested; a place not too expensive that served meat dishes, fish, and chicken. She said it was her family's favorite place. The place was quiet with comfortable booths. Nathan wanted a decent place, but not too expensive.

The small café on the main street did meet their qualifications. The food was tasty. The place was clean, and rather quiet. They decided this was where they would return for their dinner meal.

Their afternoon plan was to eat and then check out the ferry docks. How much were the ferry rides to San Francisco? Could they take the auto too, or did the ferry only take walk-on passengers? What were the time schedules?

The cook overheard their discussion and told them, "Go straight to the waterfront. There is a train terminal there. That's where you can get ferry tickets and all the information that you need." That was about all he knew on that subject. He admitted he had lived in Sacramento for the last twelve years but he had yet to take a ferry ride. He said he could not think of any reasonable explanation of why he should see San Francisco.

When they arrived at the river dock, Frank was surprised to see the sign "Ferry Tickets" right on the train depot sign. He was reluctant to go into the train station. He remembered when he jumped off the train in Weed because unknown men were wandering the tracks looking for something or someone. He didn't want to be known by the yard bulls even if it was for a legitimate reason. Without going into details he suggested that only Nathan go in and ask about ferry tickets.

Nathan was okay about doing this task. He ran into the station. Mostly he was having a high level energy day, eagerly anticipating his dinner engagement with Marie.

He came back to the car where Frank was waiting. "You want the good news first or the bad news first?"

"Just give me whatever you got."

"Well, if I take my auto to San Francisco, I have to get on a ferry in Oakland. There are no ferries in Sacramento that take automobiles. I, or we, would have to drive to Oakland and get on the ferry called the Melrose. It would cost $3.50. That is the only ferry that takes cars. Also, tickets for the ferries here are sold out for any ferries leaving tomorrow."

"So, what's the good news?"

"See that beauty of a ship over there – 'The Delta King.' It's leaving tomorrow. To have a cabin room it cost $3.50, but if you are willing to ride on the lower deck with the cargo, you can get a ticket even the last minute, for one buck."

"How long of a ride is it?"

"It's a ..." Nathan hesitated. "It's a ten hour ride."

"Ten hours? Why ten hours. It can't be far. On the map it looks so close, just across the water."

Nathan was told it might even be longer because the ship would be making stops and unloading cargo on the way, but he didn't want to upset Frank so he didn't answer.

Frank wasn't happy. Even the good news didn't seem good. They were silent in their own thoughts. It seemed that a future (like tomorrow) plan depended on how the dinner progressed or didn't progress. If Nathan still wanted to go to San Francisco, they would have to drive to Oakland. If he changed his mind (Frank was uncertain about Nathan's thoughts) and wanted to stay in Sacramento, Frank would be leaving town on his own. There was no train, no hitch-hiking travel across the Bay. His only option would be riding in a boat. He felt he would be safer riding on top of a railroad car than in the lower deck of a steam engine paddleboat. He sighed. He decided to worry about tomorrow, tomorrow.

Finding a hotel was easy. The downtown area had plenty of choices. They found one that looked clean and comfortable. Frank flopped on the bed. Nathan spent time washing up. Two hours went by, Nathan was still fussing around trying to look presentable when Frank heard him and woke up. Though it was early for dinnertime, Nathan was anxious, "Come on, man, it is time we got ready to go."

It took Frank a few moments to remember where they were going. Looking at Nathan he remembered. Nathan was a nice looking guy when he cleaned up; he asked Frank, "Do I look okay?"

Frank took a few moments before he answered. He didn't want Nathan to get too proud, but then he answered, "Actually, you look great!"

When they arrived at the café, Marie was already there, seated at a back corner table. She stood and greeted them with a smile, as if she was the gentleman instead of the lady waiting. Nathan was a little embarrassed, but he took her hand and thanked her for already getting a table for them. He introduced Frank as his best friend and traveling partner. She offered her hand to Frank too, smiled and said she was delighted to meet him.

Menus were on the table. Frank and Nathan figured they would have the same meals they had for lunch. Marie was completely undecided. She pondered over two listed meals. "I honestly want your opinion, Nathan. What should I chose? I can't decide between the steak dinner or the chicken."

Nathan knew what he would select. He also knew the prices, but tonight that didn't matter. He asked her several questions, trying to get her honest feelings. "How often do you have steak? Do you fix chicken for yourself? Did you eat chicken often when you were a child? If you had to eat dinner all alone, would you fix steak or chicken?"

Marie seemed to be enjoying this quiz and appreciated how interested Nathan seemed to be about her answers. She laughed about her cooking experiences: how easily she could burn a steak and catching and killing a chicken was too much bother. Then she laughed some more.

Nathan and Frank were laughing too. Visualizing her, in her dainty manner, chasing and killing a chicken seemed preposterous!

"I'll have chicken!" She exclaimed. "Really, I've never killed a chicken, but I watched my dad chase and kill one once." She shook her head, as if to shake the thought away. "Yes, it will be chicken. I do like chicken. What about you guys? What are you having?"

Nathan said, "We will all have good tasty fried chicken!"

Frank was surprised. He wanted a steak dinner, but to satisfy the consent, he put his menu down and stated, "Chicken it will be!"

Marie looked content. She laughed and smiled at the slightest bit of humor. When she talked she looked at Nathan and Frank, as if she liked them both. There were moments when all 3 of them talked at once either to agree on a subject or to share their life time experiences. By the time the meal was over, Nathan had talked about the lumber mill, and Frank had talked about his farming experiences, Marie talked about her father who owned a local store, her dear mother doing all the cooking, cleaning, and sewing all the family clothes. She added that she was an only child.

After dinner, Nathan suggested they walk along the water dock and watch the sun set. While on the waterfront, she held both their arms as she walked along. Frank felt like he was balancing a princess as she took her evening stroll. Frank still wasn't sure how Nathan felt about Marie, nor how Marie felt about Nathan, but it did seem obvious the evening was going well.

When the daylight turned to darkness, Nathan offered to drive Marie home. First she told Nathan directions so they could drive by the store her father owned. "He needs workers. If you come by tomorrow..." she looked at Nathan, "I could introduce you." She wrote out the directions to the place so he could find it from the hotel.

She continued on, "If you decide to stay in town, you could get a job at the store... if you really want a position." She looked directly at Nathan as she repeated this idea.

Nathan seemed elated about this possibility. When they arrived at her place, he got out of the car and walked her to the door. As he came back to the car, Frank could hear him humming a tune.

Frank didn't have to ask. Nathan blurted out his thoughts, "I'm going to hang around for a bit and see if I can get a job. I've got some money in a bank account in Weed. I'm going to telegraph Dad tomorrow and see if he will forward some to me. Marie said she knows where I could get a room to rent for a low reasonable price."

Frank nodded. He wasn't too surprised. "Guess that means I head to San Francisco alone tomorrow."

"Unless you want to hang around… I'm sure you could find work too."

"No, Nathan, I've got this goal in mind, it includes San Francisco."

Nathan drove back to the hotel in silence.

Nathan was up and gone before Frank was awake. Frank saw his note on the dresser. *I've gone to see about a job – at a store, no less. My best wishes to you, Nathan.*

Frank washed up and gathered up what little he had. The waterfront was near by; he would walk to the docks. He added a message on the same note paper: *My best wishes to you too. Frank*

As Frank walked he could remember Marie's smile. He decided what he longed for. He wanted a talkative gal that would laugh easily. The fellowship they experienced last night made for a fun evening. Frank realized he enjoyed hearing Marie jabber almost non-stop, and her soft contagious laughter.

He wished there was a train heading to San Francisco. The feel of cold air on his face, maybe even some dirt from the soot would seem okay. Definitely, he needed to be on the move and to leave Sacramento.

Chapter Twenty-Seven

Sacramento to San Francisco

Frank was able to purchase a ticket on the Delta King. This ticket meant he'd be riding on the lower deck where the cargo was stored. The walk onto the main upper deck of the ship looked inviting, but walking on the lower deck did not appear inviting. A row of windows shed some light, but they were not clean, nor clear. The view was limited. Wooden benches lined the inner wall where several men sat. They all had blankets. Frank found a space near the end of the row. It was drafty, not warm or comfortable. He debated about sitting on his jacket to make the hard wooden seat feel more comfortable, or leaving his jacket on to keep warm.

A deckhand came by and asked to see his ticket. Frank showed him his ticket. The man asked if he had a blanket. Frank answered, "No."

"We have extra blankets." Reaching into a bag that he carried, he handed Frank a comforter. "This warm material will make the ride much more cozy and warm. Just leave the blanket on the bench when you depart." Frank was thankful. He folded part of the soft cover on the seat and the rest of the folds he placed over his lap.

How he was going to make it through the next 10 hours was his main concern. He studied his surroundings. There were narrow walking paths along the deck. The pine smell of freshly cut wood penetrated the air. Heavy logs were stacked on one side. Piled high were crates and barrels lined up row by row. It seemed like a mystery as to what all these containers held. To make the trip bearable, he decided to stretch and walk around. He wondered how far he could roam on the ship with his low fare ticket.

The rhythmic chugging sound of the steam engine started up and the whistle blew a loud blare. He heard the paddlewheel turn and the water splash. Other men walked toward the end of the deck to see the big paddlewheel churn. Frank wrapped the blanket over his shoulders and walked to see the sight too. At the end of the deck he had a good view. The city of Sacramento was in sight. It appeared to be moving away; in reality he was moving away. The boat picked up speed. Frank had heard that even at top speed this boat would only go about 10 knots per hour. No wonder it would take so long to float down the Sacramento River.

This was his first boat ride. He felt the extreme rocking motion as he tried to walk straight. The movement did not really bother him; he thought it was fun to stagger from side to side, as he walked. He heard the laughter and commotion of the crowd of people on the upper floor. Many were on the outside decks. They were seeing the same sights that Frank saw, yet he wondered what else was visible on the above decks and what amenities those people were offered. He noticed a side door where crew members went up a stairway. The door appeared to be unlocked.

Frank went back to his bench seat. He carefully folded his blanket to reserve his place. Then he watched closely the door to the upper decks. When the ship had been sailing for over an hour and the door had been unused for a long time, Frank decided to do some exploring. He walked toward the door and looked around. He didn't see any crew workers. He opened the door. It was unlocked just as he thought. He walked through the door and climbed up the narrow steel steps. The surrounding area was semi-dark, but there was a rail; thus, the stairway seemed safe. He saw a doorway ahead. More stairs led upward, but he decided to walk through the first door. He didn't want to accidently open a door that took him to the Pilot House where he might meet the captain.

He realized that he was now on the first upper deck. People were mingling all about the floor. The room was noisy with talk and laughter. In this crowd he could mingle and barely be noticed. He was surprised though how dressed up everyone seemed to be. Men wore suits and women wore long gowns. Most all of the clothing was dark colors. Frank only fit in because he was wearing dark clothes too and people were so crowded together it was hard to distinguish one from another. He took off his cap and carried it in his hands. A few ladies noticed his presence and smiled. He returned their smiles. He had no intentions of getting to know anyone. He just wanted to see the action.

Many of the guests were holding glasses. He assumed they were drinking alcohol. It was still prohibition, yet on this ship, no one seemed to care. Drinking, talking and laughing seemed to be the main activity. A few stood by the rails, as they watched the water churn beneath the boat. Then Frank saw what interested him the most, a table where men were playing poker. He moved in closer. This was a serious game. Dollar bills were stacked in piles before each player. More money than Frank had. He watched for several minutes, remembering how this game went and which man was able to win. Winning meant getting all the stacks of bills. At another table there was a spinning roulette wheel. People watched as the wheel turned. These gamers loudly called out numbers; if their calls matched the spinning wheel, they would win the table money. Frank felt lucky and decided that maybe he could try. He watched several games before he made his final decision. He knew which numbers came up consistently and which numbers were seldom called. To play this game it cost twenty-five cents. Frank decided to test his luck. He placed his quarter on the table and called out his number. The wheel turned right over his number and he lost his quarter.

Then he noticed another dice game. The caller was chanting out a weird call, "Try your luck at Chuck-A-Luck!" On this table there was a small wire metal bird cage. Inside the cage were three dice. The caller kept shaking the cage and the dice rolled from side to side. Then after several shakes, the dice would fall on the table. If they called out the matching numbers, 1 through 6, someone could win the game. If there was only one matching number they still won something. The payout was good if 2 numbers matched their number and even better if the number they called out matched all three dice. Frank laid down a quarter to play the game. He called out the number 6, the number he always thought of as lucky. The man shook the small dice cage. People cheered him on to match the number. The cage opened and out fell 3 dice. Two of the dice had the 6 dots. "Six is the lucky number. You, sir…" He looked at Frank. "You won! Tonight this was a bonus roll, because sixes are bonus numbers tonight: so extra pay tonight!" He handed Frank a five dollar bill.

Frank was pleased, but decided he'd better leave the table and not try again. He really didn't want anyone's attention to focus on him. His hunger pains drove him to spend some of the five dollars on food. He went to the dining room and ordered soup and sandwich and a cup of coffee. No one questioned his presence. Enjoying the food and the water view, he slowly ate. After spending as much reasonable time as he could in the restaurant, he lingered out on the deck. He watched the waves and enjoyed the scenic views of the water and the mountains in the distance. From this deck ride, he decided maybe riding in a boat was more pleasant than riding on a train. By "on a train" he meant on top, or in an empty boxcar. He realized that paying passengers really did get comfortable seating and accommodations.

He hung around on this deck until the sun started to set. A live jazz band started playing soft music. Frank decided he needed to get back down on the cargo deck. He really didn't want to get into trouble. After watching the stairway door for several minutes, he decided it was not being used. He opened the door and started down the steps. When he was in the middle of the stairway, he heard a crew person come up the stairway. They met midway. The crewman just smiled at Frank and said, "Pardon me, sir." Frank repeated, "Pardon me!" They passed each other. Frank sighed in relief. He opened the door. He walked down the narrow wooden path to his bench seat. His blanket was still there, folded on the seat. He made himself comfortable and cozy, tucking the blanket around himself. Maybe, he could sleep awhile and let time slip by that way.

He awoke when a gentleman nudged him. "Excuse me, sir, wanted you to know we are close to port."

Frank had been lying on the bench. He sat upright and rubbed his eyes. "What time is it?"

"It's about six a.m."

"Wow, I guess I slept for several hours."

"Yeah, that can happen on a boat. The rocking motion makes for a pleasant sleep, even if you are sleeping on a board." He laughed.

Frank smiled, "Yeah, I guess you're right."

"You live in San Francisco?"

"No, sir, this will be my first time here."

"Wow, well you've got lots to see! You got a job lined up?"

Frank looked at this stranger. He looked like a hobo that would be riding a train, not a ferry boat. "I've got something in mind."

"Yeah, what kind of work are you looking for?"
Frank decided it was okay to tell this guy his idea. "I plan to work somewhere where they teach boxing – like at a gym or boxing arena."

"Well, I know a place. I have an uncle that owns a gym. He's Italian, on my wife's side. Really a nice guy. You got anything against Italians?"

Frank didn't think he had ever met any Italians. "No, sir, I've got nothing against Italians."

"Well, here's his name and his place." He handed Frank a business card. There was a picture of a building and a man's name and directions to the place. "If he can't get you a job, at least he'll let you know where you can get work."

"Thanks a lot. I'll look him up."

The boat slowed to a crawl. Frank could hear the boat plank being lowered. He folded his blanket and left it neatly on the bench. The passengers on the above decks would be let off first. Frank joined the men on the cargo deck as they lined up waiting for their turn to depart. Finally, they were allowed to leave. Frank was surprised how many men were on this lower deck. He didn't realize it before because he had only seen the ones that were near his space. As he got near the end of the ramp and was just ready to step onto the sidewalk of San Francisco, a government official, wearing a badge, stopped him. "Sir, you live here in San Francisco?"

"No, sir, I'm visiting."

"This is your first time here?"

"Yes, sir." Frank just wanted to keep walking, but the man was much larger than him and seemed to have some authority to question men as they left the boat. Frank, also, was worried if this guy knew about him winning money on the ship or not.

"You got employment or a place to stay?"

Frank hesitated, but then pulled out the card in his pocket. "Yes sir, I have a job waiting for me."

The man read the card, "Okay, sir, keep walking."

Frank sighed. He had no inkling that any authoritarian person would question why he was in San Francisco. It was like a yard bull on the railroad property. This was a "bull" on the seaport. He shrugged his shoulders and decided to forget it. He wanted to enjoy this busy city. He was finally on the streets of San Francisco!

Cable cars ran up and down the hillside right near the docks. Frank decided he had better quickly leave the seaport. Obviously, he didn't look like a paying passenger. He had noticed that all of those men were dressed in suits and ties. He figured they all had important business positions.

He hopped on a cable car and showed the driver the card with the gym's name on it. "Yeah, I know the place. Sit on one of these nearby seats, and I'll tell you when to get off. I'll point the direction for you to walk. It's not far."

"Thanks!" Frank was slightly concerned, as the cable car headed up the steep incline. The hill was the steepest hill he had seen and the cable car was full of people. He figured that these cars did these trips up and down every day, so no worries. The car moved slowly. Suddenly, there was a rough rattling sound indicating a problem. All of a sudden, the car just stopped in the middle of the street. "So sorry, folks, but it will take awhile to get the car connected to the cable again." Everyone stood up and made their way off the car with no loud complaints, as if this happened frequently. The conductor yelled, at Frank. "Sir, if you want to walk to the place you're looking for, walk uphill and count ten blocks, turn left, and walk five blocks. That will be Powell Street. You will see the place. It's not far and you'll see some beautiful scenery on the way."

Frank said "Thanks!" He could not believe that his first cable car ride was unsuccessful. Quickly people scattered, walking in different directions. The streets were busy with autos, and people walking across the roads.

Frank started the hike up the hillside. It was a cool morning; however, as he walked up the steep slopes he got warmer and took off his jacket. He was excited to be in this busy city. This excursion gave him a feel of the place. Certainly now, he knew how steep the hills were. He also enjoyed the view of the water in the distance. Breakfast: he realized he had yet to eat breakfast. Oh, well, see about a job first then eat. He kept walking.

He rested several times, sometimes sitting on a curb, sometimes on a patch of grass. The steep hills required physical energy that he lacked, especially because it had been hours since his last meal.

Finally, he saw the sign: Unione Sportiva Italiana Virtus. It was a large building. He looked at the name on his card: "Carlos." He needed to speak to Carlos.

Near the front door a young gal was sitting at a desk. Frank took off his cap and hand brushed his hair into place. He went up to the desk. "Excuse me, Miss, may I speak to Carlos?"

She smiled and said, "Yes, I will get him for you," She turned and started to walk down a long side hallway, and then she appeared to have changed her mind. She turned and looked at Frank, "You appear rather hot and thirsty. Can I get you something to drink?"

"Yes, madam much appreciated… the cable car stopped running down by the wharf and I walked here."

"Goodness, that's all up hill! Wait here I'll get you some water first, and then I will try and find Carlos. There is a chair over there, by the window, sit and make yourself comfortable."

Frank obeyed; he sat near the window and waited. The young gal returned with a glass of water and then searched for Carlos.

Carlos came into the room. He was tall with thick dark hair. He wore tennis shoes, black pants and a white short sleeve shirt.

Frank stood and said, "I've been given this card by a man that said he was your uncle. He said that you might need a worker." Frank realized he didn't know the uncle's name.

Carlos didn't seem to care. "Are you just passing through or do you plan on staying in San Francisco?"

"I want to find work sir, and I plan on staying in San Francisco for a while. I'm especially interested in the sport of boxing."

"Well, we do every sport here: football, soccer, baseball, swimming, but not boxing; however, I've a friend that has a boxing gym. He is a good trainer. He's also a good businessman. Gail, my secretary, said you've been walking the streets to get here. Let me get one of my men to drive you to my friend's place. I'm pretty sure he needs workers."

"Thank you, sir. I much appreciate the help you are giving me to get a job."

"No problem. Oh… do you have anything against Italians?"

Frank smiled thinking this question was getting ridiculous since he was in an Italian owned gym and receiving their kindness. "No, sir, I have nothing against Italians."

"Stay here and my buddy, Steve, will drive you to the boxing gym."

Frank finished his tall glass of water and waited for his ride. A horn honked outside the door. A Model T Ford was waiting. Frank stood up. He opened the door. "Are you Steve?"

"Yeah, are you Frank? You want a ride to the gym?"

"Yes, I am, and yes I do."

"Well, I'm the one to take you there."

Frank was glad to get a ride. Steve was ready to go. "Nice to meet you."

Steve opened the car throttle and sped up. He took the hills too fast. He weaved around other autos and people crossing the roads, as if they were not really there. Frank was amazed how busy the streets were. It was like Chicago only on steep hillsides.

"What do you think of San Francisco, so far?"

"Well, I haven't been here long enough to see much. Getting a job is my number one priority. So far, I'd say the city is breezy, foggy, busy and interesting. I'm anxious to see it all."

"There's plenty to see. Take in the night life too. You like any other sports besides boxing?"

"I like baseball too."

"Great, come back to our gym on Saturdays. We have baseball games on Saturdays. You might even get a job coaching kids."

"Thanks." Frank was interested. During his childhood and teen years, he enjoyed baseball. He often carried a mitt with him, in case there was a baseball game anywhere. Now his mitt was at his mom's place.

Steve stopped the auto. The entire ride only took close to ten minutes. "Here we are." Frank looked at the building. It was an older building, but still looked in good shape with red brick walls. It had one large front window. A sign hung by the front door: "Boxing Gym."

"Thank you for the ride."

"No problem. Good luck." Steve sped away.

Frank hoped there would be work opportunity here so he could find a place to stay and a place to buy a meal. As he walked through the doorway, he was greeted, "Can I help you, sir?"

"Yes. Carlos sent me over here to inquire about a job."

"Oh, yes, you must be Frank. I just got a call from Carlos. He said you appeared to be honest and a person needing work. You agree with that assessment?"

"Yes, sir, I do."

"At Carlos' place every worker is either Italian or their grandparents are. Are you Italian, or is your dad, or your grandparents?"

"I really don't know, sir… my dad left our family when I was four years old. I've never met my grandparents."

There were a few moments of silence. "Well, my name is Lewis. Here we are not so particular; we've taken young men and trained them to be boxers whether they are of Italian descent or not. If you're a good steady worker, you have employment here."

"Thank you, sir." They shook hands.

"Let me show you around."

Lewis led Frank through a long hallway. When he opened one of the side doors, Frank was surprised. The room was like a huge gymnasium. Several boxing rings were on the center of the floor. There was a row of punching bags hanging from the ceiling, mats were laid on the floor, and other exercise equipment was placed in various spaces. Heavy weights were scattered about the floor. Two men were sparring in one of the rings. Several others stood watching. They were all dressed in black pants and white tee shirts. Men were calling out encouraging cheers and direct commands. Other men stood off to the side walls of the gym, lifting weights. It was a busy room with lots of activity going on. Frank had a hard time trying to grasp all the details.

They stepped out into the hallway. Then Lewis gave a detailed description of Frank's job position. "That was just one of our gym rooms. We have four others in this building. There's plenty to do, to keep this place in order. The equipment has to be kept in working condition and placed correctly, the floors always have to be kept clean, and the locker rooms have to be supplied with clean towels. A lot of your work will be janitorial, but while you're here you'll learn all about boxing. After hours, or on your lunch break, you'll be free to use the gym equipment. It's a way to build up your muscles. Practice using the boxing bags, do whatever you feel you'd like to do. We figure if the workers know about every piece of equipment, they will do a better job of showing others how to use this gym, how to stay safe, and to keep everything in its proper place."

Frank was excited. This was the promise of a paid position to do exactly what he wanted to do: learn the sport of boxing.

Lewis asked Frank to step inside his office. It was a small room with a desk and a couple of chairs. "Have a seat."

He opened a desk drawer and took out a typed piece of paper. "Read this, and if you agree, sign your name on the bottom line."

Frank read the paper: a list of rules for the employees. Frank agreed with every statement. It appeared like a list of basic regulations: be an honest worker, respect the business and the customers, and follow the boss's rules and suggestions.

"Can I assume you will be my boss?"

"Yes," answered Lewis, "I will be your boss."

The last paragraph stated his pay would be five dollars a week, payable every two weeks.

He signed his name on the last line.

Lewis looked at Frank, "One other question. You got a place to stay?"

"Not yet, sir. I just got into town a few hours ago."

"I happen to know a lady, up the road, that has a big house. She rents some of her rooms to boarders. You might check with her and see if she has any space. It is in walking distance."

Lewis pulled out paper from his drawer and drew Frank a map. Then they walked to the front door. Lewis pointed the way toward the boarding house.

"Oh, yes, I almost forgot. Show up here tomorrow morning at ten o'clock. After work tomorrow I will give you a schedule for the week."

"Thank you, Mr. Lewis."

"You may just call me Lewis."

"Thank you I really appreciate all this..." Frank waved his hand at the boxing gym building and waved the paper to indicate what all he was thankful for.

Lewis shrugged his shoulders. "No worries, show up tomorrow at ten."

Chapter Twenty-Eight

San Francisco

Frank started his walk to the boarding house, but then he noticed a busy section with a sign Chinatown. Many shops were there, along with tall brick buildings. There were tent displays on the streets with people selling their wares. The area looked inviting. He noticed a sign Sam Lee Restaurant. The aroma of spicy, cooked, food reminded him that he needed to eat. He entered the restaurant. At a nearby table, he made himself comfortable and looked at the menu – all the items were listed in Chinese. A waiter came to the table. "What, sir, would you like to eat?"

"I don't know, but I do know I am very hungry."

"We will serve you well and give you food you like. Just wait."

Frank waited. A few minutes went by when the waiter brought a bowl of Wonton soup. "Eat, eat." The waiter placed chopsticks on the table, and also a napkin rolled up with a fork and spoon inside.

Frank unrolled the napkin and used the spoon to slurp his soup. Next he was served a large dish of chicken wings and what appeared to be pork rice noodles. Frank grabbed the fork and twisted the noodles. Then he jabbed at the chicken pieces. He ate like it might be his last meal. All the choices tasted so good, he wondered how he could have gone so many years without having Chinese food.

The waiter brought a teapot and a cup of tea. Frank would have preferred a cup of hot coffee, but instead he sipped the tea until the cup was empty. As he finished the meal, the waiter came back to his table. "Food good – you like?"

"Yes, sir, the food was excellent."

"Here fortune cookie – read your destiny."

Breaking the cookie in half, Frank read the paper inside: "Luck is near." Frank laughed. "Yes, I'd say San Francisco is a lucky place. Thank you."

The waiter handed Frank his tab. Frank laid out his dollar bill. He realized with his tip it made for an expensive meal, but it was good. He'd come again.

He picked up his piece of paper with the boarding house directions and left the restaurant.

Once again, he walked up the hilly streets. He found the house and knocked on the door. An elderly lady came to the door. She was slightly overweight, wearing a house dress, and a colorful apron.

"Excuse me, madam, I was given directions to your place from Lewis, he said you might have a place for another boarder."

"Oh yes, Lewis called me about you. You must be the man that has been walking up these hills all day. He said he gave you a job and expects you to be at work tomorrow morning. Yes, I have one available room." She smiled. "I'm Edith."

"Nice to meet you, Edith. I'm Frank."

She motioned for Frank to come inside. Once he was inside the large living room, Edith started to climb the circular stairway. Frank followed. "My rooms upstairs aren't big, but comfortable, with large windows. I believe in plenty of air. Open the windows, and bring in the air, I say."

At the top of the stairway, she paused for a breath. Then she opened one of the doors. "This room is an attic room, gets warm up here sometimes, but there's a view of the waterfront – off in the distance." Frank looked around the room. The space was small, but it had a closet, a table, chair and a large bed. "The bathroom is down the hallway. There are a couple other rooms up here. The bathroom you'll have to share with two other male roomers, but it has indoor plumbing, even hot water for the big tub!"

"Sounds and looks great! How much?"

"The rent is fifty-cents a night, but I do ask for five nights paid in advance. Can you do that?"

"Yes, Madam I can." Frank took out his pocket money and laid out the two dollars and fifty-cents.

"Okay, the room is yours!"

"Thanks!"

Edith started to walk down the stairway. Then she turned back and looked at Frank. "You got any luggage?"

"No, madam… just what's in my pockets."

"Well, I hope you plan on staying a while: lots to see and do in San Francisco. Make yourself at home."

"Thanks, I will."

Frank shut his door, sat on the edge of the bed, and took off his boots. He rested his head on his hands. He couldn't believe he was really in San Francisco. Not only did he complete the entire trip, but he had a job, and a place to stay. He looked out the window. The view was above other roof tops: water in the distance – palm trees! Grabbing the pillow, he rested his head and then stretched out on the top cover of the bed.

*****

Frank showed up at the boxing gym fifteen minutes early the next morning. Lewis greeted him and led him to the locker room. "Workers," he explained, "wear a type of uniform. It requires tennis shoes, black pants, and a short sleeve cotton shirt."

Smiling, he admitted, "Often while they work out and when they spar in the ring, they go shirtless. Over here is where you will have your own locker space to place your belongings."

A row of tennis shoes lined a bench. "Find your size. Heavy boots don't work well on these gym floors. When you're ready, come out to gym number one, and I'll get you started."

Wearing assigned attire wasn't mentioned at his job interview though he had notice employees wore matching outfits. There was a mirror on the wall. Frank looked at the stranger in the reflection. Never before had he worn tennis shoes, nor a short sleeve shirt, and tight black pants. The outfit made him appear muscular and younger. He walked out of the locker room ready to face the day.

As the time progressed, Frank was amazed at what all he could accomplish and what he learned in a few hours. His chores were mundane: fetch water buckets, pick up towels, put weights back in place, clean the locker room, sweep the gym floor, and wipe down the mats. Despite the busy chores, he also heard and witnessed techniques about boxing skills. He overheard suggestions and rules that in his mind he kept repeating.

"If you are right-handed, stand with your left foot forward, keep your left arm up and ready for defense. Remember, your right arm guards your stomach and your jaw..." Frank realized he could work and learn at the same time.

During his lunch break, he practiced with the punching bag. One of the other workers walked by and stopped to give advice. "Slow down man, take your time. Watch how the bag flows back and forth. Walk around it, over and over, see how it moves. Pay attention to your foot work before you start punching."

Another fellow worker came by. He, also, stopped and demonstrated walking around the bag, quickly moving his feet and using his arms to protect his face. He reiterated, "Body movements are important before you punch anyone or anything, including this bag." The co-worker tapped Frank's shoulder, encouraging him to keep practicing.

Frank nodded and said, "Thanks!" He paused. As if he was moving in slow motion, he started his techniques over again.

His work day stretched on for nine hours really ten hours, including his workout during his lunch break. At 8:00 p.m. he was back in the locker room changing his clothes.

On the way to the boarding house, he stopped at the nearby café and had dinner. He was tired. The sights of San Francisco would have to wait.

*****

Near the end of the second week, Frank was low on finances. Pay day was only days away, yet he had to eat. The few groceries he had purchased were gone. He decided to try the Chinese restaurant again. More than once, he had been there. He had met the owner, Chang. They had several long talks. One late Sunday afternoon Chang was outside playing the board game, Chinese Chess Xiangqi (say-on-chee). Chang invited Frank to join the table and watch the game. "I show you how to play. Then later you play too."

"Okay, sounds interesting." Frank was eager to learn something new. He sat on one of the crate boxes, as the other men did. Chang explained some aspects of the game and told Frank what the white and black ivory pieces represented. "First, notice the wooden board. This board has nine columns and ten rows. The middle row is the river. He held up some game pieces, these are soldiers. They can cross the river. This is the elephant xiang, which is what the game is called, and 'qi' means game. The elephant cannot cross the river."

As Chang talked he held up each piece: "soldiers, cannons, that jump and land on the opponent's pieces, two advisors that protect the king, and the king. The king is the most important piece of all – save your king!" Chang pointed to the other pieces: horse and chariot. "The object of the game: protect your king and capture your opponent's king!"

The men were completely silent as the game began. Frank watched closely. Laughter came as one player grabbed the opponent's piece. Some talk was mumbled as they discussed strategies of how to capture the king, or at other times, when they had to plan for several minutes on how to save the king. Mostly though, there were long moments of silence. Sometimes the players spoke in Chinese, and Frank had no idea what they were saying. After several evenings of watching the game activity, Frank felt he was ready to try. So far he had not been invited, but he hoped that he would be asked soon to join in playing the game.

It was near closing time, when Frank went into the restaurant. He sat at the table and looked at the menu. He was familiar with the meals now and he knew what he wanted. Chang came to his table. "You know what you want to order tonight?"

"I thought tonight I would order whatever you have left over – you know if you have any extra food that maybe you want to get rid of."

"Oh, you mean chop suey – chop suey is leftover food. Why you want leftovers – you on a starving diet?"

"I have a slight problem."

"Problem, what is your problem?"

"I'm broke and I don't get paid till Friday. So I thought maybe tonight I could have some food that you just want to get rid of."

"You have no problem. You know Chang. Chang owns this place. I get you nice meal – no leftovers. First, you drink tea!"

Chang left the table to bring back the table settings and a pot of tea.

Frank was thankful. He drank the tea and ate a good meal on Thursday evening, and on Friday he ate again, and paid up his tabs. It was that evening that Chang invited him to play Xiangqi with him. Chang captured Frank's king, but Frank was glad to have the experience of playing the game.

After several weeks of working at the gym, Frank heard about an upcoming party. It was near the date of the party when Lewis told him that all the workers were invited to this upcoming gala at Carlos' place. He heard there would be lots of Italian food, music, and pretty girls.

The evening of the event came. Frank dressed up as best as he could: clean clothes and polished boots. When he got to Carlos' place, the building was crowded with people. It was noisy with laughter and talking. In one corner of the large gym floor was a temporary set-up stage. Men were on the stage getting ready to play their instruments: accordions, guitars, drums and a piano. As he walked across the floor, he recognized only one person. Carlos' secretary, Gail, was standing by alone against the wall.

Frank walked near her. She recognized him, raised her glass, smiled, and greeted him with "Hey, hello! Frank right?"

"Yeah, I'm Frank, and you are Gail, right?"

Gail moved closer to where Frank was standing, "I see you're not drinking anything? Can I get you a drink?"

"No thanks, I can get it myself."

"Well, grab a drink; everything is free and available for the taking – plenty of food. It will be a fun evening. After you get your food, come back this way. I have a table saved over in the corner."

"Sounds great. I'll be back."

Frank slowly moved through the crowd of people and headed to the food table. Gail surprised him, coming up behind him, and started to fill her plate with food too. After they had their food trays full, Frank followed her back to her table.

More people arrived. Frank recognized some of his fellow workers. Couples were out dancing. A few single gals were out swaying to the music. Gail tapped her fork on the table to the rhythm of the music, "Do you dance?"

Frank looked around the room to see how crowded the dance floor was, "not really."

"That doesn't matter as you will soon see. There will be lots of group dancing tonight. Basically, there will be a big circle of people, holding hands and dancing round and round. Then couples will pair off and the men will twirl the gals and then rejoin the circle. You don't have to know what to do. If a gal grabs your hand, then just follow round and round. If you grab a gal's hand then twirl her round and round, and then join back in the circle. It will be fun!"

Frank raised his eyebrows, wondering if it was as easy as Gail made it sound.

Quicker than he had anticipated, he had his chance to find out. A large circle formed in the middle of the gym. He was still chewing his food when Gail grabbed his hand. "It's Tarantella music. Time to dance!"

She led him out to the big circle. Never had he danced so fast. There were moments of confusion, but as Gail said, more than once a gentle hand nudged him into the right direction. He swung strangers around and around, holding hands with gals he had yet to meet. Folks nodded sometimes to show him to go left or right. He had a grand time! When the music stopped, he and Gail chatted, ate more food and drank more drinks. The evening was too short and ended too soon, even though it was early morning before he got back to his room.

Chapter Twenty-Nine

San Francisco Frank's Eighteenth Birthday

September 27, 1929 Frank invited Gail to go out with him to celebrate his eighteenth birthday. Gail was excited and told Frank she would show him San Francisco. She drove up in her dad's 1925 Ford auto. She waited outside, blasting the horn. Frank grabbed his cap and ran down the stairs before his landlady complained about the noise. "You could have knocked on the door or rang the bell."

Gail was defensive, "I'd be embarrassed coming into the boarding house where only men live."

"And the landlady of the house. Don't forget Edith lives in the main part of the downstairs. You wouldn't have even seen the men. It was embarrassing hearing you blow the horn several times."

Gail laughed, "Oh, don't be silly, noises in San Francisco? No one pays any attention!"

She turned the auto away from the curb and drove down the steep hills too quickly for Frank's liking, but he trusted Gail. She was smart, reliable and not overly reckless.

"I'm taking you to the amusement park by the beach – it's called, Playland-at-the-Beach."

"Is it right on the beach?"

"Pretty much, it's across the street from the sand and the ocean. You'll smell the salt air and feel the sea breeze, but we will be walking on bricks, not the sand. You'll love it! And don't worry about expenses. My treat! It is your birthday – all my treat."

Frank protested, but compromised and said he would pay for dinner afterwards.

The evening was perfect for being outdoors. The weather was mild and it was still semi-day light. The park was decorated with lights and lit up rides. By the gate, they could hear a cackling laugh. "What's that?" Frank asked.

"Oh, that's Laffing Sal. It's a puppet – moving mechanically, waving, and laughing. She laughs all the time. Her laughter is a greeting that is always heard at this park." Frank saw the tall lady statue standing upright, with waving arms. They walked beyond the sound of Laffing Sal. The area was like a wild circus with young men yelling, "Tickets, Tickets, get your tickets here, Freaks of the World Side Show! See the Show. Step up here – get your tickets!"

Gail had to raise her voice so Frank could hear her directions. "We're going to ride the 'Aeorplane Swing!'"

"What's that?"

"You'll see, just follow me."

They weaved along the brick sidewalks until they came to a carnival swing ride. Wooden seats were swinging in the air in a circular motion. "This is what we are going to ride."

"Really?"

They walked close to the contraption. Gail paid the man two nickels. He handed her two tickets. She handed Frank one of the tickets. The swings stopped in front of where they stood. Each of them had their own seat with a lifting bar placed in front. They sat down and the loud motor started to roar. At first the swings moved slowly as they spun and swayed in midair. The ride stopped to pick up other riders. The entire set of swings went freely round and round.

Their feet were dangling. The experience was exciting, like flying in the air without being in a plane.

They laughed as they flew round and round. At times Gail screamed as the swing swayed too quickly for her comfort. Frank enjoyed the cool breeze and seeing the sights below. They swayed even higher than the large tents below. They didn't count the times the swings went around the carousel machine, but it lasted several minutes. When the ride slowed to a complete stop, they were laughing with joy from the pleasure of the ride.

Frank noticed the Shooting Gallery. He wanted to try his skill with a gun. "Step right up sir, and try your skills." Frank paid his nickel to try the game. "You get six shots, sir. If you hit that center circle you win one of those stuffed animals hanging on the wall."

Gail spoke up, "It's his lucky day. It's his birthday. You can do it, Frank. I know you can."

"Tell you what, Gail, pick out which stuffed animal you want and I'll get it for you."

"Okay. Good luck."

"Best, sir, for you, is to not depend on luck. Aim real slow, take your time and look at the center of the target. The gun will leap back at you when you shoot. Hold it firm. Aim straight at the center circle."

Frank had never held a gun before. It felt heavier than he expected. He was glad the ticket man gave him some hints. He took his time. His first shot was surprising. The gun was louder than what he expected and it did jump. His aim was off. The hole was on the paper, but below any circles. He took a deep breath.

"Okay, I know I can do better."

The next two shots were off too. Frank took another deep breath. He aimed. He stood still. He felt the weight of the gun and looked at the target. Others were standing by watching now. They, too, were silent as Frank aimed but didn't shoot. Frank froze for several more seconds. Then bang the gun went off. This time there was no jerk on Frank's arm; his arm was steady. The bullet went through the center circle right on the winning mark. Frank shot two more times and each time the hole was in the center! Gail clapped her hands and so did the ticket man and the small crowd that had been watching. "Which animal do you want?' the game caller asked.

"I'd like the kangaroo!"

Frank was surprised. There were small dogs, cats, turtles. He never thought about how cute a stuffed, smiling kangaroo would be. "The kangaroo it shall be."

Gail held her new stuffed animal in her arms. She told Frank there was another activity she knew about, one she wanted Frank to see. They left the park area and went down several dirt roads. Frank could hear autos running on dirt and sounding like they were banging against fenders. When they got close to the action, he witnessed autos crashing, but not into each other. Rather they were bumping into a huge rubber ball as if the cars were doing a sports event, moving the ball from one side of the dirt ground to another side. It was like a soccer game, only with autos moving the ball. Bystanders were watching and cheering the drivers, yelling as to which auto should win.

Gail and Frank sat on the dirt hill, above the action, watching the sight below. After the game was over and the huge ball was off to the side, one of the drivers ran up the hill to greet Gail. He called her "honey," kissed her check and thanked her for coming. Frank stood back feeling a bit awkward. He had no idea Gail had a boyfriend.

Gail turned to Frank. "Frank, I'd like you to meet Marlow. Marlow, this is Frank." Marlow seemed glad to meet Gail's friend.

He held out his hand. He and Frank shook hands. "It's Frank's birthday. I'm showing him some sights of San Francisco: sights that he might not see on his own."

"That's great, great idea. Show him around. Where are you from, Frank?"

"I grew up in Portland, Oregon."

"Oh yeah, Portland, where it rains all the time."

"Yeah, that's the place."

"Great, I've got to get back. We're gonna do another round. Stay if you like. If not I'll see you later, Gail. Nice meeting you Frank."

"Likewise," Frank mumbled.

Marlow ran down the dirt hill and got back in his car. "Isn't this rough on their cars?" Frank asked.

Gail smiled, "No, they get dirty, but the ball doesn't scratch the cars. The object is to hit the ball, not each other."
Frank wasn't too surprised to meet one of Gail's friends. He knew she was dating others and she would probably marry an Italian man. He was glad she was celebrating an enjoyable evening with him tonight.

They went back by the waterfront and watched the sunset. They talked about the differences between San Francisco and all the other places Frank had been. They went to dinner at Frank's favorite Chinese place. Frank paid for the meals.

It was after midnight, when Gail dropped him off at the boarding house. She kissed him on his cheek and wished him a happy birthday.

He felt like he had celebrated. Tomorrow morning he would call his mother and let her know he liked San Francisco.

Chapter Thirty

Changes in San Francisco

For seven months, April through October, Frank worked at the gym. On Saturdays, he went to Carlos' place and helped with the youth baseball teams. On Sundays, he toured San Francisco. He enjoyed going to the theaters, watching boxing matches, riding the streetcars, gazing at the boats, passing the street markets, listening to music, and playing pool at the bars. San Francisco was an adventurous place. Frank relished participating in the life of the city.

Trouble was coming though, and everything would quickly change. On October 29 Frank went to his job and everything was different. When he walked into the gym, he knew immediately something was wrong. The place was almost silent. There was no longer the humming sound of activity. Where was everyone? Then he noticed his fellow workers were seated on benches near the back of the gym. There were no other gym members doing their usual workouts. The employees were dressed in street clothes, not in their work attire. Lewis stood in front of them and talked, as if he was giving them important information. The workers listened quietly. Lewis saw Frank and motioned for him to come. "I'm just beginning to tell the men some recent changing events. Please, sit on the bench and join us."

Lewis continued speaking. "Today, as some of you may already know, the stock market crashed. This morning I was in a long line at the bank. As I stood there, the bank closed. The teller told us we would have to leave the premises. There was no promise of the bank reopening tomorrow or this week.

"I know that today is your pay day. I intend on paying each one of you what I owe; however, I will need some time to do so. I have

288

other funds and there are items I need to try to sell. The gym will be closing, but despite that, you will get paid. I'm asking each one of you to report back here, at the gym, in two weeks on Friday. On that day, I will pay you what I owe you. That is my promise and my word!"

The men were quiet for several minutes. Then they rapidly asked questions. Several of the guys were talking at once. Frank had no idea there was a stock market crash. He could not believe that banks were closed! His limited funds were stashed in a can under his bed. He needed his paycheck today.

Shrugging his shoulders, he sighed. He figured it was hopeless to question or argue the situation. The other men needed their paychecks too. Some of these men had families to support. Frank was on his own: he only needed to support himself. He left the gym and wandered aimlessly around town. He heard the newspaper sales boy yell out the headlines: "Black Tuesday – Read all about it!" Reading the details wasn't going to help his situation so he bypassed the newsstand and headed back to the boarding house.

Back in his room, he counted out his few dollars and his stack of coins. He would buy some food, and hope to make it until he could receive his paycheck in two weeks.

During the two weeks of not working, Frank was conservative with his money. He limited his activities to walks in the park, tossing and batting balls with the boys that hung out at Carlos' place. He also had talks and walks with Gail. They walked the sidewalks to see sights that he hadn't noticed before. Gail was worried too that Carlos' place would close as her job was already offering less hours. He tried to reassure her, that Carlos' place was well established and should survive, but as he said the words, he also worried. He saw the tension in town and nothing seemed as carefree as usual.

For days, he bought groceries, and only dined in his room. Even though he avoided spending money, at the middle of the second week he was broke and hungry. The last two days before the two weeks were finished, Frank was desperate. He went to his favorite Chinese restaurant and asked for a couple meals, without the means to pay for them. Chang served him food and treated him like a long time friend and his guest.

On the promised pay day, Frank headed to the gym. More people than usual were on the streets walking, as if they had no purpose or place to go. Frank entered the back door of the gym. The hallway was dark. He noticed most of the equipment was gone. Some rooms were empty. In one of the big gym rooms, true to his word, Lewis was passing out pay to his workers. He paid each man the cash he owed them. Each worker was profusely thankful. Unfortunately, Lewis had no hopeful words for future work or pay. The situation looked daunting.

Frank's plan was to pay Chang for the last few meals that he owed him. He folded the bills he owed Chang, and placed them in the back part of his wallet. He walked to the restaurant. The surroundings appeared different. The box seats and the wooden table, where they had played Chinese Chess, were gone. The restaurant doors were shut. There was a sign, loosely hanging on the door, CLOSED. Chang never closed his restaurant on a Friday. Frank walked around the place and could see no evidence of anyone being there. The place looked dark and empty, even though Frank had been there only a day before.

A depressing feeling overtook him. Leaving San Francisco was not what he wanted to do, but to survive he had no choice. He went back to his room. He took a bucket of soapy water and a rag, and he cleaned around the room, as best as he could. Edith and his fellow roomers were not at home. The house was quiet and empty. In an envelope Frank placed his rent money and laid it on the table with

Edith's name written on it. He also wrote a good-bye note: *I really enjoyed staying here. Frank.* On top of the envelope he laid the key.

Even though he had been in San Francisco for seven months, he had not accumulated any more than what he came with. His personal belongings still consisted of a razor, soap, and a few clean clothes. All these items were stuffed in his deep pockets. Feeling sad, he walked away from the boarding house.

Strolling through Chinatown one more time was his goal. As he walked past men that were selling fruits and vegetables, he noticed two playing the familiar Chinese Chess board game. He stopped to see the progression of the game. One player raised his head up, and below his big hat, Frank realized it was Chang! "Chang, I was so sorry to see your restaurant closed."

Chang looked up. "Frank, my favorite customer... Yes, I cannot pay my workers. It is sad. My grandfather, and my father owned Sam Lee Restaurant. The dining room was like a family place. I failed!"

"No, Chang, you had a successful business. Your food was delicious. Customers were happy. You did not fail! The world is failing us: keeping us from being able to work. You Chang... good businessman! Your place was an excellent business and had good food!"

Chang seemed pleased to hear these words. Frank opened his wallet and handed Chang the bills that he owed him. It wasn't much – not enough for Chang to reopen his place, only a small amount. Chang was a strong determined Chinese man. Yet, when he looked at the dollar bills, tears came to his eyes. He tried to hand the money back. "You keep this. I have a home, you need money to travel."

"No, it is rightfully yours. It is for you! Sometimes I need to borrow, but I always repay. And you... I hope you...win this game!"

Chang and Frank laughed. Frank tipped his cap. Chang bowed his head and placed the bills in his wallet.

Frank headed to the seaport. It was a long walk: mostly all downhill. He wanted to feel San Francisco, breathe the chilly air, and see the waterfront from a distance. He enjoyed hearing the sounds of the trolley cars, the noise of the traffic and the intermittent clopping of the horse carriages. He was leaving too soon and not entirely by choice: more by necessity. Businesses were rapidly closing. Frank figured he'd find work again in the fields, but not in the big city.

The seaport was buzzing with activity. Young men were unloading and loading crates. Large crane-like pulleys were piling crates up and onto the ships. Frank could hardly walk along the dock without bumping into a worker or stepping on loose boards or grain sacks. He saw a man of authority and he figured this man must be the supervisor. He asked, "Excuse me, sir, can you direct me to where I could get a ticket to board a steamboat going to Oakland?"

The man looked at Frank as if he was sizing him up and down. "Buddy, you don't need a ticket if you're willing to do some dock loading. See all these bags piled on the ground? Notice how they are being stacked on these flat crates. If you can do that until this ship is ready to leave, then you can get aboard with no ticket. When we get to Oakland, there will be more unloading to do. Are you willing to help us out for a free passage?"

"Yes, sir. I'm definitely willing."

"Okay, Mister, get started!"

Frank found a spot to fold up his jacket and hide it on the ground. He rolled up his shirt sleeves and started working. The job looked easy, but several times fellow workers paused their lifting to show him exactly how to stack the bags. He couldn't believe how many crates were being filled and lifted onto the boat. He had worked for two hours when the whistle blew.

The workers finished piling bags onto the last crate. They gathered their belongings and walked to the wooden plank to board the ship. Frank grabbed his jacket and followed them. He was hot and sweaty, but thankful he could ride free across the bay to Oakland. There were no paying passengers partying on this boat. There was only cargo and workers. Frank found a bench and sat down. Most of the workers were quiet, hot and tired. It was only a ½ hour break for them before they would be required to unload the crates. Then the ship would head overseas. Frank knew his voyage ended in Oakland, and then it would be a train trip across the plains.

The temperature was high when the boat docked in Oakland. Once again, Frank placed his jacket behind a corner board on the dock and he started working to unload the crates. He could have sneaked off and headed to the train tracks or just toured around Oakland, but he felt needed. Frank grabbed the bags one by one and hoisted them onto wagons. Again he worked two hours before the dock was clear. The other men boarded the ship again. Frank picked up his jacket and headed up the street, away from the seaport.

He entered a small café and ordered a sandwich, soup and coffee. The hunger pains came. He was past the point of being particular. He gulped down the coffee and gobbled the sandwich quickly. Feeling semi-relaxed, he slowly ate the beef-barley soup. A waiter stopped to refill his coffee cup. As he poured the coffee, Frank asked, "Where can I catch a train out of town?"

"Well, if you are looking for the train station, there is one at the foot of Washington Street. It's Western Pacific Railroad. Just look for the building with the clock tower."

"Thanks. I must admit I was impressed with how busy your city is. It's almost as busy here as it is in San Francisco."

"Yeah, we have lots of industry moving this way. You might not believe it, but we're building autos almost as fast as they are in

Detroit. Some folks call this town, 'Little Detroit.' Course, I don't know what's coming up. Everyone is scared… about the stock market and the banks closing and all that. Doesn't bother me too much, I never bought any stock. I don't even have a bank account. I keep my money hidden."

"Well," Frank answered. 'The changes did bother me. I was working in San Francisco. My plan was to stick around, but I lost my job. I figure now I better head out to farm country. Farmers always need workers."

"Good luck, I hope it works out for you. I hope this restaurant stays open. My hidden stash won't last long if I lose my job."

Frank paid his bill, slurped down his second cup of coffee. "Good luck to you too."

He walked a few blocks and saw where the trains were leaving the station. He was only interested in the freight trains, but he walked into the station and got a schedule. The sun was bright and the temperature was rising. He sat in the shade and studied the information. The time table listed the passenger trains, and it listed freight trains. There was information about the Feathered River Route. It sounded okay. Trains left often, headed to Nevada, and then to Utah. Maybe, by evening he could be in Denver, Colorado. He figured out the mileage. No way would he make it to Denver – that was 1,378 miles!

Changing his mind, he figured he could make it to Cedar City, Utah. On the map it looked like a straight shot cross country and only 450 miles. His estimate was about eight hours of travel. It would be night time, but that was okay. That was his plan. He would jump on a train and hopefully, end up in Cedar City.

Chapter Thirty-One

San Francisco to Utah

Frank was surprised when he hopped on what he thought was an empty car. He wasn't alone. Crouched near the back side of the boxcar were other hobos. Most of these hobos were dressed rather decent. They did not look like men that had ridden boxcars often; rather they appeared like family working men that were suddenly desperate for jobs. Frank figured that most of these guys probably had homes, and families. Maybe, these men even had good paying jobs with investments, but now suddenly, they lost their income. Like Frank, they decided to find work elsewhere, possibly on the farms, rather than the cities.

Despite the fact that these men were probably decent men just low on their current luck, Frank decided to find his own corner in the boxcar and ride alone. He decided it was for the best not to converse with anyone.

"Where are you headed?"

Frank answered, "My plan is to get to Cedar City, Utah."

"Well, this train won't go that far south. Stay on this train long enough and you'll end up in Salt Lake City, Utah."

"Really?"

"Yeah, that's where we're headed. A group of us we're going to get jobs building temples. We're Mormon – at least that's what we're gonna say when we get there. These Mormons need workers. They're building temples and interiors of temples. They need help."

"Really?" Frank didn't know anything about Mormons, but he decided not to ask. He wasn't interested in building temples; at least he didn't think that was his goal. His goal was getting to New York. Salt Lake City wasn't even on his list.

The boxcar was hot. He was leaving California, going through the desert land of Nevada. Frank took off his jacket and made himself comfortable. He pretended he was getting ready to sleep. He wasn't that tired, but he didn't like conversing with these guys. They already indicated some dishonesty by pretending to be what they were not. Frank had faked his abilities a few times to qualify for a job, but not like this group, pretending to believe religious beliefs. Stating that they didn't really accept these beliefs seemed troubling to Frank. He curled up on the hard floor, placed his jacket in a heap and rested his head on the folds of his jacket.

Hours later, he woke up sweating and feeling hot. The train moved fast. The guys were still in the boxcars. Some had taken off their shirts. They were not in one close group, as they were before. It was too hot to sit near anyone. Frank asked a couple guys, "You know how far we are to Salt Lake City?"

Two guys agreed, "Yeah, we have about four hundred miles to go. Probably get there in another seven or eight hours. You have water?"

"No," Frank mumbled. He wondered himself how he could be traveling in this extreme heat and this long distance without carrying water. Also, without realizing how far he was headed.

"We have plenty of water. Several of us came with canteens of water and tin cups. Drink as much as you want. We have more."

The water tasted cold and refreshing. Frank decided not to be as judgmental in his thinking. These guys were generous and now extremely helpful. He unbuttoned his shirt and felt a slight cooling breeze. He would have to stretch, move around, and wait.

The next time Frank woke up, he saw total blackness, it was dark, but not because it was night. They were going through a long narrow tunnel. When they got to the other side, the sun shone brightly. Frank could see the surrounding snowy mountains, bright blue sky, and lakes of water. The landscape was beautiful. The train slowed down. The other men gathered their things and got ready to jump off. "We're getting near. Time to move."

Frank wasn't part of their group, but he picked up his jacket and decided to jump off when they did unless, he saw trouble. Then he would ride further. The land showed no signs of civilization, except for the city ahead in the distance. They could jump and hopefully, there would be no other people around to even notice. The group formed a couple lines. As the train slowed, they jumped one at a time. Frank took his turn and jumped too. The leap went smoothly, like perfect rhythm. The group started their walk and Frank started his. He walked slightly in a different direction, toward town, but more to the east of where they were headed. He was going to explore Salt Lake City on his own. Hopefully, he would catch another train out of town soon.

Frank walked to a café. The city looked clean with paved sidewalks and interesting looking shops. The streets were numbered avenues, or letter names. In the section where the temples were, the simple street name was Temple Street.

Off in the distance Frank could see not one, but three temple buildings. One was like a huge church with six spire steeples. Another structure was a round dome type of building and the third edifice was also a temple with steeples.

He felt sooty, sweaty and dirty. He was sorry he couldn't clean up before eating, but his body was feeling weak and starving. There was to be no delay in getting food in his system.

Frank sat on a bar stool and ordered a meal. The waiter didn't seem to notice Frank's awful appearance. He took his order and placed the paper on the cook's bar with the other orders. Frank realized that this place had washrooms available. He went to the men's room and cleaned up as much as he could. Before his food came, Frank was wondering if the men on the train could easily find work. Frank asked the waiter a few questions.

"Any available work in this town?"

"Yes, there is always work. There's a lot of construction going on around here. You see the tallest temple out there?" The waiter pointed out the window.

"Yeah, can't help but see it."

"Right, well that's been a work in progress for over forty years since the idea developed in 1847. They finished the outside structure in the year 1893. They're still working on the inside. The Mormons are always looking for skilled craftsmen to do all the fancy work they want to do."

"Any other type of work available?"

"Yeah, our population is growing. There are lots of homes being built. The town is always a busy place."

Frank had one other question. "Mind if I ask you... are you Mormon?"

"You can ask and I'll tell you. No, I'm not. Not all of us town folks are, but I'd say the majority of the people in this town are. Do you plan on staying here?"

"No, it looks like a decent city and the surrounding mountains are beautiful, but I'm headin' to New York."

"Well, you better keep moving then because the weather will change. When that happens you won't be going anywhere. Heading to New York means going over the Rockies. It's a dangerous trip. My advice is to make sure you ride inside a boxcar, don't ride on top. There's a six mile tunnel that avoids having to go over all of the Rollins Pass in Colorado. The Moffat Tunnel is long and narrow, over six miles long. You wouldn't last if you were riding on top of a boxcar through that passage."

As the waiter left to get Frank's food order, Frank answered, "Thanks for the information!"

His food arrived and Frank started to eat his meal vigorously, like it was his first taste of food or his last. He was hungry!

Chapter Thirty-Two

Salt Lake City, Utah to Denver, Colorado

Frank wandered around the town area of Salt Lake City. The streets were extra busy with autos, street cars, horses and carriages. He noticed one store that looked interesting. Inside this two story brick building was a variety store. Clothes were hanging on racks, knickknacks were scattered on table tops, and there was a section of scattered tools.

What he needed was a few grocery items. He walked further, in this brick building, until he came to a small grocery section. There he purchased a bag full of snacks and bottled drinks. Every item he purchased he was able to stuff in his deep overall pockets. The sun was below the horizon by the time he discovered several hotels. He checked into one and that is where he bathed and slept. Sleeping on a bed was a blessing. Frank awoke the next morning early, greeting the morning sun light.

The hotel offered breakfast. It was a feast of pancakes, eggs, hash browns, bacon, cantaloupe and toast. Every bite was tasty and Frank felt satisfied. People were friendly too. Despite the ease and comfort he was experiencing, and the fact that he was clean shaven and well-fed, Frank was ready to hop on a boxcar and leave town.

The railroad went through a busy city section, but he wandered further across some fields and waited. He sat in the fields at least an hour before he heard the engine sound. The train came faster than he expected, apparently not stopping in town. Frank started running. He figured if he could run as fast as the car that he eyed, then he could jump aboard. By sheer luck, he made his jump, grabbed the grip bar on the open boxcar and landed inside.

"Mighty impressive jump, I must say!"

Frank heard the voice, but it took him a few seconds to visualize the hobo in the back corner wearing dark clothes. "Yeah, I wasn't sure myself how that was going to work out. This train was going faster than I expected."

"Yeah, these freight cars are just passing right through towns. They're trying to avoid riders like us. I heard that our population of hobos might suddenly increase due to this stock market crash. Our mode of travel might become extremely popular."

"True, I was noticing the same thing. There was a group of men on the last car I rode."

"Well, where are you headed this time?"

"Basically, I'm heading all the way to New York, but I hope this train will take me as far as Denver, Colorado."

"Oh, we'll get that far alright. Some steep climbs, rough country, but we'll make it. I've done this ride before."

Frank made himself comfortable sitting on the hard floor and padding it with his jacket as a cushion. "How long does it take to go over the Rocky Mountains?"

"Are you asking how long it takes on this freight train?"

"Yeah, that's what I'm asking."

"Well, you are in for the long haul. Between Salt Lake City and Denver, Colorado, the distance is 735 miles. On this Denver & Rio Grande Freight train the trip will take a total of thirty-five hours."

"Thirty-five hours!"

"That's what I said. But don't worry. There will be a stop and we can actually get off the train, stay in the town of Salida. That's where we will rest and get some grub. Then we will just hop back on the same train. The workers, on this freight, do it all the time."

"Won't they notice us getting on and off?"

"They might, but they really don't care. There are no yard bulls up in these mountains. It will be dark when we get there, but I know where there is an abandoned shed where we can sleep for a couple hours. Then at the first dawning light, we can go into the market and buy some food. Early in the morning, we will just hop back on the train and leave this mountain forsaken town. Matter-of-fact, the name "Salida" means exit and exit is what we will do. By the way, I'm Harry."

"Nice to meet ya. I'm Frank." Harry appeared much older than Frank and he had a long gray beard. Frank decided that whatever Harry said about train riding, he was probably right on.

Frank felt relieved. He was glad this hobo was riding. The ride would have been a long lonely one otherwise. He looked at the open doorway and could see the beauty of the terrain. Already, they were climbing upward toward the sky. He noticed his ears popped once. The ride was going to be a scenic trip. The rocky hillsides were covered in colors of rustic red and looked like layers, and layers of flat rock. Other times, he'd see a blue lake that blended in with the bright blue sky. The day was sunny, cool, but not yet cold. He was glad that he quickly made this trip and didn't wait around for cold weather. The train rambled along for several hours when all of a sudden it made a complete stop.

Frank looked over to where Harry was nestled in his corner. "Do we worry now or is this a routine stop?"

Harry had been resting, but he quickly appeared alert. "I'd say we are near leaving Utah. This is probably a routine stop of loading or unloading. A good time to stretch our legs, do a little dancing and moving around."

Unexpectedly, Harry stood up and actually did some dancing to the sound of silence: except for snapping his figures to his own beat. Frank wasn't that comfortable with dancing even if he was on a dance floor with a gal, let alone dancing alone in a boxcar, or performing in front of another hobo. He enjoyed watching Harry though. Harry appeared like he knew how to dance and entertain. Frank stood and paced the floor; pacing was his specialty. He often paced the floor when he rode too long on a train. He stretched his back into a straight position and walked, keeping time somewhat to Harry's finger snaps. They stayed upright until they heard the train whistle blow and heard the engine start up again. Near mid-afternoon the sun was still bright. "Need any food or drinks Harry?"

"No, thank you. I've got a bag lunch; guess now is a good time to eat." They both ate their own food and watched the scenery while it was still in view. There was the beauty of the high gray Rocky Mountains, with patches of snow on the tops. If they looked beside the tracks and below the cliffs, there were streams of rushing water. At other times, there would be a view of bright blue lakes. Frank had noticed that there were two locomotives on this train. Even so there were times when the train was chugging slowly on the steep upward climbs. Frank was glad that they would be getting off in a small town and walking on flat solid ground, at least for an hour or two.

Darkness had settled over the train when Frank fell asleep. Harry tapped him on the shoulder and motioned him to follow him. The train had stopped. Frank figured they were in Salida. He didn't feel completely awake and he could barely see, but he hopped off the still train and followed Harry's footsteps as they treaded through a sandy path to a wooden shed. Harry was right; the shed was empty. There were four walls, but still it was cold. He motioned for Frank to take a corner wall, and he sat in another corner. They wrapped themselves up as much as they could with their own jackets and fell asleep for a couple hours.

303

Again Harry tapped Frank. "The sun is rising, time to wake up." Frank followed Harry to a market store where they bought a few food items. Barely noticeable were other closed buildings on this main street. The town was surrounded with mountains on all sides. During this early morning hour, they didn't see any of the town people and there were no autos or even horse and carriages visible in the town. The streets were empty.

One man was running the market store and he barely spoke. He only asked one question, "Are you passing through?" Harry had answered, "Yes." Then they left the store and boarded an empty boxcar. They sat in the non-moving car for about a half-hour before the car started to move. Frank felt stiff and sore from sleeping on the wooden floor, but he also was happy that he had walked on solid ground and now he had more food in his pockets.

His current interest was in the next upcoming sight. He was curious about seeing the Moffat Tunnel that he had heard about, but if it was in Colorado and anywhere near Denver, daylight might turn to darkness when they went through the long tunnel. Not that darkness made any difference. The only difference was it would be dark before they entered and even afterwards there would be no daylight.

"Hey, Harry, you got any idea how close that Moffat Tunnel is to Denver?"

"I heard tell it is about 50 miles west of Denver. I figure it will be nighttime when we get anywhere near Denver. This tunnel has a unique ventilation system. They have doors on this tunnel and fans are blowing inside to keep the air circulating. So before a train can go through, the doors have to be opened. Sometimes the train has to wait a long time for all that to happen. Also, this tunnel is a one-way tunnel. So sometimes a train is going east through the tunnel, other times a westward train will go through. That can mean a long wait too."

Frank was thankful he was not riding on top of this freight car and hunkering down with no knowledge of the upcoming track. He agreed with the waiter in Salt Lake, this was a dangerous ride. At times he would look out the doorway. He could see that they were riding on a track that was hanging over a rocky cliff. When he looked downward, he could see the rushing creek water below. There would be no salvation if the train fell or rolled down this hillside. So far, it didn't seem like the train was speeding. At times Frank wished it would go faster, but mostly he was glad that the speed was consistent. He never felt like there was a race to get anywhere.

While the hours passed, Frank thought about his future plans. All he knew was that he wanted to get to New York, a place he had yet to see. Another plan on his mind was to see Daisy, one more time. He wanted to repay her for the money she had left in his pocket. Yes, he would have to stop in Chicago and maybe stay a few days.

He kept watching the scenery, from gray sandy steep mountains, to rocky cliffs, to rushing streams of water, to quiet lakes. Then he saw the sunset and felt the air getting chilly. He moved away from the open doorway and found a warmer corner space.

More hours went by. Frank had slept for awhile and then suddenly awoke when the train stopped again. Harry's voice startled Frank, as Frank remembered where he was. "I think this time we are in front of the Moffat Tunnel. I could see the grayness ahead from the train light as we got close."

"So is this gonna' be a long wait?"

"I have no idea, but it will be a wait. Nothing to see. It is total darkness and we are not even in the tunnel yet."

"Will we know when we are in it?"

"Oh, you'll know alright. The train will sound different – almost like an echoing sound, and the whole atmosphere will feel different. All our senses will be alert to darkness and enclosure."

Harry didn't make the experience sound inviting – at all. Frank wished it was daylight so he could see the sun now, and then see it again after the six miles of darkness. Instead, the timing made it so he was already in the dark, and it would get darker – without even the moon being aglow – and that deep darkness might seem overwhelming.

It was about an hour wait before they heard the engine roar again. They could tell the difference, by the sound and the smoky conditions inside the tunnel. They knew exactly the moment they entered through the narrow, low doorway. Frank wasn't sure of the height of this tunnel, but he figured, as with all tunnels, there would be barely enough room for the height of the train.

As the train moved slowly through, Frank often closed his eyes and tried to relax. He didn't like this close feeling and he could smell the sooty smoke. The deep darkness gave him an eerie feeling. Plus, he knew, from experience, how awful it would have been if he had been on top of the train. He imagined the effort of attempting to cover his head and breathe at the same time for this long distance. The thought alone sent him into a panic mode. He took deep breaths and tried to grasp the sensations of this once in a lifetime experience.

"Once we get through here we will only have fifty more miles to Denver. There will be some city lights and when we see those lights, in the distance, that's where we will have to jump off, or we will be caught for sure. When we reach Denver they will be checking every boxcar."

"Thanks for the information. I know we didn't converse much on this trip. I mean there was a lot to see – going over these Rocky Mountains, but I'm thankful you were riding along."

Harry was quiet for a while. "I'm glad you came aboard too. I really don't like ridin' alone even though I don't like talking much either."

"That's okay. We don't have to talk a lot just to enjoy having each other's company."

"Guess that's right. I'll let you know when we get near Colorado." The ride continued in silence. Frank really had no idea what Harry's life was like before this trip, or what he was planning for his future. Probably a lot like Frank, in that way, not too sure what the next trip or job would be like, or how long he'd be wandering. No point discussing what you don't know. Frank didn't have an immediate plan of what he was going to do next. Definitely no need to discuss present or future plans with a stranger, when he was in the dark himself. He quietly chuckled. Yes, he was literally in the dark and figuratively in the dark. Not a great place to be when one has to jump off a moving train.

Chapter Thirty-Three

Denver, Colorado

When Frank jumped off the train, the early morning was still semi-dark. He felt exhausted. He walked a few paces, found a bush and laid down on the grassy field. He rested for over an hour when he woke to sunlight. Then he walked. When he got near a paved road he followed a cement path. Ahead he saw many tall buildings. Minus the hills and the water front, Denver was a busy city, like San Francisco. Toward the west, Denver had a view of the Rocky Mountains, but the town itself was flat.

Even during this early morning time, the town was crowded. Walking on the brick sidewalks without bumping into someone was difficult. Trolley buses went down the middle of the main street, while autos, and horse and carriages passed by. Autos were parked along the sidewalks, bumper to bumper with little room between the vehicles.

People seemed to be dressed in their finest; women wore long dresses, fancy hats, and men wore suits and fedora hats. Frank realized he really didn't fit in. From the train smoke and from sleeping on the dirty ground, his clothes looked and felt dirty. His boots were dusty, and he needed to shave. He wasn't wearing a fancy hat. His head covering was a gray wool cap, like other young boys wore.

He read the signs and noticed the buildings: Larimer Square, Post Office, and the United States Mint. He wondered if this United States Mint was where they made money. He saw the Union Station and noticed the passenger trains coming and leaving.

His goal was to find a hotel, check in, clean up, find a restaurant, eat and then see a movie. He only had to turn his head to see the sign

Oxford Hotel: a tall red sandstone building. That was where he would stay the night!

He walked into the fancy lobby. The sights of the beautiful hotel caused him to stop for several moments just to look around. Off to the side he saw a fireplace with blazing logs burning. A large fabric davenport was in front of the fireplace, and several people were seated there watching the fire, while others were seated in large cushioned chairs reading their newspapers. A long dark marble desk was by the stairway. Behind the desk were desk clerks either talking to hotel guests or just standing by, ready to serve the next customer. Above the desk was a balcony with stairs on each side.

Frank walked to the front of the desk. "I'd like a room for the night please." The clerk was older than Frank and wore thick glasses. He had his hand placed on a large registration book that was on the desk top.

He leaned closer to Frank and quietly said, "I'm not sure we have a room to suit the likes of you, sir."

Frank looked at the sign that was hanging on the balcony: "80 Luxurious Rooms Available."

Looking directly into the clerk's eyes (that seemed extra large through his thick glasses) Frank firmly stated, "I'm sure one of your 80 rooms would suit the likes of me. What is the cost for a room for one night?"

The clerk seemed frustrated, but answered Frank's question.

"One room for tonight would be 75 cents." Frank knew that was a high price. Most hotel rooms were 15 to 25 cents a night.

"I'll take one room." He reached into his pocket and set down three quarters on the desk.

The clerk seemed flustered. He turned the pages quickly in his big book. "I will let you stay on the fourth floor in a corner room, and if you can write, sign your full name here."

Frank wrote his name neater than usual, but not his full name. He did not write his last name Rose. He wrote Gilbert Franklin and turned the book toward the desk clerk. While he traveled he never told anyone his last name. By not revealing his full name it helped to keep anyone from accusing him of anything, or of using his name for any falsified reason.

"Okay, Gilbert Franklin, here is your room number and the key."

Frank took the leather tag with the key. The clerk leaned over the desk and looked at the floor near where Frank was standing. "Do you have luggage?" He asked.

"No," said Frank, "there is no luggage." Frank headed toward the elevator.

"Oh, sir," the clerk yelled, "we prefer you use the stairway." He pointed to the long stairway.

"Thanks," said Frank, as he continued to walk to the elevator door. The elevator was crowded. Frank scooted toward the back and waited as the elevator rose to the fourth floor. As people departed, he was the only one left on the elevator when he arrived on the fourth floor. He walked down the long hallway and found his room number. The key fit easily and he unlocked the door. The room was lovely with a red carpet, designed with flowers and green leaves. There was also a large four poster bed. The window view was the train station. Frank opened the window slightly. He could hear the busy city sounds, and he heard a train chugging away from the station. He smiled and mumbled to himself, "This is the best room in the place, and the train sounds will help me sleep tonight."

He saw a standard note on the bed, "WELCOME Ring for service: hot water for bathing, a robe, or overnight laundry service." He knew this would involve tip money, but he wanted all of these services. Outside the door Frank rang the bell.

Shortly, a service attendant came to the door and told Frank his bath was ready, down the hallway in a small room. He handed Frank a robe, soap and a large soft towel. After taking a long warm bath in a huge clawfoot tub, he took time to carefully shave. He came back to his room and cleaned off his boots. He had clean clothes on except for his one pair of trousers. His pants would have to be laundered after he ate and went to see the movie.

He rode the elevator down to the main floor. As he left the elevator, he noticed this hotel had a dining room with a bar and bar stools and also black leather booths. He sat at one of the booths and ordered a meal. He had a chance to ask the waiter a few questions. "Excuse me, can you tell me if there are any nearby theaters?"

"Yes, we have several. What type of entertainment would you like: vaudeville acts, Charleston dancing, food eating contests, musical productions, lectures, talkies or silent movies?"

Frank was amazed at all the choices. "I was just thinking of a silent movie, I figured that was my only option."

"I heard the Blue Bird Theater is running a comedy movie."

"That's sounds good. Where is the Blue Bird?"

"It's only four and a half miles down the road – just right here in LoDo."

"LoDo?"

"Yeah, this area is called Lower Downtown. So we shorten it to LoDo. Go up 14th Street to Colfax Ave. Stay on Colfax until you see the City Park. Blue Bird is right across the street from the park."

"Sounds great. Thanks for the information."

"You're welcome. Enjoy your visit."

Frank paid his bill and took his walk through the busy town and to the quieter street Colfax. The show ticket was five cents. Frank found a comfortable seat near the back of the theater. The theater was nearly full, even with people in the balcony. The show was going with a silent Disney cartoon film. Then the movie feature started and big letters appeared on the screen: "Harold Lloyd Welcome Danger a Paramount Release."

Frank relaxed and felt ready to let his mind wander and be entertained, though he wondered how a movie with the title "Welcome Danger" could be a comedy. He was pleasantly surprised it was a talkie film, not a silent film.

What Frank didn't realize was that even though this film was a comedy, the scenes would prompt many emotional feelings for him. The first act was a stalled passenger train (a brief stop in Colorado) and Harold riding on a runaway cow. The train was headed for San Francisco. Frank was sorry he had to leave San Francisco. He came to the theater to get his mind away from the feelings of regret. As the movie continued he saw scenes in the city he had left. There was even a character with the same name as the friend he had met, Chang. Also, there was a crime incident that took place in Chinatown. Frank stared at these familiar scenes: scenes that he had left behind. The movie was funny, and ridiculous with a confusing plot, but it also was troubling and odd how this movie related to Frank's travels. The situation was amazingly coincidental.

312

The night was young when he left the theater. He slowly walked back to the hotel and gazed at the sights of Colorado. He would eat again, then request for his clothes to be laundered. He intended to leave in the morning and head to Chicago.

Chapter Thirty-Four

Denver, Colorado to Des Moines, Iowa

When the sun rose, Frank awoke. He left Denver city and headed up the fields by the railroad track and waited for a freight train. Picking up speed one open boxcar came down the track. Frank ran and jumped aboard. After a few seconds, his eyes adjusted, from bright sun to darkness. He clearly saw a group of four hobos sitting in the corner of the car. He took his place on the other side.

The way the men were seated, rather near each other, was as if they knew each other or just sat that way for comfort. Maybe they were trying to keep near one area for warmth, away from the open doorway. They were mumbling, but Frank could not hear the conversation well enough to know what they talking about. So he sat alone on the far corner and tried to make himself comfortable. Their presence made him feel somewhat nervous because they didn't seem to respond in a friendly way.

He wanted to stay on this train till he arrived close to Des Moines, Iowa. The trip would be about six hundred miles, taking at least eight hours. Before he had left Denver, he purchased some food items and a couple bottled drinks. He knew he could make the trip if there was no trouble. He really didn't want to jump off this freight. His hope was to stay on this one train car.

"Hey, you." Frank looked at the corner men

"Yeah, talking to me?"

"Who else would we be talking to? You got any smokes?"

Frank did have some tobacco in his pocket and the papers to roll, but he wasn't in a sharing mood, nor did he feel comfortable with the entire situation. "Sorry, I don't have any tobacco to share with you guys."

The other guy sighed. "Where are you headed?"

Frank answered, "I hope to get to Des Moines, Iowa.'

"Well, you got a ways to go. We, my pals and I, plan to jump off in Nebraska. We heard we can still get work there. Don't worry about us, we're not tough guys, we're just guys that need work. The trip is gonna be a long and cold, so we might as well get along – You agree?"

"Sure, I agree, no need for any disagreement." Frank thought about wanting to smoke right then, but he said he didn't have any smokes to share, so there would be no smoking on this trip.

He tried to make his area more comfortable: laying out his jacket to sit on. He wasn't sleepy. From where he sat, he could not see much scenery. Finally after several long minutes, he decided to start up a conversation; otherwise it would be a long boring trip.

"So guys, tell me what were you doing, before you jumped on this train?"

The oldest appearing man spoke first. "Well, I was busy working in Denver. I owned a store... well, I should say I was in the process of buying the store that I was calling my store. I was selling hardware, all the stuff needed for farming and for homes. My bank account was increasing and I was feeling comfortable, but as you probably could guess my bank closed down. My rent was due, I could not pay rent on my house or for the store, nor could I buy any supplies. Within weeks everything came to a sudden halt. I told my family, I would seek jobs elsewhere. My wife and my two kids are still in the house, but we don't know for how long. The store is sitting there empty, still in my name. I'm not a borrowing man. Now I'm looking for work. A couple guys, he pointed to the other men sitting on the floor, they were employed at my store. We're either going to make it, from job to job, or we go back home broke."

Frank didn't have any words of encouragement. Some businesses were still doing well – like the places he saw in Denver: the hotel, the movie house, and food stores. He didn't realize how quickly some businesses were already struggling. "Well, I wish you guys the best. I know in Nebraska, and in Iowa, they still need farm workers so I trust you will get some work. I really don't know exactly where though – I will be looking for jobs too, though my ultimate destination is New York."

"New York! They've been building skyscrapers in New York. You think you might work on a skyscraper?"

"Haven't given that much thought, but if the jobs are there then I might. I figure I can learn to do whatever they ask me to do."

"Well, with that attitude I'd hire you to work at my store, except right now there isn't a store – only an empty shop."

It was on that note the conversation ended. Frank sat still for almost a ½ hour when he decided to move closer to the doorway and see the view. The train moved fast. The view was a speeding blur of small trees, and grass appearing as tan straw sticks blowing over flat land. Sometimes there were blue lakes and small roaring rivers. They crossed over narrow bridges and went through at least two dark narrow tunnels. He saw plowed fields of loose dirt with no growing plants. Once he saw a white small church off in the distance, with no nearby houses. Staring out the doorway was causing dust and smoke to enter his eyes. He moved back to his corner and rested for a while.

When he felt hungry, he offered some of his crackers and small boxes of raisins to the other four men, who were still lingering in their corner spots. He felt somewhat guilty for hogging his tobacco, but rolling cigarettes in a moving boxcar was a hard task and not a wise idea anyway. They gladly accepted his snacks.

Hours had passed, when one of the guys yelled that he saw a sign saying they were near Lincoln, Nebraska. The guys stood up and organized their belongings. They were preparing to jump off the train. Frank advised them to wait. "As you get nearer to town the train will slow down. It's moving too fast yet. I'll tell you when."

"Gee thanks," said the older guy. "We're kind of new to this mode of travel. Getting on a sitting still train car is a lot different than getting off a moving car."

Frank stood up and got himself in a good position to watch the ground and to advise them when the right moment would be to jump. They were ready: some carrying nothing and a couple of them carrying bindle sticks. The train whistle blew indicating they were getting near a train crossing. The train slowed. Frank repeated the one word, "Wait!" The train passed the intersection and slowed down to a crawl. "Jump now!" Each man obeyed the command and one at a time jumped off the train with successful upright landings. Frank waved as they headed across the fields. He hoped the train would pick up speed and keep going to Iowa. Lucky for him the train did pick up speed. He was alone in the car, but within an hour or so he would jump off too.

A couple hours went by when he saw the sign, Des Moines, Iowa ten miles. Sunset was only about one hour away. Frank knew it was his time to jump. The train did slow down. He saw nothing around him except for fields. He stood near the doorway and watched the ground looking for the best spot and then he leaped off the train. Though he felt stiff and sore, from sitting too long, he landed upright on two feet! The air was crisp and cold; sleeping outside was not a desired option. He started walking hoping to see some nearby farmhouse. After a mile or so he did see a farmhouse up ahead.

When he got close, he noticed knife markings on the wood fence surrounding the farm house. The marking was a drawing of a man's top hat. Frank knew that meant a gentleman lives here. Anytime a hobo referred to a man as a gentleman it meant that the man probably welcomed and helped a homeless hobo. Frank felt hopeful.
He walked up the dirt path to the backdoor of a rather small house with a painted red door. Directly behind the house, he could see a large red barn. An older man answered the knock.

"Excuse me, sir, my name is Frank and I was wondering if you need any work done that I could do in exchange for some food, and one night's lodging?"

"Boy, I've got enough work to do around here for a week's worth, or hell two weeks or a month – whatever suits you."

"Much obliged sir, but I'm headed to New York, but I definitely will help if needed."

"Good, come right in. By the way, I'm Stan. You hungry?"

"Yes, I am."

"Margaret, fix some grub up we've got ourselves a working hobo for the night, and maybe one day?" He looked at Frank, as if he was pleading.

Margaret was rather heavy set with a beautiful smile and a clear complexion. She gave Frank a kind greeting and showed him the big pot of food she already had cooking, as if she was expecting company from the last freight train that Frank was on. "We have plenty. Stan, show him the bunk house in the barn and where he can freshen up."

Stan led him outside. As they neared the barn, Frank could see the acreage of land where corn, pumpkins, and apple trees were growing. "I can see you do have plenty to do."

318

"Yes, man, and besides what you see we have squash that needs picking too. I have two sons – great workers, but they went off to school, college in Des Moines. They do come home every other weekend, but in between time it's just mom and me doing the work."

The barn was warm and Stan showed him an enclosed area where there was a bunk bed. "I set up a wood stove; we keep the barn fairly warm, at least till the daily wood burns down."

There were no horses or cows, but there were stacks of hay. "You have no animals?"

"Not right now. I sold my two horses last week. Times are rather tough right now." He sighed and left Frank alone.

Frank washed up at the water pump and found the outhouse. He gazed at the land. It was a beautiful, quiet spot. Within the half hour the sun would set, but now it was still light and the sky was a bright blue.

Dinner was pleasant and before he resided in the bunk house they agreed that early dawn, 8:00 a.m. Frank would be shown what work there was to do. Between gathering pumpkins, picking apples, gathering corn, and cutting off the butternut squash plants Frank was busy. He was busy working for Stan and Margaret for five days. It was near the weekend when Stan's sons were suppose to come back home. Frank was thankful for the work and the meals. Sleeping in the barn was comfortable. Stan paid him well. He left early on a Friday morning. Before he walked through the fields, to wait for a coming train, he took out his pocketknife and marked Stan's wood fence with a circle and an x inside the circle: meaning a good place.

Chapter Thirty-Five

Des Moines, Iowa to Chicago, Illinois 1929
Eighteen Years Old

Frank knew what he wanted to do when he reached Chicago. While sitting in the empty boxcar, leaving Iowa and heading to Illinois, he fantasized visiting Daisy, one more time. His desire was to see her and to pay back the money she had hid in his pocket, months ago.

"Daisy," saying her name out loud made him smile. If she would go out with him – out away from her work place – he would stay in Chicago and spend some time seeing the sights. He visualized them walking on the water front, eating at a quiet place, dancing in the park in the moonlight: whether or not there was live music.

His thoughts were only a daydream. He was alone on the hard wooden floor of a boxcar chugging down the track, miles away from Chicago. Yes, he would jump off this moving train in Chicago, eat a meal, get cleaned up and then go to the club. Somehow he would have to get inside the main door.

Hours later, his imaginary plans came true. Dressed in clean clothes, he looked his best, as he paced the sidewalk in front of The Green Mill. The place looked the same, as it did months ago. The time was right, near dinner time. He watched a few men and several couples walk up to the door. They rang the bell. The door opened and they walked inside! The problem was Frank could not hear what they said. What pass words did they use to enter this exclusive night club?

It appeared that Daisy was nowhere to be seen, nor did he see any gals that were alone or might have worked there. He finally got up enough nerve to ring the doorbell. A gruff male voice answered, "Yes?"

It sounded like the same voice that Frank knew from before. "I'd like to enter and have dinner this evening."

"You know the password?"

"Yeah, it's keg of beer."

"Well, buddy that was the password months ago, but it's not the password this month. So I guess you haven't been around or you were kicked out the last time you were here."

"No, I wasn't 'kicked' out. I was with Daisy and she got us in."

"Really? What's your name?"

"I'm Frank." Several seconds went by before he heard the response.

"Were you Franklin Roosevelt that evening?"

Frank smiled, "Yeah, that's who Daisy called me."

"Okay, well, she liked you. Push the buzzer again and I will let you in."

Again, he pushed the buzzer. The door opened. Inside the doorway, Mack stood blocking Frank's path. "You know what, Frank? Daisy liked you! She said she hoped you would come back because she thought you were a decent guy."

Frank smiled, appreciating hearing these words.

Mack continued, "But, you know what else Frank? I'm a decent guy too. I told her I wanted to marry her and take care of her. I said

I would treat her good and she wouldn't have to work anymore. I've kept my promise. We're married and we've got a little baby boy. She's home tonight taking care of our child."

Frank was surprised. He looked directly at Mack with a more serious interest in him. Was he really the decent person and good enough for Daisy?

Mack seemed to understand Frank's concerns. "I'll always take good care of her and our son."

Frank smiled. He was honestly able to say, "I'm glad to hear this news, but I have to repay her." Frank pulled out two dollars from his pocket. "Give this to her. The dollar is repayment, when she helped to pay for my meal here. The other dollar is for whatever she might need for her child. Tell her it is from me, if that's okay with you?"

"Yes, I will give it to her, and I'll tell her that you came back to give it to her." They shook hands.

Mack said the words over again to reassure Frank. "I'll take good care of her."

"I'm sure you will."

Frank walked out the door. He wandered along the waterfront for over an hour, all the while remembering his one evening with Daisy. Now he tried to imagine her home with a child. He wondered if he would ever settle for staying in one place and having a family. He wasn't sure. He wanted to leave Chicago and head to New York.

Walking the waterfront did not give Frank peace of mind. He felt bad. Frank realized that Mack was more capable than he was of taking care of Daisy, and their baby – even if he did work in a dive. Frank came to the conclusion that maybe he needed a night's rest before he hopped on a moving train.

He headed to the Hobo Jungle. This was the place that was union organized. He hoped for a cot and a tent. A decent sleep might help Frank's pain. He remembered the guy named Beef, who collected the union dues. If he could get past Beef, he'd have a place to spend the night.

"You're back." Beef remembered Frank.

"Yes, I need a place to sleep."

"Okay, sign here." Beef stood by the small box "table" while Frank signed his name. "Follow that trail and you've got tent number fifteen."

Frank was surprised how many tents had been added to the camp. He didn't make it directly to tent fifteen. Two men were boxing right on the grass and several other men were watching. Frank stopped. These guys were good: boxing like trained boxers. He stood and watched their every move, evaluating which one could win a match. He observed how they hit or dodged from being hit. These guys wore boxing gloves which also gave them a look of being professionals.

As the fight wore down, neither one winning or being injured, Frank asked one boxer a question. "You do professional boxing?"

The boxer stopped and answered, "Yeah, I do, but I only get to do a few matches these days. I've done several in the past-won some and lost a few."

Frank was ready to fight. He wanted to fight the world and circumstances, but since he couldn't do that, he decided that fighting with a pro boxer might be okay. "You feel like fighting me a round or two?"

"Are you also a professional boxer?"

"Not a pro, but I've done some boxing."

"Well, I'll tell you what. I'm near broke right now so if you want to make a wager on this 'practice fight' I'll bet some money on a round or two."

"Sounds good to me."

"Okay, I'm Stan, what's your name?"

"I'm Frank and I bet five bucks I can win this match."

The pro boxer looked at Frank. "First, one question, are you right handed or left handed."

Frank wondered where this question might lead, but he answered truthfully. "I'm right handed."

Okay, Frank, you will only have to put up two bucks. If I win you only pay me two dollars. If you win I pay you three bucks; however, through the fight you have to lead with your south paw – got it!"

Frank knew this was a great disadvantage, but he also knew that while at the gym in San Francisco he practiced boxing with his left hand leading, at other times, with his right hand leading. He was praised for being able to fight either way. "Okay, it's a deal."

Stan asked the other boxer to loan Frank his gloves. Many of the hobo men were listening and watching this whole interaction. They were anxious to see how this would play out.

"Wait a minute;" said the fellow boxer as he handed the gloves to Frank, "You guys need a referee. I'll be the caller. How many rounds are you going?"

Stan held up three fingers. "Okay Frank?"

"Yeah, I'll do three rounds."

"Okay," said the newly self appointed referee.

They laid down their dollars under a nearby rock, a total of five bucks. The referee reminded them: "Winner takes all!"

Frank took off his jacket and one of his extra shirts. He definitely was in a fighting mood. He wanted the pile of money.

They stood facing each other. More men gathered around the circle area to watch this bout.

Stan was heavier than Frank, but Frank was taller. Both men had muscular arms. They touched their fists together, then stood back, and looked into each other's eyes.

The referee put his lips together and made a whistle sound – indicating the fight started.

The two boxers surrounded each other – going in circles with fancy footwork for several seconds, waltzing together without touching. The sideline men were yelling: "Jab him, jab him! Don't just dance around – let's see some action!"

Then Stan slugged Frank in the jaw. The crowd yelled, "Good going, way to go!"

Frank felt the pain, but it didn't deter his movements. He quickly slugged Stan back, one good slug on Stan's jaw. Stan punched back. Frank blocked the punches with his gloves. Several punches only hit each other's gloves. There were more fast jabs, back and forth: jaw, cheek, chest, stomach. The whistle sounded. Both men stopped and moved to opposite corners.

Frank was in pain. Not the mental anguish he felt earlier, now he was in physical pain. This kind of pain wasn't new to him. He had fights before and he knew pain came with boxing.

Second round: Stan started immediately hitting hard, a fast right at Frank's face. All of a sudden, Frank tasted blood that was coming from his lip. The whistle blew. "Want to call it quits?" the ref asked.

"No, why?" asked Frank. "We agreed to 3 rounds."

The referee blew the whistle again. The hobos were cheering and making their own bets. Mostly betting that Stan would win, but also betting on how that would happen.

Both fighters hit hard and fast. The hardest blow came from Stan: a smack right at Frank's nose. All of a sudden, Frank remembered Mr. Steward. He aimed directly at the side of Stan's jaw and slugged hard. Amazingly, Stan fell backwards to the ground and did not stand right back up. The men echoed the same chant: "Get up man, get up!"

Stan was conscious, but looked dazed and kept moving his head back and forth, as if to decide if his neck was still able to turn. The ref started the count down. At ten he blew his whistle and held up Frank's hand. "I declare this hobo, Frank, the winner!"

Frank's nose was bleeding. Someone picked up his extra shirt and handed it to him. He held it tightly on his nose. Stan slowly stood up. He took off his gloves, picked up the money. He helped Frank to get his gloves off and then handed Frank the money.

"You did a great fight, using your south paw!"

"It was a good bout. Thanks," answered Frank.

Frank headed to tent fifteen. He won the bet, but he did not look like a winner. His face was bloody and he could feel his nose swelling. He feared he had a broken nose. One of the hobos came to Frank's tent. "I've had some training as a medical doctor." He peeled back Frank's shirt and looked at Frank's nose. "Yeah, probably broken, but not crooked so lucky for you, it will probably heal. I'm going to bring some buckets of water in here. You soak your shirt in the cool water and keep holding, keep holding your wet cold shirt on your nose!"

Frank spent most of the night tending to his injury. The process helped to take his mind away from his troubling thoughts of Daisy and his current status of life. Through the night, he only had one concern and that was his constant physical pain.

Frank was surprised how much blood he had in his system. He slept in late because mostly he was up all night holding his cold wet shirt on his swollen, bleeding nose. Finally after several hours, the bleeding stopped. He was ready to rise and eat, but not ready to hop on a freight train.

By the time he left his tent, the breakfast meal was over, but something was cooking. He wandered over to the fire. As he got closer, he knew it was a pot of stew. Stew at the hobo jungle was always a bit iffy. Stew could actually have beef or chicken, but it could also have dandelion leaves or stems, and other unrecognizable plants. Some stews had mushrooms, bread crumbs, and/or cooked oatmeal. Usually, he was hungry enough that he really didn't care. Not caring was how he felt this early afternoon.

"Here he is, the man of the hour. Welcome, boy. Come join our feast."

Frank was surprised that these men looked at him, in a respectful way: jumping up and ready to serve him a meal. "Sit down lad; we will bring you the food and a cup of coffee. Just relax."

Frank sat on a nearby log. He was glad to sit down. He felt weak and somewhat dizzy. During the boxing round, last night, he wasn't

327

knocked out, so why he felt dizzy made no sense. Drinking the hot coffee did help. Eating the stew actually tasted good and smelled like fresh chicken.

"Man, this stew is good: plenty of chicken bites."

"Yeah, while you were hiding in your tent last night, we had some action here."

"Really," asked Frank, "what happened?"

"Well, Max and Slim, over there," (both men raised their hands to identify themselves) "decided late last night that they wanted chicken. So they went off across the fields. They wandered down this dirt road until they found a farm house. Slim knew exactly which farm house was raising chickens. Right, Slim?"

Slim nodded his head, "I'm somewhat familiar with places around here."

"Slim and Max went in the hen house and grabbed a couple big fat chickens! That's what you're eating. Trouble is that ruckus woke up Farmer Brown. He called the sheriff."

"Really?"

"Yeah, the sheriff showed up here this morning with Mr. Brown."

"Wow!" Frank looked over at Slim and Max. "How come you guys are sitting here eating when you should be in the poky?"

Max spoke up, "Well, as luck would have it, Mr. Brown said he would give us chickens if we would just knock on his door and ask. He doesn't want us going in the chicken coop and disturbing the hens and causing chaos. His exact words were: 'Don't steal my chickens!'"

"We promised no more stealing chickens: least not from Mr. Brown." Frank just shook his head in disbelief and continued eating the delicious tasty stew.

"You got plans for the day?" Beef asked him.

"Yeah, I think I will wash my clothes in the river, and stay put for a couple days, if you don't mind."

Beef rubbed his chin and took a close look at Frank. "I think that is a wise decision. Stay put. Truthfully, you still look like a mess."

Frank hadn't looked in a mirror, even though there were a few mirrors hanging on the trees. Washing up, even shaving, might help his appearance, and how he felt. While eating, he made a firm decision to relax, get more sleep, and forget about travel, at least for a couple days.

It was three days, before he felt decent enough and strong enough to depart from the camp. In between time, he had talked to the guys about his trip to New York. He even walked to the train station and got a schedule of departing trains. He learned that the distance to New York was over seven hundred miles. Train travel time could take up to twenty hours, maybe more if the train made stops along the way. He also was told that riding via rail was the most scenic route compared to hitching a car ride. Of course, he always preferred train travel over hitchhiking.

On the second week of November, during the early cool morning, Frank left the hobo jungle and headed to the grassy knoll where he knew he could catch a freight train. When he heard the engine, in the near distance, he raced down the hill. His jump aboard felt easy; surprisingly, he felt okay. His strength was back to normal.

This boxcar was not empty. Several men sat in one corner of the car. Frank gave a semi-friendly wave. A few of them waved back, a slight sign of welcome. "How far are you going?" One of the men asked.

Frank found a corner and sat down. "Well, I'm heading all the way to New York, but for this round I think I'll stop in Cleveland, Ohio. I decided it's too far to make one long trip to New York."

One of the hobos got up and walked toward Frank. He was older than Frank and had the appearance of being a well versed traveler. His coat was long with pockets and a hood. His hair was rather matted and long, and he hadn't shaven for quite a while. With his gray looking beard he appeared like a rough guy.

Frank felt a little leery about him getting too close. The man sat on the floor. "Let me tell you a little bit about traveling to New York. After you leave Cleveland you will be going through the Allegheny forest. You will see the most beautiful countryside. Now is the perfect time to see the fall colors. That is, if you don't stay in Cleveland too long. Have you heard about the Kinzua Viaduct?"

"No, can't say that I have."

"Hey guys, this hobo doesn't know about the Kinzua Viaduct!" The men, in the other corner of the boxcar, started to snicker. One yelled out, "Guess he'll find out soon enough."

The hobo turned back and looked at Frank, "Well, man, the Kinzua Viaduct is the highest rail viaduct in the world! Scary, but also you'll see the best view of all time, especially this time of the year. Riding on top is where you get the best darn view of all." Then he started laughing and went back to his corner.

Frank wasn't sure what to think of this conversation. He decided to ask at least one question. "You guys know how far it is to Cleveland?"

The same man who had spoken to Frank answered. "About 340 miles and takes about six hours. It's where I'm headed. Just watch when I jump off. I've done this trip many times. If you're asleep, I'll wake you."

"Thanks," said Frank. "Sounds like a good plan. I'll watch."

Chapter Thirty-Six

Chicago, Illinois to Cleveland, Ohio

Frank did not watch. He fell asleep. Hours later, the old man stood above him and calmly said, "It's time to jump." Frank awoke somewhat startled, trying to focus as to his whereabouts. Then he remembered. He quickly stood upright ready to leap off the train.

Both men walked toward the open doorway. Frank looked out at the ground and then down at the blurry tracks. The cold wind blew in Frank's face. He had to yell to be heard. "We're going rather fast, don't you think?"

"Around these parts this is as slow as it gets, unless you want to be seen at the station house."

"No, I guess this will have to do."

Frank preferred to make his own decisions about jumping on and off trains, but he had asked this hobo to show him when to leap, so now it was up to him to decide on his own, or take this guy's advice. He believed him because he could see the town, yet the train kept its speed. This freight train may not stop. It might breeze by and unload up the tracks a ways.

The old man yelled back, "There's a grassy knoll ahead, that's where we'll jump."

They were getting in position to make their leap when another hobo got near them. "I'm jumping here too."

The old man looked at him, somewhat surprised. "I thought you were going farther east?"

"I was, but I changed my mind, thought I'd see some of Cleveland."

The old man looked suspiciously at him. Frank wondered if some sort of secret, or plan, was exchanged by their private glances. Despite this concern, his main worry was not what these two men might know, that he didn't know, rather his main thought was leaping off this fast moving train safely. All three men stood upright ready to leap.

In less than a minute the older man leaped, then the second hobo leaped, and finally Frank. All three of them landed flat on the ground, with their faces in the dirt. Frank brushed the dirt off his clothes and touched his arms and legs to feel for any broken bones. He felt somewhat dizzy as he wiped the dirt away from his face. When he realized he was okay, he looked at the other two guys. The younger one was giving a hand to the older hobo. The other hobo had a bindle stick that had fallen away from him. He reached for his stick. Suddenly with a quick motion, the younger guy grabbed the bindle stick and said, "Before I give this to you, you have some explaining to do."

Frank wasn't sure if he should hang around and watch this confrontation, or head up the road. The younger hobo looked at Frank. "Hang out here – till we settle this, because this involves you too. You see this old man here, whose name is Jim, he's a pickpocketer and he picked your pocket while you slept. Tell me how much money you had, Frank, and I'll show you where it is. I will bet the exact amount will be in this bindle stick."

Jim and the other hobo froze in place as they waited for Frank to check his pockets. He knew exactly how much money he had. The amount that was in his pockets was thirteen dollars and seventy-five cents. He had more dollars stashed in his boots, but he always slept with his boots on. He wasn't worried about his boot money. He checked his pockets, and with his fingers dug into the deep grooves.

His coins and dollars were gone. "I had a ten dollar bill and three ones and three quarters."

The young hobo reached into the bindle stick and pulled out a ten, three ones and three quarters. He handed the money to Frank. "Well, what do know?"

Frank was surprised. "Here you keep the three bucks for your effort and watchfulness." Frank tried to hand three dollars to the young hobo.
"No way – it's yours. By the way, I'm Ken."

"I'm Frank and I appreciate your help." They shook hands.

They both looked at Jim. Ken went close to him. He handed him the bindle stick. "Now you, old man, you are getting on the next train and leaving town. If not, you will be in jail for the night. Got it?"

Frank thought about the possibility of losing his funds and he decided the old man needed more of a lesson than just an easy escape. He walked directly in the old man's path and blocked his way. The old man had a fearful look on his face. Frank grabbed Jim's shirt collar and held his tight fist in the man's face. "I could beat you to a pulp and leave you lying here. I've worked hard for every cent I've earned. When I've had to borrow, I've paid back. Not once have I stolen from another man and taken his earnings. Mister, you need to clean yourself up. I assume stealing is your way of life. You need to learn a new way of living. Beg, or earn a living, but don't steal! If I see you again and I hear about you pick pocketing another man, I won't hesitate to teach you a lesson." He loosened his grip.

Jim was shaking. He wiped his brow. "You're right stealing has been my way of living, taken many beatings for it too. I'll try what you say. I've got family in Pennsylvania. I may try to reach them. I really don't like this way of living." He straightened up his clothes and headed down the grassy field following the tracks.

334

Frank breathed a sigh of relief. He really didn't want to get in a fist fight. His nose was just beginning to feel normal. He did want to scare the old man though, and he thought what he did was right. He looked at Ken. "Now what do we do? Shall we walk into town together or you want to go your own way?"

Ken looked up the road, "I've been here before, there's a hobo jungle that I know about at the edge of town. You need a place to stay tonight?"

Frank wanted to sleep in a hotel. "You know any decent, yet reasonable hotels in town?"

"Oh yes, there are many hotels in town, but they are all fancy and cost a lot. If you intend to go to New York City, you had best stay at the hobo jungle tonight. They've got tents and running water. Basically, Cleveland doesn't like hobos in their town. They expect everyone to be working. If you don't have a job and need a place to stay, they suggest the county jail. There you're fed bread and water. Have no fear, I know where the Hobo Jungle is, the police probably know too, but they don't care as long as we hide behind the trees. Just follow me. We can clean up there, by Lake Erie, and then if you want to see the town, go for it. Just don't appear or act like a hobo. Save your dough for New York."

Frank was happy to hear all this advice. "Okay," Frank relented. He thought about the situation that Ken described. If what Ken said was true, the attitude in this city was different than Chicago or even San Francisco. Jails were not feeding the hobos in those cities; if bread and water can be called "feeding."

Together Ken and Frank walked along the city streets, but avoided going into the shops. As they walked through the town, Ken described all the scenes of the city: the tall fifty-two story train terminal tower, the Playhouse Square theaters, and the Arcade Shopping Area. Frank walked the streets in awe of the amazing sights. The city was crowded with people, autos, and streetcars. No one was paying attention to these two men not wearing suits or top hats, not hurrying off to work, but leisurely seeing the sights.

They walked until they were near the outskirts of town, along Lake Erie. Hidden behind bushes, beyond the trees, they saw the campsite. A few tents were lined up. "Here is where we can stay tonight," Ken stated as Frank looked around. The place seemed okay to Frank. A smaller camp than Chicago, but similar with trees, mirrors hanging on branches, tubs for washing, clothes lines, a fire going, some tarps and blankets laying about, and Lake Erie with plenty of water. All he wanted was a place to clean up. He intended to head right back to downtown Cleveland and see what was going on in town tonight.

During the early afternoon, Frank freshened up, and changed to a clean shirt. He was anxious to eat, see the sights and maybe catch a show.

A kid on the street corner, selling newspapers, yelled out his sale pitch: "Read all about it. Stock Market News of the Day!"

Frank stopped. "Say kid, you know a good place where I can get a good meal?"

"Sure, you want to read about the Stock Market news?"

"No, not really – I've got no stock so no need to worry whether the news is good, or bad, or whether the stock is up, or down."

"Okay," the boy lowered his arm and set his papers on a wooden box. "I'd say the best place to eat is New York Spaghetti House, which is right here in downtown Cleveland. I'll even draw you a map." He took a pencil out of his pocket and a piece of paper.

"Also while you are drawing, could you please give me directions to a nearby theater – I want to see a movie tonight."

The kid looked up from his drawing. "Why do you want to see a movie when the play Dracula is in town?"

"What's Dracula?"

"What's Dracula? Where have you been? Dracula is the scariest play of all time and the lead actor Bela Lugosi is playing tonight! Everyone wants to see him act. He thinks he really is Dracula. Get there early and you might get a ticket. It's at the Liberty Theater. Before you do all this, check out the arcade walkway – it's just down the street. Do you see those glass walls? That's the arcade."

Frank thanked the newsboy and followed the boy's written directions. He saw the sign The Arcade, Built in 1890. He walked through the glass swinging doors. This was an indoor shopping area – a huge building with walkways and many shops. There were passageways that went over streets and a high arched roof. Frank was impressed, but he was also hungry. Looking at his drawn map he headed to the Italian restaurant. While walking on the city streets, he looked up at the 52 story train terminal. Everything in this town was amazing, almost like he imagined a small New York would look like.

The New York Spaghetti House looked like a brick house amongst the tall surrounding buildings. As soon as he entered the large room, he felt like he was among his Italian friends in California. He could hear the waiters yelling to the chef the orders in Italian. The food was the best spaghetti he had ever tasted. "Excuse me," he addressed the dark haired waiter, 'what makes this spaghetti taste so good?"

"Oh, we serve a special brown thick sauce, it's a secret recipe, and no one complains. People just come again and again to eat the spaghetti. The owners, Mario and Maria Brigotte, make this sauce. Mario used to work in an Italian restaurant in New York so that's why the name New York."

"Did this use to be a house, because it feels and looks like a home instead of a restaurant?"

"Oh, yes, sir, this house belonged to the Zion Lutheran Church. This place was the church's parsonage; where the preacher lived. Now it's Brigotte's parsonage, the waiter chuckled. In this home we've added Turkish coffee and Turkish cigars. If you want, try some after you finish your meal."

"Thanks, I appreciate the offer, but I'm headed to the Liberty Theater. So I better not sit and enjoy coffee and cigars."

When Frank arrived at the theater, there was a long line of people. Frank joined the line. He didn't have a ticket, but he had coins in his pocket and thought he could buy a ticket.

When he got near the entrance an usher stopped him. "Do you have a ticket, sir?"

"No," answered Frank as he jiggled the coins in his pocket.

"Well, you can purchase a ticket for 75 cents." Frank knew this was a high cost. Usually, he could see a movie for a nickel or a dime. "75 cents?" he questioned.

"Yes, sir, 75 cents!" Frank felt for his three quarters and handed them to the usher.

"Very good, sir, here is the program with some viewing information. Please read through the material before the first scene."

"Sure," said Frank. He found a wooden folding seat near the back of the theater. The place was huge even with a balcony. The ceiling was decorated with stars and painted clouds. The stage and high ceilings made the theater appear as a castle. It smelled like an old castle too, rather musty.

He decided to read the paper, he was handed. As he read the words, he could not believe what he was reading. There was an extra free ticket, labeled 'A Faint Ticket' in case... "you, as the guest, faint during the play Dracula."

Frank snickered and stuffed it in his pocket. He knew it did not apply to him. He would not faint and he probably would not return to Cleveland to use the ticket anyway. Then he read the long paragraph, "In connection with this presentation of the Vampire Play, Dracula patrons are notified that they will be admitted at their own risk. A duly qualified, trained nurse will be in attendance at each performance, but it must be distinctly understood that the undersigned accept no responsibility whatsoever."

Responsibility of what? Frank wondered. What reaction did they expect from these audience members? He glanced around the auditorium to see if he could spot a nurse in a white uniform. He wondered if she was young and pretty enough that he should faint. He shook his head and said out loud, to no one, "What a bunch of baloney!"

The lights dimmed and the play started. As the scenes progressed, the audience and Frank felt the tension. The same moment the actress on stage screamed, the women in the audience screamed. When Dracula hypnotized his victims, against their will, Frank felt nervous. Another shocking scene was when Dracula's image did not appear in a mirror. The revelation was clear, Dracula was not human!

Despite these incidents, Frank did not feel an urge to scream himself. Stage life was make-believe, dramatic, but still make-believe. He knew that when he left the theater he would be back to real hard life of basic survival. There would be no threat of Dracula after his blood, but there would be real challenges of getting to New York, finding a job, and a place to keep warm. As the play ended, Frank considered his plans for the next day.

Early the following morning, before Frank hopped on the train, he wrote a letter to his brothers Millard and Lou, and dropped it off at the post office. *I advise, don't see the play Dracula – a bunch of nonsense. P.S. I'm in Cleveland, heading to New York.*
Love, Frank

Chapter Thirty-Seven

Cleveland, Ohio to Jersey City, New Jersey

The boxcar that Frank hopped onto was crowded with traveling men. He decided to ride on top. The weather was mild and at the time it seemed like a good idea.

The train was going at a moderate speed. He climbed up the side ladder and pulled himself upward. He was the only hobo riding on top. After walking across the roof a short distance, he sat.

Pulling his jacket up around his neck and ears gave him some protection from the cold wind and the bellowing smoke. He didn't know how far he was from the beautiful Allegheny Mountains, that he had heard about, or the Allegheny Forest that he would be going through. Now the view was rather dismal: flat plains, dry grass, and off in the distance the gradual disappearing city of Cleveland.

A mixture of feelings overtook him: loneliness, adventure, and yearning. He wanted to be in New York, get a job, and maybe, see his grandparents, aunts and uncles. He felt he was akin to family members, that he had yet to meet.

Riding on the train usually pacified his restless spirit, but today he was anxious. Not anxious because something bad might happen, but anxious to see New York. He wanted to explore the big city – a city he felt attached to even if he had yet to be there.

His thoughts were interrupted by the engine sounds: the continuous drone of the chugging, chugging, and the occasional whistle sounds. The discomfort was sitting on the hard boards, and trying to avoid the heavy black smoke. The cold wind bothered his eyes and penetrated uncomfortable coldness to his skin.

After an hour or so of travel, the scenery changed to a massive forest of surrounding trees. The train slowed down. Then, all of a sudden, there was a dramatic change of scenery. Instead of being next to a forest of trees there was a canyon, and the train was on a viaduct above the forest. Frank estimated the train was on rails over 300 feet in the air! Frank remembered what the hobos had joked about – riding over the Kinzua Viaduct on top of a train car. He stood up for only a moment to see the surrounding view. Immediately, he sat down. His body shook, as his mind realized that if he slid off the top of this car he would die. He would not fall only from the height of the boxcar he would fall into this canyon hundreds of feet.

No one would find his body. The train slowed to a crawl as it crossed the viaduct. The slow speed indicated to Frank that not only was he scared of this experience, so were the engineers. They were creeping across these rails as if the weight or swaying of the cars could cause a complete collapse. Frank figured this was a short-cut, but he was amazed that it was even possible for men to build such a viaduct over this deep canyon of forest trees, let along have trains cross it successfully. Of course their plan wasn't for a rider to be on top of the one of these cars. And here was Frank, the one rider on top.

He decided he might as well look at his surroundings. He tried to see the beauty rather than look at the scene as a death trap. The trees, at the peek of their foliage, were beautiful with dazzling colors of red, green and shades of yellow and gold. With all the different rays of color and the blazing sun shining on the leaves, Frank thought the scene would make a great movie picture show. He had to laugh, yes if this was a movie scene he would appreciate it more. Now the experience was reality and the height was genuine, the slow chug, chug sound of the train was authentic. The train moved, as if it was using all its power to cross this canyon, or did it have the sound of struggle only because the engineers were using less power because it was the only way they felt safe crossing these high narrow rails? Either way Frank was nervous. The canyon crossing was close to a mile. Frank felt like the distance was the forever mile.

Once across the canyon, the train picked up speed again. Frank wasn't sure how far it was before the next stop, but he decided however far, and however long, he would jump off even if he wasn't in New York. He would jump off and figure out where he was when he got there.

Frank straightened his legs out and tightened his jacket around himself. These attempts were to make him feel more comfortable as he got into a crouching position. There was no choice except to keep riding until the train slowed or stopped.

Thankfully, he was no longer over a canyon, but he was also exhausted from not being able to walk or stand. His muscles felt stiff and sore. This position and anxiety continued for over an hour when suddenly, for what seemed like no apparent reason, the train slowed down. Frank stood up and viewed his surroundings. There was a huge water tank ahead. The train was going to refuel with water. Here was his chance, not to jump off and start walking because he saw no roads or towns, but to at least get into the boxcar and stretch his legs.

He walked across the car's roof. When he reached the end he grabbed the ladder rung, swung his body off the top of the car, placed his feet on the rungs and climbed downward. Now he was on the couplers. When the train was close to an actual stop he jumped off. Then he ran beside the slow moving cars and jumped onto the open boxcar. Once inside he flopped onto the flat wooden floor exhausted. His muscles ached.

The car was not full with men, as it was when he first got on the train hours ago. Some riders must have gotten off before the viaduct ride; however, there were eight guys in the car. They saw Frank flop on the floor. One of the men asked, "Where did he come from? We're out here in the boondocks; nothing's around here and all of a sudden he shows up?"

A few moments went by in silence while Frank took time to sit upright, and breathe.

One guy came close to him with a thermos in his hand. He took off the lid and handed it to Frank, "Here buddy have something to drink." Frank slowly sat up and reached for the thermos. He was surprised how thirsty he felt. After several satisfying gulps of the cold stale coffee, he handed the thermos back. "Thanks, I guess I really needed that."

"I got a sandwich to share too if you tell us where you came from. Falling into the car, the way you did, it appears you came out of the sky."

Frank laughed, "No, though I saw lots of sky, I was ridin' on top."

The guys were all quiet and just stared at Frank, like he was talking crazy. "You mean you rode on top over the Kinzua Viaduct?"

"Yeah, that's right. I did."

The hobo reached into his pocket and pulled out a ham sandwich. "Here you deserve a meal, but this is all I have got."

Frank took the sandwich and ate it quickly before he even said "thanks" and asked his pending question, "How far it is to New York?"

Oh," answered the hobo, "You headed to New York? This train won't take you there. This route will end in New Jersey, but there's work to be had there, if you want work. The next stop will be Jersey City, just stay on the train about four or five more hours."

Frank sighed and leaned against the wall. He felt exhausted. The men still looked at him as if he was an odd fellow. Frank didn't care. He took off his cap, placed it behind his head for a pillow, and leaned against the wall. With his eyes closed he folded his arms together, braced his knees up against his body and dozed off. Miles and hours went by before he woke up.

Chapter Thirty- Eight

Jersey City, New Jersey

When Frank jumped off the train he walked across some fields. He saw a road sign, Jersey City, 10 Miles. He realized he was in New Jersey. The realization was okay. New Jersey was across the river from New York and he was excited to be so near his destination.

He decided he would try hitchhiking into the city. Maybe, he could get some information before he arrived in the big city. Since he had hopped off the train he had only seen one auto go by. He wasn't too concerned; figuring he only needed one auto. After he had walked about 25 minutes he heard a car coming down the road at least 25 miles per hour. The car whizzed past him. Then a few feet ahead it stopped. Frank ran to the car. A middle-aged looking guy opened the side door, "Need a ride?"

"Yes, sir I do. I'd like to go to Jersey City."

"Well, that's where I'm heading so hop aboard!"

Frank sat on the leather seat, "Much obliged. I really appreciate the ride. I rode on top of the boxcar and I still feel stiff and sore."

"You rode on top?"

"Yeah."

"Isn't that rather dangerous?"

"It sure can be, but I made this trip even over the Kinzua Viaduct and over the Allegheny Forest. Sorry, I'm so dirty. You know a place where I could get cleaned up?"

The man thought for a few seconds. "Yeah, I know just the place. I belong to the Dewey/Kennedy Supper/Athletic Club. They have showers there, locker rooms and even cots to rest on. There's also a basin to wash clothes. Course, you need to be a member to get in but, I'm a member. I'll let you in and you can freshen up."

"Wow!" This was more than Frank expected.

"By the way, where are you originally from?"

Frank decided to be truthful with this helpful gentleman. "Well, my name is Frank and I'm from Portland, Oregon Though I've done some traveling and even stayed in San Francisco for a while."

"You said Portland, Oregon?"

"Yeah, Portland, Oregon."

"I had a restaurant in Portland for several years; Dave's Steak House. Not my name, just the name we called the place. Ever been there?"

"Can't say that I have, but I worked for Swift Meat Packing Co. and I think they delivered meat to Dave's Steak House."

"You're right, that's where I bought all my beef. Do you know…?"

Suddenly, this helpful gentleman and Frank discovered they knew many of the same people – workers, and salesmen from Portland The conversation was lively as they discussed these other men's personalities and idiosyncrasies. By the time they reached Jersey City they were laughing together as long time friends might. The city was not as large as Cleveland, or San Francisco, but it too had busy streets with streetcars and autos parked along the borders of the sidewalks. There were only a few tall buildings.

Together they walked into the fancy restaurant in a tall brick building. A maitre d' met them at the door, "Welcome Robert."

Frank heard Robert's name for the first time. He realized they had jabbered several miles and yet he didn't know the man's name was Robert.

Robert spoke quietly to the host. Then he turned to Frank "I will show you where the shower rooms are and I'll also give you a set of clean clothes. "Actually…," he looked up and down at Frank's height, "we look about the same size. I'll give you some clothes from my locker. After you clean up and wash your clothes meet me at this dining hall. Don't worry – every cost will be on my bill."

Frank was so amazed how this day was progressing he barely nodded a thanks and followed Robert to the men's locker room.

After he got cleaned up, washed and dried his clothes, and placed his clean clothes in the locker, he met Robert at one of the dining tables. Robert looked at Frank. "You look like a different man – not a hobo, but like a business man!"

Frank laughed. He had never been referred to as a business man even after getting cleaned up. Of course, Robert's pants and shirt were perfectly ironed and felt and looked dressier than Frank had worn before. "Keep the clothes." Robert said. Then he added, "While you were cleaning up I talked it over with some members here – nobody likes it when it's their turn to clean up the place. So we decided that if you want to clean up every night you could stay here at nights. Not only can you stay, but they offered to place money in a can that's on the piano. Whatever they volunteer to give will be your wages. Do you agree to that?"

"Sure," Frank was delighted to hear this plan – it was like his lucky day!

That night he did some cleaning, and found a janitorial closet with supplies. This was a lot like his job in San Francisco. They also had a workout room with mats and weights and boxing rings. Frank felt like he was at a second home. He followed the pattern from his last job. Basically he mopped floors, took out the garbage, swept the floors, and washed down the mats. After closing time he vacuumed the dining area. Everything was clean by 2:00 a.m. Then he rested on the cot and used one of his shirts as a blanket and soundly slept.

When he awoke it was 11:00 a.m. He heard sounds. Men were already in the work out room, showers were going, and the dining hall was a busy place. He didn't want to push his luck or be greedy so he headed to a nearby café and ate his breakfast. While there he asked directions to the ferry terminal. He could ride a streetcar to the dock. His plan was to see Brooklyn, and go into Manhattan. A ferry ride was only 5 cents round trip. This was an exciting day. This would be his first experience of seeing New York City.

The city of Manhattan was flocked with people. Constantly people were busy moving on the sidewalks and on the streets. They all seemed to be in a hurry. Children were on the sidewalks playing: jumping rope, bouncing balls, and in some places throwing balls in basketball hoops.

The noise was loud with autos honking and the chugging sound of auto pipes making their steady rhythm sounds. The streetcars had their motor noises too and bells clanging as they made their frequent stops. Even horses were clogging down the streets and pulling carriages.

There was much to see. Store fronts were side by side with walls touching their sides to other buildings – no separation between. Street vendors were selling their wares under tents right on the sidewalks. They were yelling, "Get your canollies they are the best, beautiful scarves sold here, help the artists, wait till you try our fresh fish eggs and eels in the pan." Only three words described the scene: loud, busy and crowded. Frank walked the streets for hours, enjoying all the views.

In midtown Manhattan, Frank walked through Grand Central Station and collected train schedules, not because he was leaving soon, but just in case. He spent over an hour wandering around Central Park. He bought his lunch at the hot dog stand. Amazingly, the brightness of the night lights made it feel like daytime. The night felt cold when he caught a ferry to return to Jersey City.

Chapter Thirty-Nine

Jersey City to New York

"Stocks, bonds, dividends, preferred stock, trades, profits, investing, exchanges, ticker tape, corporations," these words were being jumbled together. Frank sat on the ferry listening to the conversation of a group of talkative men. They all wore suits, Derby hats, long suit jackets and carried leather satchels. Often they would open these leather cases and sort through their long rolls of paper. At times, it seemed that no one was listening; rather they were loudly accentuating their points, whether anyone heard them or not.

Frank tried to pay attention to this chatter, but he didn't understand their discussions. From their demeanor, he knew the men were frustrated, anxious and definitely opinionated, but Frank had no idea whether their ideas were right, wrong, helpful or detrimental. He also didn't know why the steadiness of stocks, the rising and financial gain seemed to now suddenly be falling. He had seen the headlines of the New York Times, "Stocks Collapse, Brokers, and Bankers Optimistic to Continue." What did all this mean?

As the ferry docked in Manhattan, the stock broker gentlemen all departed, in one large group. They walked fast while continuing their conversations. They seemed oblivious to their surroundings, pushing pass people as if they were the only ones on the wooden gangplank.

Frank slowly walked off the boat. As he walked and observed the other passengers, he got an idea. He noticed one woman with three small children struggling to keep her group together. There were also several elderly people struggling with their luggage. Frank decided he could help. An older lady was near him toting a large leather piece of luggage. "Pardon me madam, could I be of service carrying your bag to the sidewalk?"

The lady stopped her pace and looked directly at Frank. She would have to decide quickly because many people had to change their direction to go around Frank and this lady. Their stopping caused a slowdown

Frank smiled and pointed to the bag. "I'll carry it for you and walk your pace just to help you through this crowd."

"Thank you, sir, I would appreciate the help."

Frank picked up the bag. The luggage was heavy, but less than any weights he had lifted in the gym. As he suggested, he slowed his pace. He walked right beside her so she would not fear that he was taking her bag away. When they reached the main sidewalk where the taxies were waiting, Frank set the bag down.

"Thank you, kind sir. I'm most grateful." She handed Frank a quarter. Frank was surprised, but pleased. He realized that he could earn some money by doing this service. He tipped his hat and said, "thank you!"

"No," she said, "Thank you! I wasn't sure how I was going to manage today. Your help was appreciated."

She raised her hand toward the cab driver. The taxi driver hopped out of his parked car. He grabbed her luggage and loaded it into the trunk.

Frank looked back. More people were still walking on the long ferry dock. He noticed the same mother that he saw before, with her three children. He walked back, and offered to help her with her bags. She nodded in acceptance. He carried all three bags and she grabbed the hands of the two youngest children and told the third child to follow Frank closely. She said she had an auto and her sister was waiting for her. When they arrived on the sidewalk, she saw her sister. She stopped and reached into her purse and paid Frank

50 cents! Frank was pleased and told her how grateful he was for the generous tip. She laughed. "No, I'm the grateful one. Watching three children with my hands full was an impossible task. I'm much obliged for your help!"

Her sister walked toward them. They hugged each other and laughed, before they even started to talk.

Frank set down the remaining last bag near her and quickly walked away. He realized this experience could be a side job for him. If he helped some folks and he didn't receive a tip that would be okay; however, on days when he could receive compensation it was definitely worth a part time way of earning money.

His goal for the rest of the day was to see more sights of Manhattan. As the ferry crowd thinned out, Frank started to walk away from the dock. Today, seeing sky scrapers, museums, the library and maybe, viewing the inside of one of these huge churches, was his goal. He also needed to find a post office. He wanted to let his mom, brothers, and his friend Tommy know that he was in New York City!

Chapter Forty

Sights & Sounds of New York City 1930

Frank spent months living in Jersey City. He worked during the late night hours cleaning the club. In the early afternoons, he came to the New York Harbor and carried luggage for passengers. The waterfront was an active place. Not only were there ferries, there were huge ocean liners, going to and from Europe. Smoke and steam poured out of the boats like tea pots steaming on a stove. Tug boats pulled them out to sea away from the port and led them into the port. This spring day Frank decided to spend time walking the streets of New York, to capture the feel of the big city. There was so much to see and to do. "Busy" was the one word Frank had used to describe the area, when he wrote to his mother. Everyone seemed to be in a hurry.

Men and women dressed fancy. In the summer, some women wore large flowery hats, high heel shoes and long dresses. Other young gals wore shorter dresses, just below their knees. Frank even saw girls wearing blouses and long slacks as they skated on their roller skates down the sidewalk. Men wore white shirts, ties, black shoes and carried their briefcases.

He remembered how different the attire was during the winter, when women wore flat hats, long coats with fur collars and black boots. Men wore over-coats, fedora hats, black leather shoes, and neckties. No matter the season, men always carried briefcases.

Often men were on the streets and sidewalks selling wares and food items from carts. A mixture of food, gasoline, and dusty street smells lingered in the air. The vendors yelled out to advertise their products: "Roasted peanuts, hot dog with mustard and relish, deli sandwiches, coke a cola, canollies-they are the best, eels in the pan, get your newspapers here!"

The streets bustled with traffic. Double-decker buses, automobiles, taxi cars all hurried past one another, with no regard to which side of the road they were to use. They quickly zipped around each other, honked their horns loudly and frequently, to clear a path. Pedestrians often dangerously dodged the street traffic to cross a corner congested with vehicles.

Trotting horses and high wheeled buggies were also part of the chaotic madness. Above the road, was the El (elevated) subway. This train did circles around town avoiding accidents and giving smooth rides. From the sidewalks, the sky could barely be seen. Instead of white fluffy clouds or the bright blueness of the horizon, there were ninety-five steel silver skyscraper buildings, close together and reaching to the heavens. Often Frank leaned back and gazed upward, admiring the pointing spirals of cement. Store fronts stood side by side with cement walls touching their sides to other buildings.

Church steeples towered higher than Frank had seen before, except maybe the temple steeples in Salt Lake City. Here the church steeples mingled with the other tall skyscrapers. The Woolworth building stood 792 feet tall. This building was 60 stories and considered one of the tallest buildings in the world! Frank discovered that the architect's name for that building was Cass Gilbert and the millionaire five and dime store owner was Frank W. Woolworth, matching his own formal name, Franklin Gilbert! Frank also heard that the building had an elevator, its own water supply and electric power. He planned to go and see that place floor by floor.

Frank read the theater signs and was overwhelmed with choices of movie titles. Famous names were lit up with neon lights. Names such as: George & Gracie Allen, and Fred Astaire. Movie titles like, "Damsel in Distress" and "A Featured Newsreel." There were also flashing lit-up advertising signs, and snack signs advertised in neon

355

letters: "Coca, Cola a Cool Taste," "Spearmint Gum Steadies the Nerves." Bright colorful lights also flashed restaurant signs: "The Hollywood Restaurant, Lunch 40 cents, Supper 85 cents," "The Cotton Club."

As Frank walked past the stairways to the subway stations, he thought about the times he used this means of transportation. Riding a subway train was like being placed in a long tube. The ride reminded him of how a postal package might be airmailed from New York and zipped through the skies to San Francisco. Being in a subway train meant being transferred across town. This ride could include going in an underground, and/or an underwater tunnel. While above ground, Frank could see the double tracks and watch how fast the cars traveled. He remembered seeing a train on an adjacent track whiz by so close, it felt within touching distance of passing the one he was riding. No one could jump on or off these trains as Frank had been doing on the boxcars. These tracks were surrounded by cement walls so when Frank rode under water he didn't even realize he was underwater. All he knew was he crossed a river and he and his fellow passengers did not use a bridge.

Two places that gave Frank a peaceful rest in this busy city was St. Patrick's Church and Central Park. After walking for over two hours, he entered St. Patrick's church to rest his body. He sensed the quietness and respect that people gave to this structure. He noticed that people often stopped and made hand motions by a table near the door. Frank wondered about these gestures. A priest stood nearby so Frank asked, "Excuse me sir, may I ask you something?"

"Certainly young man, what is your question?"

"What are people doing when they stand by that table and do these hand motions?"

"Let me demonstrate and explain what this gesture means." The priest went to the table. "This is a way of prayer and also a sign of faith in believing in the trinity, that is God as the Father, Son, and Holy Ghost. This water is 'holy' because it has been blessed by a priest. A person will dip their right hand fingers into the bowl and then place their fingers on their forehead like this." The priest demonstrated. "This touch is acknowledging God as our Father, then we touch near our heart to acknowledge the Son (Jesus), then touch our left shoulder as we say Holy, and touch our right shoulder to say Ghost. Any believer can do this gesture to start and end a prayer. We as Catholics, do this also as we enter and leave our church. Are you a believer, sir?"

Frank had not been asked that question before. He hesitated. "I do believe there is a God and I figure He has protected me at times. And heaven knows I will probably need more protection in times to come."

"Do the gestures if you feel like doing so. It is one outward sign of belief and respect for God Himself and what this structure represents – a holy place."

"Thank you, sir, for your explanation," Frank did the gestures. He knew that God was not only in a holy place like this castle church that he was viewing, he also knew the Lord had been with him on his previous train journeys. Visuals came to mind of when he fell and landed on the couplers, when he rode on the train that was speeding way too fast, and when he rode on top of the boxcar over the Kinzula Viaduct. Surely, God had been with him.

He wandered down the aisle to an empty pew. There was no service going, but a choir rehearsing could be heard behind the walls of the altar. Their singing and the organ playing made the atmosphere seem peaceful. He rested and listened to the musical sounds. Tourists wandered around the church – some even used cameras to take photos of the painted glass windows, and the high ceiling, but Frank just sat still. This was the largest church he had ever seen. Many wooden pews lined the chapel. The long rows of benches looked like a setting of a large theater auditorium. The floor and doors were made of marble. High white pillars reached upward toward the arched ceilings. The artist glass stained windows were long and narrow. Numerous tall, life like, marble statues stood in various corners of the church. One statue appeared as Jesus. Everyone in the area was being quiet and respectful. He could hear their shoes tap on the marble floor, otherwise only the music could be heard.

He had heard that this church was built in 1858 and wasn't completed until 1879. There was one man with the dream of finishing this cathedral. This man's name was Archbishop John Hughes. People thought his dream was crazy. They called the idea "Hughes Folly." Frank had heard that St. Patrick's Church was the first erected building around this area. The structure took up the entire block. There were no other skyscraper buildings in the area then. No one dreamed that the big city of New York would be built around this same church. Now its steeples were competing with other high rises. Frank stayed for a half-hour sitting in the pew and looking at his surroundings. When he left the church, he felt energized to walk the mile to Central Park.

This was the other place that gave peace amid this busy city. Here was an eighty-four acre park with trees, and even sheep grazing on the grass. The paths circled around a lake with swimming ducks, a fountain spraying water and wooden park benches.

Frank often went to the park and participated in afternoon chess games and at times rented a bike to ride the paths. Today he heard music play and saw a crowd gathering to dance. It was at that moment he met Anna. "Hello, my name is Anna."

Frank turned his head to see a tall, brunette gal smiling at him. "Hi Anna, I'm Frank."

She was slightly swaying her body to the rhythm of the music. "Do you like the music?"

"Yes, I think the band sounds great and it looks like you are enjoying the sound."

"Yes, I like the idea of dancing in the park, dancing outdoors; especially on this warm sunny afternoon." Couples were gathering on the wooden stage and dancing. Frank decided to jump in, like diving into a pool. "Would you like to dance with me?"

Anna smiled, "I certainly would." He reached out for her hand and escorted her to the wooden platform. They danced several dances from slow to fast and back to slow when the band took a break. Then they sat on the park bench and finally introduced themselves. "I'm from Portland, Oregon. Where are you from?"

"I'm from St. Paul, Minnesota. Tell me, Frank, what did you do in Portland?"

Frank started with his childhood stories. He told her about playing baseball as a kid, running through the fields in Portland and even about winning a spelling contest.

She told him about living in Minnesota, about the freezing cold winters, the lowest temperatures, even colder than New York, ice skating on their front yard, and playing ice hockey on their icy driveway. Frank was just beginning to feel relaxed and hoped the band would start playing again when she told him she had to leave. She said she had to meet her parents at a nearby hotel. They were leaving New York the next day.

Frank sighed, many times he'd meet someone in New York and they would admit they were only tourists, there for a couple days, or leaving on the next train or plane. Anna and Frank shook hands, smiled and said good-bye.

Frank left Central Park. Even though Anna had left quickly, it was fun to dance with someone and to enjoy his day in the big city. He felt energized and connected to his surroundings. There was something about New York that was like a magnet pulling him to stay. Maybe, he would figure it out if and when he met his grandparents. Yes, he would try to find his grandparents who lived in Long Island. This plan would not happen today, but seeing his relatives was his goal for his next adventure.

As he neared the water front, the night turned dark and cool. He caught a ferry for his return to Jersey City.

Chapter Forty-One

Long Island, New York Summer 1931

Even though Frank worked most of the night cleaning up the club and the dining area, he woke up early. He had plans for the day. This was the day he planned to meet his grandparents.

His mother had given him their address. Yet, she did not share any other information. Frank did not know any details or family history. He could only surmise that when his mother left home, at the age of nineteen and married his father, there was conflict between her and her parents. Evidently, it was not a time of blessings and fond farewells. Was it his mother who would not reach out to her parents, or were the parents not willing to communicate with their daughter again? Distance and time apart had a major impact on this relationship. Still, Frank was nineteen now and old enough to search for the truth on his own.

He took the early morning subway from Jersey City to Manhattan. In Manhattan he went to the huge Penn Station. While there he got train schedules (for future reference – he always wanted train schedules.) For today's venture he also got bus information.

He discovered for 25 cents he could take a bus from Manhattan to Queens Valley, to Amityville, to Bay Shore, and to Sayville. The ride, including stops along the way, would take up to 2 hours and 42 minutes.

As he wandered the neighborhood streets of Sayville, thinking he was near the exact address, he heard a voice, "Who are you looking for?"

Frank looked at the neighboring house. A tall man was standing on his porch staring at Frank. "I'm looking for the Benjamin Family."

"Well, you're standing in the right place, right in front of their home."

"Really?" Frank took a second look. The house was white with a large front porch. Whicker chairs were on the porch and a swing was hanging from the rafters. This was a two-story house with a white garage in the back of a long driveway. The home looked inviting and comfortable with thick green grass and a flower bed by the walkway to the porch.

"Yes, they live here, but they are out of town. I'm kind of watching the place while they are gone. You know, picking up the mail and watering the plants. Are you related to them?"

"Yeah, I guess I'm their grandson."

"Interesting, you guess you are their grandson? Where are you from boy?"

"I'm from Portland, Oregon."

"Wow, that's a long way from home. Gilbert and Ella will be back, but it will be in a couple weeks. Come back in two weeks."

Frank was slow to answer. He was shocked that his Grandpa's name was Gilbert. That was his formal birth name. His mother never told him that her father's name was Gilbert. She only told him her maiden name was Benjamin. Frank was pleased that he was named after his grandfather. His mother must have respected her father.

"Can you tell me anymore? I really know little about them. My real name is Gilbert too; Gilbert Franklin Rose."

The neighbor came closer and shook Frank's hand. "Glad to meet you Gilbert."

"Really, I go by Frank now."

"Okay, Frank, I'm Sam. Gilbert and Ella are good people. Come sit on my porch a while. At least we can chat some before you head back."

"Okay, thanks."

He and the neighbor sat on the porch. Sam offered Frank a glass of lemonade and a plate of cookies. Frank learned he had uncles: Norman, Louis, Ralph, Walter and an aunt named Anna. Frank's brother was Louis. Maybe that name (his brother's name) was in honor of his uncle. Sam wrote out their names and gave Frank Norman's address. He suggested Frank visit his Uncle Norman. "They all live in Sayville."

Frank repeated the name, "Sayville."

"Yeah, Sayville. Years ago when they were deciding what to name this area they selected the name Seaview, but the guy that sent the information to the post office didn't know much about spelling. The story goes that he misspelled Seaview and spelled Sayville instead. Then when the town's people tried to change the name they got a letter back from the head postal service saying that there were too many towns called Seaview, so they had to keep Sayville. I think now the people like the name Sayville. We don't get confused with the other similar town names."

Frank and Sam laughed and shared more stories about Sayville. Also, Frank shared a few observations about Portland and how it was a growing waterfront town. Then he thanked Sam and headed back to the bus stop.

He promised himself that he would come back again. He truly wanted to meet his grandparents, his uncles and his one aunt. He visualized sitting on one of their porches while sipping a drink and eating cookies. He thought about long visits of chatter, laughter and creating memories of family history. Yes, he figured the day would come…

Chapter Forty-Two

Still in New York 1932 Age Twenty

"Hey, you!" Frank stopped walking and looked around. Two police officers, in long coats with guns in their leather holsters, looked directly at Frank. Frank could feel his heart beating faster than normal. He had committed no criminal act; he hadn't even been in a fight lately, so why were they coming close to him in an authoritative manner?

"Are you carrying identification, a driver's license to prove who you are?"

"No," answered Frank. "I don't own a car so I have yet to get a license."

"You have proof of where you are living – a rental receipt or a house payment slip or any such proof?"

"No," answered Frank.

"Where are you residing?"

"I'm working and staying at the Dewey/Kennedy Club in Jersey City."

"Jersey City?"

"Yes, Jersey City."

The officers looked at one another and nodded.

Frank offered more information. "You could call there. They would verify I'm really staying there."

"Who would you suggest we call Mr. Dewey or Mr. Kennedy?"

"No, sir, but a member by the name of Robert, knows I've been staying there. He was the one that helped me to get employment at the club."

"Does this 'Robert' have a last name?"

Frank realized he never asked for Robert's last name. Silence.

"Jersey City is basically out of our jurisdiction; however, all cities and states are investigating this crime scene."

"What crime scene?"

"The Lindberg kidnapping!"

"The what? Has Lindberg been kidnapped?"

"Sounds like you don't read the news either. No, Charles Lindberg's kid has been kidnapped from their home, which happens to be near Jersey City."

The officers moved closer to Frank and then both of them pushed against him, turned him around, pulled his arms back and snapped handcuffs over his wrists.

Frank didn't try to fight, but he argued. "Wait, you've got the wrong guy. I've never kidnapped anyone. I've got a clean record. I haven't committed any crimes."

"We didn't say you did. We're just taking you in for questioning."

"You already questioned me and I was truthful."

"Yeah, maybe, but we'll do more questioning at the station."

They walked to the end of the block, an officer on each side of him. A large flat-bed truck was parked at the corner. Other officers were sitting on wooden benches in the back open aired truck. The vehicle looked like a fire truck, but it had written on the side the letters: 'New York Police.'

Frank had seen these police transports going up and down the streets of New York, always with several officers. He never imagined he'd be riding in one of these mobiles. They put on the loud siren, and zipped quickly around autos, buses, and taxies.

The whole situation was unbelievable to Frank. Did they think he was a dangerous criminal that needed to be quickly hauled off to jail? He wished he had worn Robert's pants today, and he wished he had bought a longer business looking coat, as other men were wearing, and a Derby hat as the stock brokers wore. Maybe, if he wore business-like attire they would not have questioned him. Now he didn't know what to do. Even if they granted him one phone call he wasn't sure who he would call. He didn't have phone numbers with him. His family (mother and brothers) wouldn't come to New York to bail him out. They could not afford to do that, nor would he want them to know about this predicament.

They arrived at the station house and escorted him into the front office. One of the officers undid his handcuffs. Frank had to take off his jacket, empty his pockets, take off his boots, and hand over his coins and dollar bills. Then they escorted him to a cell. The cell had iron bars on the swinging door, gray steel walls, and a gray cement hard floor. Inside the cell were two cots and mattresses, and one toilet against the back wall. Frank hesitated. One officer gave him a slight push into the cell, and slammed the cell door.

"Now what? When do you guys ask me more questions and find out the truth that I've got a clean record and haven't committed any crime?"

"We will be questioning you more later. We'll let you know when."

Frank sat on the cot. He didn't even have his jacket or boots. He wanted to request for his jacket to use as a blanket or pillow if he had to spend the night. Surely, they would figure it out that he wasn't the man they were looking for.

When did this crime happen? How did it happen? Why haven't they got the devil that did this horrendous act? How old was this kid? All these details Frank didn't know. There was a story about Lindberg. Frank heard a news boy yelling the Lindberg name. He figured it was all about another famous flight by Lindberg, not a terrible story about his child.

Frank felt extremely restless and somewhat claustrophobic. He heard sounds in the distance: prisoners yelling, officers walking the halls with heavy boots, even traffic noises from outside. He felt like he was placed in an area where no other prisoners were near.

He couldn't believe that he was thinking and referring to himself as a fellow prisoner. He had committed no crime so why was he here in New York in a single locked up cell?

The afternoon hours went slowly by. Dinner time was near. Frank heard the sound of heavy boots coming near the cell. Surely, they had figured out their mistake, will apologize (or not), and let him out.

An officer carried a tray of food. "Stand back against the wall," he yelled at Frank. Frank moved against the wall. The man unlocked the heavy iron bar door. He placed the tray on the cot. "Eat, and when you are through, slide the tray under the door." He left and slammed the iron door behind him.

"Wait," called Frank. "Have you heard if I'll be released? Did they call and find out that I really have been staying at the Dewey/

Kennedy Club? And could I get my jacket back – for a pillow or something?"

The officer walked away not answering any of Frank's questions. Frank looked at the tray. It had some sort of meat, white mashed potatoes with no butter, one piece of bread, and a cup of water and one napkin. Frank looked at this free meal. He didn't want even one bite. He sat on the cot and bent low, cupping his hands around his face while rocking back and forth, trying to comfort himself. He felt like a child that needed rocking: rocking from his mother or a father who would say, "it's okay, you are innocent, you did no wrong, and no one can punish you for doing no wrong."

After several minutes of this rocking motion, he came back to reality. He had better eat. The situation appeared that he would be locked up all night. He didn't want to lose strength. He needed to be strong, determined and ready to leave when they said he was released. He ate the dinner, drank the cup of water, and slid the tray under the door. When someone, anyone, came back for the tray, he would again ask for his jacket.

Early the next morning, Frank woke up hearing banging noises. At first he could not remember where he was. Then he felt the shock again that he was in a jail cell. His tray, that was under the door, was gone. He had missed the opportunity to talk to anyone. He wondered if he had missed breakfast too.

He yelled, "Hey, anyone around? Anyone? Can you hear me?"

"Yeah, we hear you. Shut up. No one wants to wake up this early."

"What time is it?"

"It's 7:30. Shut up till breakfast comes."

"What time will that be?"

Frank didn't receive an answer only another command. "Shut your trap until then!"

Frank sat on the bunk and listed in his mind all he planned to do when he was released. He may have lost his trustworthiness by not cleaning up the club last night- he'd probably have to find another place to stay. He would try for a higher paying job, and find a decent place to rent. He loved New York; at least he loved New York up until yesterday. Now he wanted to be anyplace other than where he was.

This time a man dressed in a green shirt and khaki pants came to the door and ordered him to stand against the wall. Frank moved back and quickly asked his questions.

"Is there a place to wash up in here? Do I get my jacket back? Has anyone called the Dewey/Kennedy Club to verify my character and whereabouts?"

"Sir," the worker actually stopped in the cell and looked at Frank. Then in a calm voice he answered Frank's questions one at a time. "We have wash-up time at 11:00 a.m. every other day. This jail has been remodeled. We have new sinks, tin tubs and some shower stalls. You'll be able to wash up at 11:00. I can bring your jacket to you before this evening, as I leave my shift. I don't know about the phone call, but I'll check. Enjoy your breakfast." He walked out and shut the door.

Frank felt somewhat comforted to meet a nice worker that didn't fear him and treated him like a fellow honest man. Frank sat on the cot and ate cold scrambled eggs, with a piece of dry toast, drank the cream-less, sugarless coffee. He slid the tray under the door.

Five long days and five long nights went by. Frank was still alone in the cell. Close to 3:00 p.m. Frank got a visitor. Not a guest to see him, but another arrested man to share his cell. At first, he was overly concerned. Frank wasn't sure if this situation was a blessing or a curse. The cell was small, not roomy enough for two men. This meant getting along with a stranger in a small space.

Surprisingly, in a matter of minutes Frank realized the bum looking older man that was shoved into his cell actually had a familiar face. After the stranger had tossed his hair back off his face, and rubbed his beard, Frank realized his roommate was the man who robbed him months ago on one of his last train rides.

"Well, what do you know? Evidently you didn't get with your family in Pennsylvania."

Jim looked at Frank. He walked backward against the wall.

"Don't worry I'm not going to beat you up – though you probably deserve a good thrashing. What did they get on you?"

Jim relaxed. "Oh, the usual. I swiped some food off some grocery carts. You know a man has gotta eat."

Frank smiled, "Yeah, we gotta eat." He pointed to the empty cot. "Well, sit down and make yourself comfortable."

Jim looked at Frank. "What did they get you for?"

"They got me as a suspect for the kidnapping of Lindberg's kid."

"His baby?"

Frank was surprised to hear that the crime was of a baby kidnapping. "Yeah, his baby."

"I could testify you wouldn't do that. You're a decent guy. I know a decent hobo when I meet one and you're a decent hobo."

"Well, that's great, but they don't know I'm a hobo. Your testimony would probably not do me a bit of good, so pretend we just met."

"Okay, if that's what you want."

Jim dug down into the cuff of his pants. He pulled out a deck of cards. "Want to play some poker?"

Frank raised his eyebrows and smiled in a pleasant, surprised expression.

"You got a deck? How come? They took everything that was in my pockets."

"Oh, they did the same with my stuff. I didn't have a deck of cards. These were on the sergeant's messy desk under a pile of papers."

"You stole them!"

Jim started to shuffle the cards, like an expert card player. He sat on the edge of the cot. "I borrowed them. Want to play?"

"Sure." Frank nodded. Time passed quickly as they owed each other imaginary coins and dollars.

On the fifteenth day of confinement, two officers came to the cell door. "Both of you stand back against the wall." Both men did as they were told. "One of you brought Cooties into this jail. We don't like Cooties. We had a nice clean place, now you guys messed it up. You are going to the shower rooms, take off your clothes and leave them on the floor. Then you will soak in the tubs and you will shave. You will be given green night gowns tonight, and be placed in a different cell. We have to fumigate this one. Tomorrow you will get your own disinfected clothes back. We don't want you here anymore."

The officers never cracked a smile or demonstrated an ounce of kindness. They acted like telling them they would be released the next day was like giving a mean, firm order. Really it was a jubilant message. When they arrived at the shower room, Jim insisted on using a private toilet area. He was granted permission. Frank figured Jim had to dispose of the deck of cards somehow.

When they finally got into a different cell for the night, they danced around the space, laughed and hugged each other. Frank said, "I don't think I ever had cooties."

"I don't think I did either," said Jim.

"Probably you," said Frank. "You looked like you just got off the train when you arrived."

'True, but you weren't looking much better: thin, scrawny, long hair, not shaven for days. Actually, I'd bet it was you. You got to admit you were looking bad."

Frank nodded. He really didn't know how he was looking. He hadn't seen a mirror for two weeks.

Early the next morning before their breakfast arrived, they were handed their clean clothes, boots, jackets and even their money. They were told to "get lost!"

As they neared the front desk, Frank noticed the deck of cards barely visible under a pile of papers on the sergeant's desk. Jim was good; maybe he should keep his profession of stealing.

Outside, Jim and Frank shook hands and parted ways. Frank wasn't sure where to head next. Maybe, it would be a ride on a boxcar.

Chapter Forty-Three

Leaving New York City 1933
Age Twenty-One

Frank had a premonition that something might go wrong. He shrugged his shoulders in disbelief. Life had already gone wrong. He had spent two weeks in jail – how could life get any worse? He chuckled; riding in a boxcar full of hobos wasn't as bad as being locked up in a small cell with one thief, and no hope of release.

After being released from jail, he went back to the Dewey/ Kennedy Club. Robert told him he had lost his work position, and his place to stay. They had to hire another man while Frank was gone. He was near broke spending his last remaining money staying in hotels.

He searched for work, but even though New York City was a busy place, many people were without income. Since 1932, New York City had changed. Central Park was not the beautiful green scenic oasis that Frank knew. Many people now were destitute either from stocks collapsing and banks closing, or from losing farm lands due to the dust storm conditions. They came to New York from other states looking for hope.

For months individual folks and families were making camps in Central Park. They called the area 'Hooverville' because they didn't feel former President Hoover did them right. They felt the working class needed help. Government aide was not available.

In March 1933 President Franklin Roosevelt became the new president. He promised major changes. Frank noticed the beginning of these changes. Hooverville, in the park area, was being cleaned up. Still there were long food lines and jobs were scarce. Future promises were being made. There was hope for jobs and improved conditions. Yet, between Frank's changing circumstances and the city's struggles, Frank's previous longing to stay had changed. He knew the time now was to head back home

He jumped on a train that would take him from New York City to Chicago. He was surprised, but not really concerned that the car was crowded with hobos. The ride was uncomfortable. All the men were crowded together in the boxcars. The day was hot and humid.

As the train neared the Chicago station, they heard the call, "Water, there's water!" All the men moved quickly. The train kept moving, but they leaped off one by one. Frank was ready to jump off the moving train too. He slithered between the men to the doorway. Then he felt resistance, something was holding him back. A metal clip hanging on the doorway caught his overall strap. He pushed forward, ready to leap. He hesitated before he jumped. He felt the tearing of his overall bib. These seconds of delay hindered his movement. Knowing he had to leap away from the train wheels, he gave himself an extra push of momentum.

As his feet hit the ground, he tripped. He fell forward, and landed with his face in the dirt. Only semiconscious of his surroundings, his body was limp and not moving. He heard a repeated yell. "Move your legs, man, pull your legs in!" The loud roar of the engine echoed in his ears as the warning voice shouted one last time, "For God's sake, move your legs!" He heard a blasting train whistle. Something was on the tracks. Where was he and who was yelling? Think, Frank, think!

After moments of dangerous hesitation, he came to his senses. His landing wasn't on the track where he had jumped from, instead, he landed on adjacent tracks, and another oncoming train was headed directly at him. The train whistle blared again. Reality! He jerked his legs off the rails and slid his body back away from the track just seconds before the train passed. The noise was deafening. He held his knees close to his body, still protecting himself from the nearness of the passing train. A gust of dusty air blew at him like a strong gale of wind. Despite the dangerous situation he was in, he was safe!

He checked his body as the train passed. He was not injured; he felt no pain. Sitting upright, he breathed a sigh of relief. He stood on the adjacent tracks, stepped off the tracks and slowly walked along the dirt to the flowing water stream. Men had gathered there to get water. One of these men had been the one that had yelled at him. One of these men had saved his life and/or at least saved his legs and feet from being mangled by the moving train. No one looked directly at him. He could not begin to guess which man was his hero. He whispered a prayer of thanks. Cupping and dipping his hands into the water he took gulps of drinks and splashed water around his face and arms to cool off. He would get back on the next train and head to Portland.

Chapter Forty-Four

North Dakota to Montana-Heading Home

Frank knew what it was like to go to bed hungry and then to wake up in the morning still hungry. Often Mr. Steward would punish the boys by sending them off to bed with no dinner. The discomfort of stomach aching pain, was familiar to Frank.

So when he had his own freedom, while riding the boxcars, he quickly learned that in order to prevent hunger cravings he had to always eat before he went to bed, and be prepared to have some money for a meal in the morning. His goal was to not go to bed hungry and not to wake up without means of getting a breakfast.

Now he was traveling through the plains of North Dakota heading back home. Not only was he without funds, it seemed the whole nation was devastated. He saw farm lands that were empty. Farm equipment sat still on deserted properties. Many plots of land were not plowed or green, but gray with sand from previous dust storms. He rode among a large group of hobos that were traveling place to place, going somewhere hoping for help. Sometimes families rode inside the boxcars. If the hobos noticed the families, they would let the family have the boxcar to themselves. Frank had heard that many families were headed to California.

On this boxcar, Frank had spoken to a young kid, who said his name was "Slim." Frank figured his name fit his appearance as he was as tall as Frank, only much thinner. The kid admitted he was seventeen and he had run away from home. They had lost his dad when he was ten. His mom was the only one bringing in money for the family. Two younger brothers were still at home. He knew they were about to lose their house, so Slim decided to seek work. So far, he had earned five dollars. He confessed that money was spent days ago. He also said he hadn't eaten for three days.

It was early morning, when the train slowed down in the middle of Montana. Frank realized he had to help. Somehow, he had to feed himself and this kid. "I know a place where we can eat. Let's jump off the car right when it gets near this upcoming town." Slim agreed, he grabbed his knapsack and got ready to leap off the train. The train slowed down. They both jumped off.

The day was hot. Frank knew about this area, from passing through this town before. They walked over a mile to a small town. Frank noted the street name and found the café he was looking for. Sweating and feeling weak they walked into the "Pit Stop Café." They were the only customers.

The place seemed empty and quiet, but they could hear rustling noises in the kitchen. Someone moved the pots and pans. Frank sat on the counter bar stool and the kid sat beside him.

When the cook came to the counter, he took one look at Frank and said, "Hey, I remember you. You were here a year ago. Are you still hopping on those boxcars?"

"Yeah," said Frank.

"Ain't it time to land somewhere?"

"That's exactly what I plan on doing. I'm heading back home. On the way I met this kid here, and dog-gone it, we're hungry."

"Well, I can solve that problem. I've got plenty of grub here. No workers today, except me, but I can do it all. It's too darn hot today for customers. Actually, I'm surprised that you two made it from the railroad tracks. There's a water pump outback. Why don't you freshen up and when you come back in I'll have pancakes and bacon for you. Does that sound okay?"

Frank smiled, "That's sounds more than generous."

Frank and Slim went to the water pump and poured water over themselves. The water spray alone gave them some energy.

The food came. The cook stood by and watched Frank and Slim as they eagerly shoveled the food into their mouths.

"Hey, guys, slow down. Enjoy the food. No point hurrying. I won't shut this place down."

Frank agreed. He didn't want to feel sick from eating too fast. "Yeah Slim, let's slow down and enjoy this meal."

Then the long conversation began. Al, the cook, was glad to have company. "Have you seen the devastation of the farm lands? Can't believe what is going on. People losing their land, heard tell some are heading to Alaska – free land up there. Not so much for the Montana people – I hear tell they are giving free land to people that come from the cold states, like Minnesota, North Dakota and Wisconsin. I guess they figure if you survive there you can survive in Alaska. Haven't been to Alaska, but I hear tell it's colder than Minnesota and I know it's freezing there."

Frank listened as he continued to gulp his food. He knew they had to leave soon, walk back to the tracks and catch the next passing train. Plus he had to figure out a way to get out of the restaurant without paying. The cook was a heavy–set guy. He could turn on Frank and get him and the kid arrested if he was desperate for his pay. Frank could not let this happen. "I think I could use another round of those flapjacks. You got any more of that pancake batter?"

"Sure, you want more?" Al had already been generous with the order, but he also noticed how hungry they both appeared to be.
"Yeah, I sure do and a couple more bacon pieces too." Then he looked at Slim. "You want more too?"

"Guess so" said Slim, if that is okay?"

As the cook headed back to the kitchen, Frank yelled, "more for the kid too." The cook was whistling "Oh Suzanna" as he stood by the iron plate stove. The bacon sizzled. Frank turned to Slim. "I'm leaving now – I don't have any money to pay for this meal. You can leave with me, or stay here and talk your way out of this."

The kid looked at Frank in disbelief. He really thought Frank had the money to pay. Frank stood up and headed for the door. The kid grabbed his knapsack and followed. As they opened the door, a bell on the door rang. The cook didn't notice at first. Frank and the kid were a good 50 feet away, going as fast as they could when they heard the cook yell, "Hey, aren't you gonna pay for your meals?"

Just as they got near the tracks, a train came. First Frank, and then Slim grabbed the side rail and hopped aboard. They sat down on the side of the car with the least number of hobos. The kid was still panting. Frank was panting too, "Well, you feel better? Did that meal satisfy you?"

"I don't know. My stomach feels so nervous now. I don't know if I feel worse or better with, or without hunger pains." Frank's answer to the kid was "Well, a man has gotta eat!"

Chapter Forty-Five

Montana to Spokane, Washington

Frank arrived in Spokane. He was broke, dirty and hungry. First, he went to the river bank and washed up as best as he could. He had a bar of soap, one item he always carried with him. After drying off in the sun, he ran his fingers through his hair. Using dry leaves, he brushed the dirt off his boots. With confidence, he walked to the Davenport Hotel. He didn't want to infringe on his friends, but he was desperate.

As soon as he walked in the doorway, he noticed extreme differences from when he had been here before. Instead of the lobby being a busy place, there were no guests sitting on chairs visiting, the fire was not lit in the fireplace, and the area seemed ghostly quiet. He went to the front desk and asked if he could speak to James, the bellboy.

The desk clerk appeared somewhat taken aback, "You mean James, the manager?"

Frank wasn't surprised that James had gone up in status. "Yes, I guess, that is exactly whom I'd like to speak with."

"Well sir, he is in a meeting right now, but if you would like to wait, in the bar room, I could direct him there when he is finished with his meeting."

"You have any idea how long that meeting will take?"

"I'd guess probably about a half-hour."

"Okay, please let him know that Frank, the hobo showed up. I'll be in the bar room."

Frank sat on one of the leather bar stools. The huge room was nearly empty. One couple was seated at one of the dining tables and two other males sat at the counter. The waiter came to take Frank's order. He recognized Frank immediately. "Frank, what brings you back this way?"

Frank remembered the waiter and realized he never did catch his name. "Remind me your name?"

"I'm Matt." They shook hands.

Frank answered his question, "I'm heading back home."

"I heard that story – let me think… back in 1928. You were heading back home then."

"Yeah, well, I did make it home, but then I left and I've been across the United States since then. Now I'm heading back home again."

"You hungry, Frank?"

"I'm starving, but I'm also broke."

"Well, I've got food, so tell me your order." He handed Frank a menu. Frank looked at the cheapest prices.

"Anything you want, don't worry about prices."

Frank laid down the menu and looked at Matt. "Before I order, I want you to know I've paid all my debts during these years. I've had work. On this last trip, I now owe for two meals in Montana, and if I eat here I will owe this meal. I will pay it back. I have no intentions of leaving IOU's unpaid!"

"I believe you Frank. I'll decide your meal. Just stay put."

Matt went back into the kitchen. The day was young. Frank figured he'd be served a hearty breakfast with coffee and orange juice. Within ten minutes, he was right.

Matt served the food and sat on the bar stool next to him. He wanted to hear all about Frank's travels. So as Frank ate slowly enjoying each bite and letting his stomach digest the food, he told his stories. The tale started with the sights of San Francisco, to the towering temples in Utah. He talked about his ride over the Kinzula Viaduct and the beauty of the Allegheny National Forest. In detail, he described the many buildings and skyscrapers of New York.

He did not tell about his days in jail, or the disappointment of leaving New York without visiting his relatives. Neither did he talk about the downturn of the city with Hooverville Villages, nor the deserted farm lands across the prairie states.

Matt told Frank about James' promotion, but how the depression kept the hotel at a standstill. There had been no improvements and few overnight guests. He explained, "...the results are vacant rooms, wasted food and continuous meetings of how to improve conditions and rise above these depression days. If Franklin Delano Roosevelt does what he is promising maybe there will be hope and changes."

As they were lamenting on sad, worrisome current conditions, James walked into the room. He too greeted Frank warmly and immediately offered him a room for the night. Frank accepted the offer with the condition of repaying with funds that would be mailed back.

That night, Frank slept comfortably in a warm room. He dreamt about trains. The vision included many trains in long lines with open doors enticing hobos to ride. He saw himself going from car to car, not being satisfied, and not climbing aboard. In the middle of the night, he woke up frustrated like he needed to go somewhere, but how and where? These were troubling questions. He fell back to sleep.

When he awoke the second time, he was ready to leave. Matt had given him a bag of muffins, a couple bananas and a bottle of apple juice. He left the hotel with his food bag and caught a train heading southwest.

As he jumped aboard into an open boxcar, filled with many hobos, the realization hit him; this could be his last train ride. At least, the last time he would hop on and hop off a boxcar. Maybe, the last time he would witness a group of men huddled in a corner of a boxcar trying to keep warm from the morning dew and mist. He wanted to capture all that he was sensing.

The boxcar smelled like wood and the lingering smells from being a previous cattle hauling boxcar. There was also the odor of men, a mixture of cigar smoke and the smoke from the steam engine. The sounds were a continuous drowning rhythm of the clickety clack, clickety, clack of the train wheels. The loud bells rang and the long whistle sounds echoed when they neared the intersections.

He wanted to intently observe the views as if he had never seen them before. In his mind, he wanted to compare the view of Washington and Oregon to the beauty of the Allegheny Mountains, and to compare the land of the Northwest to the flat prairie. He remembered the plains when they held the beauty of growing crops, but on this last trip he only witnessed the scene of desolation from the dust storms.

As the train traveled, Frank was wide-eyed gazing at the sights. These views were common for him; he grew up in the Northwest; however, now each view was a sight from an open boxcar doorway and that was what he wanted to remember. The view moved quickly; some were views of tall green grass blowing in the wind, other places were scenes of golden, dry grass. Cliffs stood tall with wide waterfalls flowing downward on the rocks. He noticed a rainbow crossing one of the waterfalls. The colors glistened in the sunlight. Green monstrous fir trees grew right on the rocky hillsides, as if they didn't need fertile soil, only a space to reach the sky. The blue of the lakes and rivers, maybe not as long as the Mississippi, were still impressive. The sky and clouds above could be seen, as there were no skyscrapers hindering the view. He whispered to himself, 'remember Frank what this is like to feel the breeze hitting your face and seeing the countryside, not through a window pane, but right here on the ground speeding down the railroad tracks.'

When he arrived in Portland, he rode across the bridge and then, as he did before, he hopped off the train, and walked the sidewalks to his mother's place. He visualized his mother and then later his brothers welcoming him. This time he didn't tell them the day or time he would arrive, they will be surprised. He was anxious to see his family again.

*****

"Mom, I'm home!"

"Frank, Frank Gilbert is that you?" Mary threw off her apron and ran the few paces from the kitchen to the living room. In her haste, she knocked over a table lamp – that Frank caught just as it was about to hit the floor.

She ran into his arms. "Goodness, gracious, I would have baked a cake, had I known you were coming.

Oh, my precious boy. I cannot believe you are really here!"

"Yeah mom, I'm really, really home. I'm tired, hungry and sorry to say…broke."

"Well, don't worry son. You are home. We can change all that." They hugged again.

Mary fussed with her hair, wishing she was more presentable. "Right now I'm fixing dinner. I will add another potato. Use your

385

room; it is still available just for you. We'll eat and then we will talk."

Frank kissed her on her cheek and headed toward the bedroom. There was a sense of comfort of returning home.

Chapter Forty-Six

Portland, Oregon

"There's a dance tonight at the Crystal Ballroom." Lou mumbled this information, as he glanced at the sports page. Frank sat across from him on his mother's davenport. He was reading the headlines of The Journal Newspaper.

Frank laid the paper down. "So?"

"So, let's go and meet some gals."

"Really, you are going to the Crystal Ballroom to dance? Isn't that the same building called the Cotillion Hall?"

"Yeah, that's the place, only now it is called the Crystal Ballroom. They usually do square dancing, but tonight there will be a real band playing. They have a mechanical floating dance floor. It actually has a bounce to it. They say it is like 'dancing on clouds'."

Frank eyed Lou, "And you know how to dance?"

"Yeah, I've been practicing." Lou stood up and showed off his dancing skills. He danced around the room doing the quick steps of the jitterbug and raised his arm pretending to twirl a girl around.

Frank was impressed. He knew Lou was into sports, especially golf, but he never saw his brother dance before, with or without a partner. Frank sighed, "I don't know. Doesn't the Crystal Ballroom require a suit, tie and all that jazz?"

"If you can dance with your boots on, then all you need is a clean shirt, and a bow tie." Lou reached into his pocket, pulled out a bow tie, and threw it toward him. Frank caught the black tie. Lou continued his plea, "Don't worry about a suit jacket, they take your jacket at the main door. All you really need is a clean shirt and wear black pants."

Lou grabbed his overcoat. He was ready to leave. "I'll be back around 7:30 to pick you up."

Frank hesitated, "You know what… I think I'll ride my bike there. I need some exercise."

Lou stopped. "Okay, brother, but pack a clean shirt."

"Don't worry, I'll clean up."

Lou raised his eyebrows in disbelief and headed out the door. "I'll see you there!"

Frank was amazed as he walked into the huge brick building. The ceiling was high and the side windows were huge. He took an elevator up to the dance floor. He could hear the lively band music and the chatter of the crowd of people. Chandeliers hung from the ceiling. A gal at the front desk smiled, "Your coat/jacket, sir, and your cap?"

"Oh, yes," He reluctantly took off his jacket, cap, and handed them to her. He started to walk away. "Sir, you will need a ticket to get your items back."

"Oh, yes, thank you." Frank felt bewildered by the whole situation. The music was loud with a fast swing rhythm. He felt like he should head back home. He hid his bike, behind some garbage pails, but now he worried about that decision. He felt edgy until he saw her across the room. She was about 5'7", with light brown hair, and was rather thin. Her dress was slightly short, below her knees, and swayed back and forth. Her black heel shoes kept rhythm with the music. Continuously laughing, she appeared to be enjoying the rhythmic sounds.

She danced the Charleston steps with a couple surrounding gals. They were kicking their legs, moving their feet backward and forward, and clapping their hands to the beat of the music. This was a faster dance than Frank wanted to do. He'd have to wait for a slower song. He stood against the wall watching her sway, listening to her laughter, and felt a connection. There was a crowd of people mingling, dancing, and sitting at tables, but Frank kept his eyes only on this one gal. He waited through three dances before a slow piece played.

He figured she might be ready to sit down, have a drink, and relax. Yet he stood beside her and asked, "Will you dance with me?"

She hesitated, smiled, and took his hand. They danced three songs – to a slow beat and used slow steps. A lady singer came on stage on the third song. As they waltzed, Frank listened to the words: "We strolled the lane together, laughed at the rain together..." Frank felt like he wanted to be "together" with this gal forever. The sensation was strange since he hadn't even talked to her yet.

As the music suddenly changed to a faster tempo, she suggested they sit down and talk. The conversation continued until midnight. She shared her life story of marrying young, traveling across the United States via car and train, as part of her work in sales. She hesitated. "I have a daughter; she is now seven years old." Frank was silent. So she continued. "While I work, she stays with my aunt. My aunt takes care of her, by her I mean my daughter, Susan. You see my husband died two years ago, from a heart attack. It meant I had to work and support myself and Susan."

Frank understood this situation. He remembered how his mother had to board out her three sons and go to work. He nodded his head. He took her hand and looked directly into her eyes. "It is wonderful that you have a daughter. I'm sure she is the joy of your life." She sighed and smiled!

He talked about his previous work at the meat plant, and about traveling across the United States via car to California, and by trains too, but not as a paying passenger.

At midnight Frank saw Lou. Lou was with a gal and they were leaving. He waved and Frank waved back. Frank lingered longer still visiting with his new friend. They had shared many story experiences, yet they hadn't introduced themselves, name wise. Frank heard her name when another gentleman came to the table. "Pearl, can I escort you home this evening?"

The man was tall, dark haired and fairly good-looking. He appeared somewhat tipsy. Frank stood up. "I can take you home Pearl." She answered him, "I'd appreciate that…" She paused, and slightly laughed realizing she still didn't know his name. Frank nodded and quietly said his name, "Frank."

She took his hand, "Yes, you may take me home, Frank."

The other gentleman shook his head and left the table. Frank suddenly realized he had offered to take her home, but he only had his bike, and he had no idea where she was living.

"I'm staying at the Benson Hotel, I work there and they have living quarters for their maids – so I stay there."

Frank was relieved; the Benson Hotel was less than a mile away. He figured this would work out. They got their wraps from the counter, and went outside. "Where did you park?" she innocently asked.

"Well, I parked my bike behind some garbage pails at the end of the block."

"Your bike?"

"Yes, it is a new bike – you'll like it." Her reply was only a laugh. "Wait here for only a moment." Quickly he retrieved his bike. He placed his jacket over the handlebars and then before she could protest, he carefully lifted her onto the handlebars.

"Comfortable?" he asked.

"Amazingly, it's okay," Frank placed his foot on the one pedal, and swung his leg over the seat. They rode near the curb of the dark streets of Burnside, and then right by the movie theater lights on Broadway. He rode the bike directly to the front door of the Benson Hotel. "May I call on you sometime? Sometime, soon?"

"Yes," she smiled. "Just call the Benson Hotel, after five. They will call me to the phone."

"I'll do that. By the way, my name is Frank Rose."

"And I am Pearl Yambert."

"I'll be calling you, Pearl"

Chapter Forty-Seven

Portland & Seaside, Oregon 1933
Age Twenty-One

Pearl anxiously waited for Frank's arrival. They had dated several times and this time she had something special in mind. He greeted her in the lobby of the Benson Hotel, by the fireplace. She was anxious to tell him her idea. "This Saturday, let's take a train ride to Seaside, an afternoon at the beach!"

"You mean as a passenger?"

"Yes, of course, how else?"

"Well," Frank laughed. "I've never been... a ....well...a real passenger, before, really."

Pearl wasn't sure what he meant, though she knew he had been a hobo, she didn't really know or understand the way of the hobos.

She slowly explained, "Well, it's easy. I'll buy us the tickets and meet you at the depot. Saturday morning the train leaves at ten. Dress casual. We will enjoy a day at the beach. You can meet my daughter Susan, she has been staying at my aunt's place, but she will be with me this weekend."

"Okay, yes, okay. Are we still on for dinner out tonight?"

"Yes, definitely!" They hugged and left the lobby of the Benson Hotel for a downtown evening of dinner and dancing.

On Saturday at Seaside beach there was a slight breeze and the air smelled fresh. Many folks walked along the promenade. Bicyclists weaved around the autos on the road, and a few rode on the wooden sidewalk boards around the slow paced pedestrians. The area was busy with people enjoying a sunny day at the seashore.

Susan walked between Pearl and Frank. She looked up at Frank.

"I'm Susan." She held up seven fingers.

"Yes Susan, and are you showing me that you are seven years old?"

"Yes," Susan pointed at each finger and counted them slowly, "one, two, three, four, five, six, seven!"

"That's very good counting Susan."

They reached the end of the prom and went down the stairway to the sandy beach. Susan smiled as she ran to the swings. Frank and Pearl ran too. When they reached the swing set, Frank gently placed Susan on the wooden board seat. He slowly pushed the swing back and forth. Pearl found a nearby log to sit on and watched them.

"My daddy died from a heart attack."

Sympathetically, Frank answered, "Yes, Susan...I know that." Susan kept swinging back and forth, as Frank continued to give her swing gentle pushes.

"Do you like my mother?"

"Yes," Frank turned his head toward Pearl. "Yes, I like her very much."

"What is your name?"

"You may just call me Frank."

"I like you, Frank."

"You know what? I like you too, Susan."

While watching, from her nearby distance, Pearl wrote her thoughts in a small notebook: *Is Frank to be my future husband, would he be able to provide for me and for Susan? He's been a wanderer. I'm older than him, by several years. Yet, he seems mature for his age. Will he stay?* She added her last thoughts. *He is good looking, tall and muscular. He seems to have a kind heart. I want to be near him all the time. Oh dear, I think I love this man.* She laid down her pen.

Susan ran across the sand holding Frank's hand. They were both barefoot. Pearl laughed and enjoyed watching the sight.

That evening, Frank proposed to Pearl. I will find steady work, save my earnings, and I will return to you. You, I, and Susan will get a place to live. I will stay in Portland, be your husband – no longer will I be a hobo - hopping off and on trains."

They held hands. They were silent, thinking about these upcoming changes in their lives. "Please Pearl, wait for me."

Chapter Forty-Eight

Portland, Oregon 1933 Age Twenty-One

Frank wandered along the Portland streets. Poverty was evident. Men were living on the streets, as it was in New York City. In northeast and in southeast Portland there were homeless camps, not hobo camps, but camps for the homeless. These places were called Hoovervilles and Shantytowns. Folks had built places to reside in from scrap wood, tin pieces and even cardboard boxes.

Frank knew if he went to work at the meat plant, where Lou was working, he would get hired, but he was restless and wanted to try something different. He went by the railroad yard. Hobos were still jumping on and off the trains. Being a transient would not be the answer anymore. To have a wife and raise a child (Susan) he'd need a steady income.

Then he saw the office door and a sign: "Join the Army, Uncle Sam Needs You."

The army – he had not thought about this possibility before. He was strong and able bodied. He didn't mind work. He knew the pay and the benefits were good. The country was not at war. Maybe the Army would be the right choice. He walked through the door.

A man in uniform sat at the front desk. He handed Frank a folder of papers and a pen. Please be seated and answer every question on these forms.

Frank hadn't done any paperwork since his school days. He started the process. He gave his mother's address as to where he was living, and noted that he had completed his eighth grade education. Next he listed three major work places: Lake Farm Dairy. Swift Meat

Packing Company, and the Boxing Gymnasium. There were yes and no questions. "Have you ever been arrested?" YES "Have you done jail time?" YES, Frank was truthful.

He returned the papers to the front desk. Next he was called for the physical exam. After this procedure he was told to wait.

He waited over fifteen minutes when a sergeant called his name, "Gilbert Franklin Rose." He followed the officer into a private room. The sergeant sat behind his desk and motioned for Frank to sit in the chair in front of the desk. "Your name is Gilbert Franklin Rose?"

"Yes, sir!"

"You passed your physical."

"This paper states you are twenty-one years old." He continued looking through Frank's answers. "You've been arrested?"

"Yes, sir, I was arrested in New York."

"Did you spend time in jail?"

"Yes, sir, I spent time in jail in New York."

"Well..." he looked at Frank's paper work again, "we don't need ex felons in the service, but we have a place for you in the CCC program."

Frank was immediately relieved. Even though he went through the paper process he really didn't want to ever fight a battle in the army. He wasn't sure what the CCC program was like.

"You know about the CCC program?"

"No, sir, I don't."

"I'll give you a brief explanation. The C's stand for the Civil Conservation Corps. The program is part of Roosevelt's New Deal program getting men jobs and improving our country at the same time."

Frank wanted to explain that he could get his own job, and that he was not a felon, but he had a hunch this might be the opportunity he needed. The sergeant continued. "Wherever you are assigned you will have to work for a period of six months; however, you will be paid during that time. I think the pay is around thirty dollars a month, and twenty dollars a month will be sent home to your family. He looked at the paper work again. I guess that would be your mother. He shuffled his pile of papers and stamped the top of several pages, stapled the pages together and handed the pile to Frank. "Here is some information about the program and your assignment number. Read through this when you get home. In about a week, you will get a letter in the mail. That letter will tell you exactly when to report and where you will be sent. Do not ignore this letter. You are dismissed."

Frank left the room with a pile of papers that he folded and stuffed into his pocket. He felt relieved figuring he got a break. He didn't realize that the assignment to work for the CCC program would be extremely difficult, and far from his hometown, Portland.

Chapter Forty-Nine

Seattle, Washington to Juneau, Alaska 1933
Age Twenty-Two Years Old

During the late fall, the official letter came in the mail. Frank read all the pages carefully. Some of the information included details about the Civil Conservation Corps. The last page included only a few details, but the information was clear and concise. Frank was to report for duty early Monday at 7:00 a.m. on October 30, 1933. He was to board a ship in Seattle, heading to Alaska. The exact port number and directions were listed.

Frank's first thought was to jump on a freight train and go to Seattle. Instead, his mother paid for a ticket on the passenger train. Frank had his second experience of sitting on a cushion seat and riding inside a passenger car. She also gave him money to stay at a motel so he could arrive early at the seaport. The ride and the night stay went well. That experience would be his last pleasant experience of comfort for the next six months.

Early that cool, foggy morning Frank boarded the huge ship. Many men rode in the lower deck. All of the men were reporting for duty for the CCC program. Immediately, they were given orders. They were told where to sit, how, and when to mingle with others. They were also advised how far they could roam on the ship, when they were to eat, and where they were to sleep. There were also assigned meeting times, which would be conducted while at sea.

Frank felt somewhat overwhelmed, but at least he would enjoy sights that he had yet to see. He always thought he would like to visit Alaska. Leaving Seattle via ship was exciting.

The trip started out okay. Frank thought about his brother Millard when he stayed on a ship for months and went as far as China. Working on land seemed like a better option. At least on land, Frank would not fear high waves or the thought of possible drowning. He knew where the life jackets were kept, but he wasn't sure how many life jackets were on this ship. There were at least 2,000 non-army men/boys aboard. All of these men were assigned to be workers of the CCC program. There were also army officers in uniform. On this trip Frank didn't have the opportunity to browse from deck to deck. At times he felt like a prisoner, being told what to do and when to do it.

Early the next morning, a loud whistle blew. Every man was to rise, eat their breakfast, and then meet in the lower deck to get information about their assignments. After breakfast, they all sat on wooden benches and faced one direction. An officer stood in front of them and held a megaphone and spoke loudly. "Welcome aboard men. I will give you information about this voyage. As you can see, there will be some rocking and rolling. I'm sure that last night you all felt the waves while we traveled over the Strait of Juan de Fuca. They don't call that an "earthquake fault" for nothing. But, we don't have to worry about those waves again. We passed that section. Though I must tell you there are big waves yet to come, and if there are storms we will experience more rocking and rolling.

"We will be going about ten knots and will be following the inside passage. The entire trip will take about four to five days. As we arrive at certain CCC camps, some of you will be let off according to your assignments within three days, if all goes well."

He pulled down a huge map that was taped to the wall. He took a long wooden stick and pointed to Seattle. "Here is where we started," He moved his stick over the names: Victoria, and Vancouver. He called out each name and continued his stick upward passing over: Prince Rupert, Ketchikan, Wrangell, and Petersburg. Then he moved the stick to the side of the map, to Sitka and then back to a straight upward line to Juneau. Next, he moved his stick to the left and pointed to Cordova, and Kenai Lake. Then he took a black crayon and circled Ketchikan, Petersburg, Juneau, Cordova and Kenai Lake. "These places are CCC camps. Each of you have been assigned to one of these camps. Each camp will have about 300 workers. Your jobs will be assigned when you arrive at the camps."

Men quickly raised their hands. They had questions about the time it would take to get to their particular camp. What provisions were supplied? What was the weather like in these areas? Would there be phone service? What about medical supplies, available doctors? What would happen if they got sick? What would their duties be? The questions were coming quickly, but the answers were non-existent or very vague.

Frank decided not to ask – he would just wait and find out what each day would bring. He had his pillowcase with him and it was packed with a few supplies. His brother Millard helped him by packing gloves, warm shirts, socks, toothbrush, soap, a warm jacket and a warm wool cap. He also had a decent pocket knife, matches, tobacco and rolling papers for smoking. He was expecting the CCC program to provide him with the tools he would need, daily food, board and room.

The nights were okay. Frank didn't mind sleeping on the hard benches. He laid out his jacket to cushion the rigid seat, and covered his face with his wool cap. The movement of the ship rocked him to sleep. The ship did dock in Ketchikan, but only the assigned workers to Ketchikan left the ship. Everyone else just stayed aboard and waited until the ship left port. The men noticed the change of weather. The temperature in Seattle was around 57 degrees when they left. The air felt like at least 20 degrees colder. Frank wore his jacket.

The next stop was Petersburg. It was pouring rain with a strong wind. Every man was bundled up as much as they could be to provide for their warmth. A number of men got off the boat and saw flat land with an overgrown jungle-like atmosphere. The area did not look inviting. Frank figured his assignment would be Juneau. He had heard that Juneau did have a lumbermill. That news was encouraging. With the mill and the abundance of trees, they would be able to build structures. What he did not realize, was what all they would be required to build.

The waves between Petersburg and Juneau were rough. The weather was stormy. The duration was an eight hour trip. They had left Petersburg during the early morning hours, but now it was eight hours later. Frank knew it was still daylight, but the day was dark with clouds and heavy rain. When the ship stopped at port, Juneau did not look any more inviting then the muddy area of Petersburg. Mountains surrounded the area, but they were semi-covered with fog so even their whiteness looked drab. The entire scene looked dismal. As they walked off the wooden plank, all they could see was muddy ground, huge trees and rocky land. The question was where were they going to stay and how were they going to survive? They walked through muddy fields. There was one large tent and that was their meeting place. Inside the tent, were wooden tables, and hard wooden benches. The men were asked to be seated. One of the officers, soaking wet and carrying his suitcase over his head as he walked through the deep puddles, decided he did not want to stay in this "God-forsaken mud hole!" He loudly announced that he was going to "return to Seattle on the ship that was still at the dock."

Frank and most all of the men overheard the conversation. He too felt like leaving, but he figured that for him there was not an option, but maybe the officer had the power to do as he wished. Another officer of higher rank stood directly in front of the persistent first officer and announced loud enough for all to hear, "No, sir, there will be no extra persons leaving on this ship. This ship will only leave with their crew and the men that are headed to their assigned camps. Those are the orders!"

The first officer was out ranked and outraged! The men that heard the conversation were basically quiet. They now knew that they too were going to be stuck in Juneau for the duration of their assigned time.

The top ranked officer turned his attention to the men waiting to hear their fate. "Attention men!" The men were silent, realizing this program was going to operate like an army base. "For starters, you will be camping in tents until you can build barracks. You will also be assigned to build outhouses. Until that time, make do as you can in the wooded areas. There are no roads in or out of Juneau. Ships and planes are the only way in and out. For now we are basically here to stay and get the work accomplished that we will be assigned daily to do."

There was silence in the tent as the men contemplated their assigned miserable future fate. Orders and directions continued. Frank heard most of the long list of duties: "building docks, warehouses, roads, runways…" The list went on, but he was thinking about barracks and outhouses.

"Don't be too concerned men, we have plenty of lumber. We have an abundance of trees, as you can see. There is even a working sawmill. You will be supplied with work clothes and gloves. You will be well prepared! Report back here in this mess hall for dinner in two hours. You are now dismissed."

What did "dismiss" mean? Frank thought what a crazy suggestion. There was no place to go. The land was all muddy. He would rather stay in the mess hall and wait for the food. Instead, they all scattered to the make-shift tent city. Canvas was placed over lean-tos from the tree boughs and inside each canvas tent was a cot and mattress. Frank had to laugh. He knew the hobos were having better living conditions than what he had just been offered.

At the dinner hour, they were told their work schedule. Starting the next day they would be working eight hours a day, seven days a week. Their first project was to build log bunk houses and wooden outhouses.

Early the next morning, Frank started to chop a tree. As he was chopping, using the axe that was provided and wearing the gloves that he was given, a man started working on the other side of the tree with a crosscut saw. He was sawing away without saying a word until Frank stopped to look at him.

"The tree falls best if you do a V cut." He demonstrated with his hands. "We will cut perpendicular to the wood grain. Let me show you." He took the axe from Frank and started to cut the tree diagonally. "I will cut this side, and then I will tell you when to stand back. Together we will yell timber and the tree will fall." He handed the axe back to Frank, and started cutting again with his saw.

Frank knew this young man was not one of the CCC men. This worker was a native, living here in Juneau. He knew about cutting trees, he understood the land, the weather and all the conditions that Frank didn't know. Frank didn't ask any questions, he just kept chopping.

"Timber!" The tree fell. They looked at each other. "My name is Toklo – it means I am spontaneous and versatile. What are you called?"

Frank shrugged his shoulders. He wasn't sure how to define himself. "My name is Frank. The word Frank means honest and candid. I'm an honest man."

"Shall I call you honest or Frank?"

Frank gave a semi-smile. "Just call me Frank."

They shook hands and started to work on the next tree.

Toklo and Frank sawed down several trees. Finally, after many hours of working in the rain and the soggy mud, they stopped and sat on the wet ground under the protection of a large tree. Frank spoke first, "I'm from Portland, Oregon."

"I've lived in Juneau all my life. I have a wife and two small children. We want to help you men. We need roads and a good seaport. America came to help. Thanks.

"We build our own boats, we fish, we hunt. We know how to make it here. You seem like me. You took off your gloves when they got soaking wet. Good man. We don't wear gloves. That's crazy. Too wet for gloves."

Frank laughed. "Man, it's too wet for anything! Do you ever have dry, sunny weather?"

Toklo laughed, "Oh yes, nature gives us all we need, when we need it. You have wife, children?"

"No, but I have a girl waiting for me. I hope to marry her when I get back to Portland."

"Where is this Portland?"

"About four hours south from Seattle."

"Oh, yes, Seattle. We get supplies from Seattle. A good city, Seattle." Toklo and Frank went back to work.

The rain and the work were consistent. Frank felt like he would never get use to the conditions. Though he came from a city, where the rain was consistent, but he had to admit not as often, nor as cold as it was in Juneau.

After several weeks, the men actually built a long bunk house, bunk beds and a row of outhouses. From staying in makeshift tents to now sleeping in a wooden framed long house everyone was in a better mood.

"How are you doing?" Toklo asked Frank one morning.
"Actually, I'm doing okay. A lot of these guys are young, but eager workers. In the evenings there is good conversation and sometimes singing and some music. A couple guys have banjos and harmonicas. The talk and music livens up the mood."

"What projects are you working on next?"

"Tomorrow and the next few days we are working on paving some roads. We heard there might be a few dry days. Do you agree?"

"Oh, yes, I agree. Maybe, three dry days. Good days to pave a road."

Day after day and month after month they worked in freezing temperatures and plowed their way through deep snow. Finally, Frank was into his sixth month. The weather was milder and the work had slowed down. The area looked different than when he and the other 300 men had arrived. He wasn't sure what the bunk house would be used for after they all left. Toklo wasn't sure either.

There were useable roads, instead of flat muddy paths, and a few more decent docks. The operating sawmill was busy with native workers. This asset was a foretelling sign that more needed structures would be built. Yes, Frank was proud of what he had learned about carpentry, road paving, and building aspects in general. The experience was good. He was satisfied that he was part of a team of workers that accomplished so much.

Toklo was thankful and told Frank that the native people were glad for what the Americans had accomplished to help their tribes. Those words alone made Frank feel that the challenges were worth the efforts.

Frank had sent a letter to Pearl, he hoped she received it. *My dear Pearl, our work is almost finished. By the end of April, I should be home. I am anxious to hold you in my arms again. Please Pearl, wait for me to return. Frank*

Chapter Fifty

Portland, Oregon June 1933

"Heard you've been ridin' in the boxcars?"

Frank walked up the familiar front porch stairs. Mr. Steward was waiting on the porch, leaning over, and holding a cane.

Frank continued his walk up the steps, "Yeah, where did you hear that?"

"You're friend Tommy. He found out somehow."

Frank remembered he did send Tommy one postcard when he was in New York. He never guessed that Tommy would spread the news. Frank stopped on the porch and took a good look at Mr. Steward. No longer was Mr. Steward strong, as Frank had remembered. His hook arm didn't look like a weapon anymore. Frank figured he could easily grab that steel hook and toss Mr. Steward to the ground. This weak man before him was no longer a threat.

This past foster parent no longer looked stern. He didn't even sound threatening. Mr. Steward seemed now like a man that was just tired, not caring much about life anymore. Certainly, he was not the disciplinarian, nor a parent figure. Matter-of-fact, he appeared fragile, like a child.

Mr. Steward sat in the wooden rocking chair and rocked back and forth. "I've never been to New York. Yeah, Tommy showed me that post card – all the way from New York. I couldn't believe it!

"What did you see in that big city? What work did you do there?
Did you visit your relatives? I heard they pay big money in New
York. I've never been to New York. That's really something! You
went all the way to New York!"

Frank sat down on the porch swing. He breathed a long sigh.
He felt relieved. His revenge and rage, that burdened him for years,
disappeared. There was no need to beat-up Mr. Steward. Mr. Steward
had been hit years ago, long before Frank knew him. He had been
bashed by a train; he had lost a leg and lost an arm. Frank knew the
dangers of trains. He could have been a victim too. If so, he might
have been mad at the world as Mr. Steward was. Frank shook his
head, saying no to these thoughts. He knew that no matter how mad
at the world he might be, he would not punish a child with whippings,
or kill a dog for his own revenge. Yet, maybe now, Mr. Steward had
changed.

Frank took tobacco from his pocket and the paper sleeve to roll
a cigarette. He looked toward Mr. Steward, "New York City is the
busiest, largest crowded city I've ever seen..."

End of Book II

Frank's parents
Sylvester and Mary Rose

Frank and his brother Lou

Frank's brother Millard in goat cart

Lou and Frank in the goat cart

Frank Rose (age 19) with friend

Pearl's daughter Susan and her dog Chink

Pearl

Frank Rose in later years

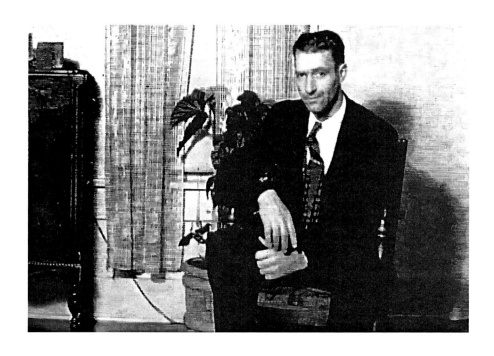

A Special Thank You to

Artist and support person, Ron Walker
Editors, Patsy Walker and Lynette Miller
Formatting genius and on-call IT support, Selena Hansen
Cover art and graphic layout, Sandra Putaansuu
Publisher, Karen Bonaudi

Writer friends who gave me dead-lines, encouragement and corrections

Sally Jones
Donna McLain
Mary Lyons
Gloria Sanders
Connie Budge
Marianne Brown (in memoriam)
Margaret Barton Ross
Alan Rose
Lori Steed
Elaine Cockrell
Carrie McKinnon
Jaimee Walls
Suzanne Loeb
Michael Kruger
Debz Briske

Many other friends and relatives that kept asking, "When is the book going to get finished?"

References

Tapes

Gilbert Franklin Rose life stories, Walker Production video tape recordings, Ron Walker, 1991

Books

Allsop, Kenneth, *Hard Traveling, The Hobo & His History*

Britannica Junior Encyclopaedia Vol. 6 1975 Ref: Copper

Hanson, Erica, *A Cultural History of the United States*, Lucent Books, 1998

Freedman, Samuel, New York Souvenir Album, *Camera Masterpieces*, New York Magazine, 2016

Provost, Stephen H. *Highway 99: The History of California's Main Street*, Craven Street Books, 2017

Mulvey, Deb (Editor), *We Had Everything But Money*, Reiman, 1992

The Chamber of Commerce Handbook for San Francisco, *San Francisco Bay Ferryboats -- Yesterday*

State Farm Road Atlas, State Farm Insurance, 1994

Websites

"Allegheny National Forest" *US Department of Agriculture Forest Service*, https://www.fs.usda.gov/allegheny

"Meatpacking" *Encyclopedia of Chicago History*,
http://www.encyclopedia.chicagohistory.org/pages/804.html

"Great Depression" History Channel,
https://www.history.com/topics/great-depression

"Model T Ford Forum: What are all these pedals?" *Model T Ford Club of America*, 2005,
http://www.mtfca.com/discus/messages/29/6815.html

"The Dustbowl" National Drought Mitigation Center,
https://drought.unl.edu/dustbowl/

"Saint Patrick's Cathedral" https://saintpatrickscathedral.org/

Skaret, Morey, "Riding the Rails in the 1930s"
https://www.historylink.org/File/3369

"The Hobo Ethical Code of 1889: 15 Rules for Living a Self-Reliant, Honest and Compassionate Life" *Open Culture*, 2016, https://www.opitenculture.com/2016/11/the-hobo-ethical-code-of-1889.html

"Moffat Tunnel" *Uncover Colorado*
https://www.uncovercolorado.com/activities/moffat-tunnel/

"1920s Men's Fashion Style Guide" *Next Luxury*
http://nextluxury.com/mens-style-and-fashion/1920s-mens-fashion-style-guide/

"Ford Cars 1903-1917" *YouTube*
https://www.youtube.com/watch?v=42C7GiJnE0I

"A Day in New York 1930's in color" *YouTube*
https://www.youtube.com/watch?v=65Deh9u2pLw

Readers Group Guide

Questions & Discussion Topics
Book I

1. List differences between the times when Mary was a single mother seeking employment compared to mothers in recent times seeking employment.

2. What child care options do parents have today? Is there still a need for more options? How should these options be improved?

3. As described in Chapter Three, discuss the actions of the characters, Mary, Anna, Ruby, Millard, Lewis, Frank, the household servant, and the police.

4. From the story in Chapter Five, what is Frank's reaction to Mr. Steward's punishment? What advice does Lou give to his brother? Give examples of other ways, besides harsh punishment, children can learn lessons.

5. List ways that Miss Brown showed fairness and kindness to her students.

6. Millard goes off to work at a young age; list the good and negative aspects of this concept. Give examples of other situations where youngsters started work at an early age.

7. Frank won an eighth grade Spelling Bee Contest; give examples where school success transferred into long-lasting adult learning, or helped in successful work experiences.

8. When Frank left school what troubling choices did he have to make?

9. What are some of the challenges facing teenagers today as compared to the years that Frank was a young teenager?

10. Why did Frank think jumping on a train was safer than hitchhiking?

11. List some lessons he learned about hobo riding, that he heard about on his first train ride.

Questions & Discussion Topics
Book II

1. List reasons why Frank decided to travel again on the boxcars.

2. Explain why Frank wanted to learn the sport of boxing.

3. What did the waiter say to Frank about boxing?

4. List reasons why Nathan and Frank made good traveling companions.

5. What were some of the differences between road travel then compared to road travel today?

6. What aspects did Frank like about San Francisco?

7. Tell about the scariest movie or play that you've seen. How did it compare to the Dracula Play?

8. What did Frank like about New York City? Tell how and why New York City changed while he was there.

9. What difficulties did Frank encounter while working for the CCC program?

10. Frank's attitude changed toward Mr. Steward, what caused these changes?

11. List lessons we can learn about forgiveness.